UNION OF JEWISH WOMEN,

CENTRAL COMMITTEE

FOR

JEWISH EDUCATION.

RELIGION, NATURAL AND REVEALED

RELIGION

NATURAL AND REVEALED

A SERIES OF PROGRESSIVE LESSONS
FOR JEWISH YOUTH

BY

N. S. JOSEPH

REVISED EDITION

The three great words of Religion are—God, Duty, Immortality
SCHILLER

London
MACMILLAN AND CO., LIMITED
NEW YORK: THE MACMILLAN COMPANY
1906

Printed by BALLANTYNE, HANSON & Co.
At the Ballantyne Press

PREFACE TO PRESENT EDITION

THE first Edition of this work was published about twenty-seven years ago by the Trustees of the Jacob A. Franklin Fund, who purchased from me the copyright, subject to certain conditions. The copyright having reverted to me under one of those conditions, I have lately been urged to prepare a new Edition, with such changes as naturally result from the advance of knowledge and the changes of view consequent thereon.

My dear and revered friend, the Rev. Simeon Singer, minister of the New West-End Synagogue, whose recent decease has bereft the Jewish community of a religious teacher unequalled in nobility of character, high ideals, and scholarly attainments, was foremost in urging me to undertake this task, and his wish was seconded by his learned kinsman, Mr. Israel Abrahams, M.A., Reader in Rabbinic to the University of Cambridge. Both assured me that they had, for many years—and, indeed, until the book had gone out of print—found it of great value in their practical work as teachers of Religion.

The changes necessary to a new edition of a religious text-book that would be abreast of recent knowledge, and of those modern ideas shared by the majority of intelligent men, seemed to me to involve a labour and responsibility beyond my powers, especially having regard to other duties lately undertaken by me. Hence

I at first declined to entertain the project; but, after much hesitation, eventually yielded to the persuasions of these two friends, they promising their good counsel and active aid.

Both have most amply fulfilled their promises; and I have, further, had the advantage of the assistance of my esteemed friend, Mr. Claude G. Montefiore, M.A., Hibbert Lecturer (1892), who generously lent his aid by perusing the entire work, and by criticising my revisions and additions. I deem myself fortunate in thus having had the benefit of the scholarly knowledge and practical experience of these three distinguished religious teachers and preachers; and the best indication of my gratitude to them is that I have adopted most of their invaluable suggestions. None of these kind advisers, however, must be held responsible for the work as it stands.

It is a great grief to me that my ever-to-be-lamented friend Mr. Singer has not lived to see the publication of the book, which he incited me to reproduce in the revised form. It is right I should add that, following his advice, I have made as few revisions as possible—fewer, indeed, than I had originally intended. Many parts of the book would probably have assumed a different character if I had now been writing it for the first time.

It will be found that, in various places, I have added sundry notes and quotations, so as to give increased force to the text. I hope that these, being chiefly the thoughts of great thinkers, will enhance the value of the work.

October 1906.

PREFACE TO FIRST EDITION

THIS book has been written in scanty moments of leisure, snatched from the pursuit of an arduous profession. It therefore, doubtless, contains many imperfections, which would not have existed if the work had been the result of a steady and continuous effort.

It was commenced some years ago, at the suggestion of a dear departed friend, the Rev. BARNETT ABRAHAMS, and was discontinued when his death deprived me of his promised co-operation. It was resumed a few months since, the necessity of such a work having been, for many years, constantly pressed upon me, first, during my connection with many of our communal institutions, and lately in the education of my own children. This last exigency gave the most powerful impulse to the progress of a work for which a too scanty leisure hardly qualified me.

While there is no lack of excellent books professing to teach our Religion, they all partake of a more or less dogmatic character, little in harmony with the inquiring spirit of the age. The rationalistic tendencies of modern thought have administered a rude shock to all religions. They have caused many good, truth-loving parents to be less zealous than of old about the religious education of their children, the modern notion being that Religion and Reason are in some degree antagonistic. Children, hardly free from the restraints of the nursery, quickly imbibe, or perhaps inherit, the prevailing spirit of inquiry, and ask intelligent questions which would have surprised and horrified our grandfathers, but which must yet be answered.

The day for dogmatic religious teaching is at an end. For infants it may suffice. In the undeveloped intellect of the little child it may fill a temporary gap ; but to the mind of an intelligent child, accustomed by the modern system of education to the exercise of the reasoning faculties, the teaching of Religion by a purely dogmatic method is useless, perhaps mischievous. The lesson, if swallowed, is not digested. If retained in the memory, it is, perhaps, retained only to crop up in years of maturity, not as a part of a living Faith, but as a pretty fiction, an exploded belief of credulous childhood.

With our Holy Religion this should not be. For, starting with few postulates, it makes but small demand on blind faith, and is essentially a reasonable Religion, that can bear the bright glare of inquiry. There is, therefore, no excuse with us, as with other creeds, for dogmatic teaching.

The object, then, of this work is to present a rational view of our Religion—to give the " reason why," wherever possible, for its principles, its ordinances and practices, and so to raise our Faith to the higher dignity of a firm, intelligent Belief.

Although the principal ceremonial observances ordained in the Pentateuch will be found to have a place in these pages, the work must not be regarded as a compendium of our Ritual. It would have been impossible to render it such, without touching upon debatable ground, and alluding to points upon which our co-religionists are not altogether unanimous. The

omission of these debatable subjects (which probably
few will notice) is therefore not accidental but intentional, the work having been written in a sense that
may render it acceptable to Jews of all shades of
opinion. The omission, however, to those who notice
it, will be useful, as showing that the differences which
divide the Jewish camp are really insignificant, and
that upon all truly important points of doctrine and
observance, Jews are unanimous.

A few words must be said about the scope of the
work, the style, or rather styles, in which it is written,
and the mode in which it should be studied. The book
is intended to teach our Religion *progressively*, under
the two heads—Natural and Revealed Religion. The
first principles and most important observances and
laws, enunciated in the simplest language, suitable to
the capacity of the youngest children, will be found in
the earlier Chapters of both parts of the work. As the
work progresses, the subjects become less easy ; and
as those subjects are not intended for the perusal of
very young pupils, the child-like language of the earlier
Chapters is dropped, but a sufficiently simple style is
preserved. The later Chapters (except Chapter XII.)
and the Appendices, treating of subjects of inherent
difficulty, are meant only for the perusal of advanced
pupils, and consequently no attempt has been made to
couch these in language of strained simplicity. Hence
the variation in the mode of treatment, which, though
it may affect the unity of the style, will probably
enhance the utility of the work.

CONTENTS

PART I

NATURAL RELIGION

PART II

REVEALED RELIGION

APPENDICES

RELIGION, NATURAL AND REVEALED

PART I

NATURAL RELIGION

CHAPTER I

THE EXISTENCE OF A GOD

EVERYTHING in the world must have had a maker. You cannot imagine it possible that anything, however simple, made itself.

If I showed you a piece of stone, and told you that the stone made itself, you would laugh, and tell me that you could not believe such nonsense. And you would be quite right. You would tell me that the stone had no power to move, or to think, or to do anything—much less to make itself.

And if I showed you a plant, with some beautiful flowers growing on it, and I told you that the plant made itself, you would laugh still more, and would say that you knew better. You would tell me, perhaps, that the plant had grown from a little seed, and that the little seed had come from another plant, just like the plant I was showing you; and that the first seed that ever became a

A

plant, could never have been clever enough to make itself in such a wonderful way that the seed should bring forth a plant, and the plant a flower, and the flower a seed, and the new seed a plant again, and so on, year after year, till now.

And if I showed you an animal—say a bird—and told you that the bird made itself, you would laugh at me again. You would tell me the same as you told me about the plant. You would say that the first bird could never have been clever enough to make itself in such a wonderful way ; and that if the bird had made itself, it would have been clever enough to keep itself alive for ever, which we know no animal can do. And of course you would be right.

But, suppose some one told you that all the world, as you see it, came by chance—that the mountains and valleys, the beautiful trees, and the sweet-smelling flowers, the beasts of the field, and men and women, and you too, all came by chance, you would think this idea still more laughable. You would say that chance never did anything half or quarter so orderly. You would call to mind that when you upset your desk by accident or by chance, the contents tumbled out in the most disorderly way, and you would have been very much astonished if it had been otherwise. You would call to mind that the things you see in the world are very regular and very orderly. You would remember that you never saw trees grow upside down, or the sun shine in the middle of the night, or anything heavy refuse to fall to the ground—all which might happen, if things were arranged by chance.

You would also remember (and if you did not, some one ought to remind you) that all the things we see around us on this beautiful Earth, seem to be arranged for one *design* or purpose, for the good of living creatures, and above all, of man. And we know very well that if there is a design or purpose in anything, that thing cannot be said to be the work of chance, but must have had some one to design it.

I dare say you have, at some time or other, closely observed a steam-engine ; and if you have, I doubt not that you have thought it a very wonderful thing. Even if you look at it from a distance, as it almost flies along the iron rails, dragging after it waggons piled with goods, and carriages full of people, it seems a living wonder. But if you walk close up to it, while it is standing still, you will think it yet more wonderful. For you will see that it is made up of an enormous number of parts, some very strong, and some very delicate ; and if you ask how many pieces there are in it, you will be told that there are nearly four thousand, and that each one of those four thousand pieces is necessary to make the great giant move. And then you will think to yourself how clever the men must be who could make such a wonderful machine.

And if any one were to tell you that the steam-engine came together by chance, or that it was not made by an intelligent or clever maker, you would tell him he was a stupid fellow to talk such nonsense. You would say, " I see here four thousand pieces of metal of different shapes and kinds, some large and some small, and I see that they fit into one another exactly ; so they could not possibly have come together by chance ; and I see also that there is a design or intention in their being so put together—namely, *to move ;* and as there is a design or intention, there must have been somebody to design or intend, and that person, whoever he was, may be termed the maker of the engine, without whom that engine would never have been made." And this would be a very sensible answer for you to give.

I have been talking about a steam-engine, because it is a thing that most people have seen and looked at closely, and because also they know (or can learn by asking) how or by whom it was made.

But now I am going to talk of engines much more wonderful than the steam-engine. Perhaps you may see them with less wonder, because they make less noise ; but when you look at them attentively, you will see in them even more to admire. And the more you look, you will find there is the more to be seen ; and though, unlike the steam-engine, you will not find the maker's name written in letters of brass upon them, you will not be slow to find out who was the maker.

The engines I mean are the glorious sun and the tranquil moon, the twinkling stars, and the beautiful Earth on which we live. And I call them engines, because they are known to move, to be always moving ; not like the steam-engine, by fits and starts, when water is poured in and heat applied ; but ever moving, ever working, never stopping to take rest, never even slackening speed for an instant.

Then, too, there are engines on the Earth itself, which we may look at more closely than we can at the sun, moon, and stars ; such, for example, as the animals that live on this Earth. Yes ; these, too, are engines, and many of them have more parts than the steam-engine itself, and these parts are much less likely to get out of order, and they need fuel or food less frequently, and they are capable of repairing themselves over and over again, when they wear out or get damaged, till they get so old that there is hardly anything left worth repairing.

Now, as we cannot talk of more than one of these engines at a time, let us take one as an example, one with which I believe you are better acquainted than any other ; I mean—*yourself*.

You will remember that the steam-engine is a running-machine. It moves, and drags a train after it ; but it can do nothing else. You, however, are something more. You are a reading and writing machine, a tasting and smelling machine, a seeing and feeling machine, a hearing and talking machine ; but the greatest wonder of all is that this machinery of yours is under the control or management of a something within you, which you cannot see, and which is called the *Will*, and that this Will is guided by another unseen something within you, which we call *Reason*.

But as we can see neither the Will nor the Reason, we will let them alone for the present, and talk about the machinery only.

Look at your hand. How beautifully it is fitted for its purpose ! It can carry your heavy load of books, and it can thread the finest needle with the finest thread. It can hurl a heavy cricket-ball a very long way, and it can make the thinnest up-stroke with the finest pen. It can throw ; it can carry ; it can pull ; it can push ; it can lift ; it can crush ; it can bind ; it can loosen. Look at that great stout workman. He has just been lifting a hundredweight of grain with his brawny hands ! Look at him now. He is using the same hand to take out a little particle of dust that has been blown into his fellow-workman's eye !

I called you just now an engine. I think I must have been wrong. Why, your hand alone is a hundred engines all put together ; for it can do a hundred *different* things, and many quite *opposite* things.

Just look at your hand, and ask yourself if you think it became a part of your body by chance, or without design or express intention. Of course you will reply, that it was designed for the express purpose of doing all the things which we see it doing, just as the steam-engine was designed for the express purpose of *moving* and *dragging*. There-fore, we cannot help saying at least the same of the hand as we felt obliged to say of the steam-engine, that the hand must have had a very clever maker ; and I think you would feel inclined to add that, as the hand is so much more wonderful than the steam-engine, and as no man, however clever, can make a true imitation of a hand with all its powers and movements, the maker of the hand must be far more clever than he who invented or made the steam-engine.

Now the hand is only one part of you. There are hundreds of other parts of the body quite as wonderful ; and the more you look into and investigate these matters, the more you will see to admire, and the more certain you will become that the maker of all these wonderful contrivances of your body must be a Being of mighty skill.

Perhaps you never thought before what a wonder you are. If not, I hope what I have told you will not make you conceited ; for let me tell you that there are other animals which, so far as their bodies are concerned, are quite as wonderful. There is the elephant, for example ; he has a trunk which can tear up a huge tree and can also pick up a pin. There is the camel, too, with an extra stomach, capable of holding enough spare water to enable him to travel a long distance in the desert without drinking.

There is not an animal that can be named, whose body is not truly wonderful in every point of its structure. And then, if we look more closely into the peculiarities and habits of each animal, we shall find how beautifully the body of each is suited to the climate in which it is to live : how some are clothed with fur, others with wool, others with bristles, according to the heat or cold to which each is likely to be subject.

Then also we see how wonderfully it is contrived that life should be preserved as long as possible. For example, we know that all animals are liable to accidental injuries, and that they would soon die if those injuries were not repaired. But we see that the animal has in itself the materials for its own cure. If part of a steam-engine be broken or damaged, engineers must come with tools to mend it. The engine cannot mend itself. But animals are machines that can and do mend themselves. If the skin be broken in a living animal, or the flesh torn, there is a matter produced by the wound itself which heals it. Even if the bone of a living animal be broken, the broken edges give forth a liquid which soon hardens into solid bone, making the broken parts, if placed together, stick to one another, and form one sound bone again.

Is not that wonderful ? And wherever we look we find something to admire, something to wonder at. I do not mean to say that we can always tell the design or object or use of everything, when we see it. But that is caused by our ignorance. At one time, people were much puzzled to know what could be the use of certain poisonous plants ; but now they have found out that these plants which destroy life may, if used in a particular way and in very small quantities, serve as medicines to cure disease and so preserve life. And thus it may be with many other poisons and many other things whose object we cannot at present understand. Perhaps, when the world becomes wiser, we shall know all about them too.

And, after all, those things which puzzle us are not the greatest or the most important points in the universe. The things we see every day are the greatest wonders. Sunrise and sunset, rain and snow, wind and hail, the change of the seasons, the growth of plants and animals—lifeless seeds becoming living flowers; lifeless eggs becoming living birds; life everywhere, in the sea, in the fields, in the rivers, in the forests, in the air; living things made to last till their place is taken by other living things like themselves; and every one of these living things full of machinery which seems perfection—these are wonders indeed!

You will remember we made up our mind that the steam-engine must have had a very clever maker. Now what shall we say of the World?

Do you know that, when I ask myself that question, I begin to have quite a poor opinion of the steam-engine? For I never knew a steam-engine to lay eggs, and bring forth a brood of little steam-engines, like that fine old hen with her large family of chickens. Nor did I ever know a steam-engine that was capable of doing anything else than *move ;* nor did I ever know a steam-engine, that was out of order, get itself in order again without being doctored by an engineer. And still the steam-engine is a very wonderful thing, and must have had a very clever maker.

Well, what shall we say of the World?

I am sure you will agree with me in coming to this conclusion, that the World and its contents must have had a maker possessed of an intelligence, power, and cleverness, to which the intelligence, power, and cleverness of the engine-maker cannot bear the least comparison.

This great and wonderful Maker of the World and its contents we call GOD ; and what I have tried to prove to you is THE EXISTENCE OF A GOD, who designed and created the World.[1]

[1] See Appendix I. (intended for teachers and advanced pupils)

CHAPTER II

PERHAPS you may ask, How am I to know that the world had only *one* Maker? How am I to know that there is only *one* God?

You might perhaps point to the steam-engine I talked about, and tell me it was made by several makers, and you might ask how you are to know that each wonder of the World had not a separate maker.

You would not be the first person who asked such a question. Indeed, in olden times, there were several nations who believed in almost any number of gods.

I am going to prove to you that these people were very foolish, and that it is right and reasonable to believe that there is only one God, the Creator of the whole World and of everything therein. This is what is meant by the Unity, or oneness of God.

Let me take you back to our old friend the steam-engine. Now, it is certainly true that the engine was made by several people; but one man only designed it. That is to say, there was one man only who first made a drawing or picture of it before it was begun. And that same man it was who settled how large it should be, and how strong it should be, how much weight it should be able to drag, how fast it should be able to run, and how large and how small every one of the four thousand pieces of metal should be. And all the men who were employed in making the engine were just like so many machines, obeying the orders of the master-engineer, not daring to disobey, but following exactly the picture or design he had set before them.

It was only by this strict obedience that the engine could ever have been finished, and turn out to be a moving machine; for if one of the workmen took it into his head to make one of the parts larger or smaller than was intended by the master-engineer, the engine would have turned out weak or unruly, or perhaps would never have been able to move at all.

So you see, after all, the whole engine might be said to be the work of one man; for, in making it, the common workman, who put it together, had no more to do with the *design* or *intention* than the miners who dug out of the earth the metals of which it was made.

Indeed, if we look at the finished steam-engine, we shall at once see that one man only must have had the arrangement of it. If it were not so, the enormous number of parts would not fit into one another so exactly.

It is this exact fitting of the various parts, all pointing to one object or intention, which makes us feel sure that, however many hands put the engine together, one master-mind designed or arranged it.

Now, if I can show you that the Earth, nay, that the whole World is in this respect just like the steam-engine, that every little or great part exactly fits into some other part, and that each part, as well as the whole which is made up of the parts, points to one great object or designed intention, I think you will believe that, however many powers may have been used in making the great World, there was only *one God*, who was the Master-engineer of the World, who designed, ordained, arranged, and regulated it all.

Let us begin with the Earth itself. What do we find therein ? We find coal in abundance, to warm our homes and cook our food ; then iron, the material of all those tools with which we till the ground, make our clothing, our furniture, indeed everything that has to be shaped ; the stone to build our houses, and lime and sand to join the stone together ; and then, not the least of the treasures of the earth, we find springs of pure water bursting out of the hard rocks, flowing in little streams, and swelling into large rivers, always ready and at hand to quench our thirst. All capable of being used for the good of the inhabitants of this Earth.

Then let us consider the Sea. It is the great cistern, from which the sun and air draw up moisture. The moisture collects into clouds, the clouds fall in refreshing showers of rain upon the fields and forests, making the earth bring forth corn, and fruit, and flowers in abundance. And then the surplus water runs into rills, and the rills run into ditches, and the ditches into brooks, and the brooks into rivers, and the rivers into the sea ; and so the water which came from the sea returns to the sea, so completing its circle of usefulness, and ready to begin anew a like circle of silent, useful work ; and all capable of being used for the good of the inhabitants of this Earth.

Next, let us consider the living things that swarm in the sea. There are shoals of fishes which yield food, sea-monsters which yield oil, and sea-weeds which manure the fields near the sea-coasts ; all capable of being used for the good of the inhabitants of this Earth.

Then let us consider the Air. How wonderfully it is arranged ! We are always breathing a part of it. So, too, are the plants. Now you might think that, in course of time, all the air would be spent, or would become impure, through so many plants and animals breathing it ; and so it would, if it were not for a very beautiful arrangement.

The air (which, you know, you cannot see, and which you only feel when it blows against your face and when you call it wind) is made up of several parts, or different kinds of gas or air, mixed together. One of these parts (oxygen) animals inhale or breathe *in*, and when it has passed through their lungs, fanning and keeping alive the flame of life, they exhale it or breathe it out again, and it is then found to be entirely changed, and to be exactly like another part of the air (carbonic acid gas) which the plants breathe. And so, you see, the animals breathe out the very kind of air which the plants require.

But I have not told you all the wonders yet. This carbonic acid gas, which the plants and trees breathe, also becomes changed in passing through them, and when they have done with it, and exhale it or breathe it out (for plants, and trees also, breathe, although with organs quite unlike our lungs), it has become changed back again into oxygen — the very kind of air that we and all animals require to breathe.

Now, is not this wonderful ? You see it cannot matter how many animals there are upon the earth to be supplied with air. For, however impure they make it, the plants and trees are quite sure to set it right again.

Surely such a fact as this is quite enough to show that the animals, the plants, and the air they breathe must have had one and the same Maker. For how could we imagine it possible that the animals were made by one maker, the plants by another, and the air they breathe by a third, and yet that this clever and beautiful arrangement could exist.

The example which I have here given is not an exceptional instance, but is one of many instances showing that, throughout the world, things depend one upon the other ; and—still more wonderful— that what is useless to one object is thrown off from it, but is immediately taken up by another object, to which it is not only useful, but positively necessary.

And this is the great fact that we find in nature —*there is no waste*.

Now, if you inquire into the cause of this, you will find how it is that there is no waste. You will see that the objects of the animal kingdom, the vegetable kingdom, and the mineral kingdom—in plain words, animals, plants, and the lifeless materials of the earth—have a way of changing places one with another. I will explain what I mean by an example.

Suppose we sow some beans ; the rain moistens them ; in course of time they will sprout. There is something in the seed which we call *life* (but which we do not at all understand), giving it the power of taking up a portion of the air, and of the water, and of the lifeless earth, and so the seed grows into a plant. It becomes larger and larger. At last it flowers ; then the flowers drop off, and gradually the beans appear in their stead. A stem, a root, a number of leaves, a flower, and a quantity of beans (themselves seeds for a new crop of beans) seem all to have come from a simple seed. But they have really come from many things besides the seed. Something has come out of the earth, and something out of the air, and these some-things, which were before lifeless, have mixed with the little seed, and become part of the living plant. How, we do not know, and perhaps never shall.

Now, what becomes of the plant ? Let us watch and find out. Suppose a horse eats the beans. The beans will become part of his flesh and blood, and muscles and bones, and so such part of the plant as is useful for food becomes part of an animal. As for the remainder, it is not wasted.

The leaves will fade and the stalks will wither; but the leaves will crumble into dust at last, and become part of the earth again—a very fertile part, known as leaf-mould. The stalks and roots will do the same, if left to themselves; but the farmer will perhaps burn them, and use the ashes for manure, which brings them to the same useful end; for they become part of the earth again, ready next year to serve the same useful purpose; perhaps not as part of a crop of beans, but for wheat, or barley, or mangold-wurzel, or something of that sort.

And, pray, bear this in mind. It is the *same* earth, the *same* lifeless soil, which becomes part of the beans, or part of the wheat, or part of the barley.

We have seen how the lifeless earth changes into, and forms part of, the living plant, and how a portion of the living plant changes into, and forms parts of, the living and moving animal. Let us watch the further changes.

The horse which ate the beans, of course, breathes; and it has been found that part of his food goes to form the air which he exhales or breathes out.[1] So certain portions of the beans go back to the air, which, you will remember, was part of the nourishment of the growing bean. And more than that, as I told you before, it goes back just in the very state, fit and ready for the plants to breathe.

Then the ordure from the horse will contain

[1] Namely, the carbon of the carbonic acid gas which he exhales.

B

those portions of the beans which were not able to be changed into flesh or blood or muscle or bone ; and we know that this is turned to a very useful account as manure, forming part, and a very fertile part, of the ground, although so nasty and offensive to the smell.   And perhaps, after all, the nasty smell is an advantage ; for it is a hint to us to bury the offensive matter in the ground, where it may be useful.   Otherwise we should probably let it lie about, and it would not only be of no use, but would render the air of the neighbourhood unhealthy.

But what becomes of the horse ?   In course of time it will die of old age.   Its skin will be used for one purpose, and its hair for another, and perhaps its flesh will feed other animals ; but its bones will be burnt and ground for bone-earth, a most valuable manure ;   and such parts of the poor old horse as cannot be turned to some pro-fitable purpose will be buried in the earth, where it will become dust, very fertile dust, ready, like the bone-earth, to grow a crop of beans, or wheat, or barley of extra-fine quality.

So you see the changes take place, but never come to an end ; for nothing is wasted.[1]   One thing depends upon the other, like the links of a chain.   The chain is complete between the animal, the vegetable, and the mineral creations.   They change places over and over again.   It is the same

[1] " Nothing hitherto was ever stranded—cast aside ; but all, were it only a withered leaf, works together with all ; is borne forward on the bottomless, shoreless flood of action, and lives through perpetual metamorphoses."—*Carlyle*.

matter, the same substance—call it what we may —mineral, vegetable, or animal. Only, in one case life is wanting ; in the other two life is present.

Now let us sum up the few facts we have noticed. We have found that the same matter runs through the earth, the plants, and the animals ; that these make all sorts of exchanges one with another ; that all the exchange-process is transacted by that wonderful agent which we call life ; that during all this never-ending business nothing is lost, but that what one throws away as useless is immediately snatched up and used by another.

Does this look as if these things had more than one Maker ? If there were two or more makers, would it be likely that the work of one would exactly fit into the work of the other in every respect ? that the object or intention of one would exactly agree with the object or intention of another ? that the material used by the one would be the same as, or capable of changing with, the material used by the other ?

If there were more than one Maker, would it be likely that the earth and every particle in it would be acted upon by one fixed and never-changing law or rule ; that the great planets, which twinkle only like little sparks in the sky, would (as we know they do) all follow the same law or rule ; [1] that all the animals would be made in such a way as to breathe *one* air, and all the plants in such a

[1] The law of gravitation. And modern discoveries by means of spectrum analysis have shown that the same chemical elements that form the material of the earth, form also the material of stars whose distance is beyond computation.

way as to breathe one *other* air ; and, above all, that there would be plain and evident in all the works of creation on our earth *one* main object, namely, the good of all living creatures ?

The thing is impossible. Two or more makers cannot be. If such a work as the steam-engine required one master-mind to design it, what shall we say of the world, where we find thousands of objects—each more wonderful, more lasting, more perfect than the steam-engine—and all fitting exactly into one another, and pointing to one object—*Life ?*

There can be but one conclusion—that the world must have been designed by *one* Master-mind ; that there is but *one God*, the Creator and Ruler of all things created.

After reading all this long argument, and coming to this conclusion, I dare say you wonder how it was that, in olden times, there were so many people—and some very clever people, too—who believed in several gods.

I will try to explain to you how it was. And when I have finished, I think you will find that the explanation affords another proof of the Unity of God.

The nations who worshipped several gods saw the works of the Creation with eyes like our eyes, but not with thoughts like our thoughts. They would view the sun as the source of light, which made their fields fertile and their gardens gay. Then they would view the rain as a source of gloom, and as an enemy of the sun, because it often, when in excess, spoilt their crops, undoing all the good which the sun had accomplished. Then they would consider the wind as an enemy of the rain, because it dried it up, and thus undid the rain's work.

So when they saw the different powers of nature fighting with each other, and one undoing the work of the other, they thought each power had a separate god which ruled it.

And this idea they carried still further. They saw that men were ruled by different virtues, vices, and passions. They saw one, all of whose deeds were caused by the ruling passion of Revenge, another actuated by Love, another by Hatred, another by Ambition, another by Avarice, another by Patriotism, another by Philanthropy, and so on ; and they found such very different results produced by these different men, that they imagined the various virtues, vices, and passions which led them or drove them on to these different results, must each have a different god.

Besides, they often saw in one and the same man, perhaps in themselves (as we find in ourselves), good passions and bad passions fighting with one another, sometimes the one and sometimes the other gaining the victory.

And thus it happened that they had a multitude of gods—a god of the sun, a god of the rain, gods of the winds, and a god of the waves ; for they saw so many different and opposed effects produced, that they were led to think each effect must have had a cause which was itself a distinct creator.

Of course you and I know this idea to have been very absurd. And I really think that many of the clever people of those days must have thought so themselves ; for some of them, in their books, made their gods cut a very funny figure, representing them as doing all sorts of ungodly things. But certainly there were millions who really believed in all these gods. And we must not laugh at them ; for, in truth, they knew no better.

You see how their idea of a number of gods arose. They noticed the sun, and noticed the rain, and noticed the wind ; they saw the effects of each, but did not think of the effect of all put together. They saw that one power moistened the earth, and the other dried it ; that one parched the earth, and the other cooled it ; but they did not see that it was the moistening and drying, the parching and cooling, which, all put together, made the crops grow.

So, too, in the affairs of men ; they saw the love and the hatred, the charity and the revenge, the avarice and the ambition, the good and the evil, pulling different ways ; but they did not see that all these opposites put together kept the world of men always in movement, always in that state of activity of mind and body which is a necessity of man's nature. In a word, they did not look at the world as we have been looking at it—as a *whole ;* and did not notice—indeed, did not know —how all these parts fitted into each other, and formed the whole.

But, happily, we know better. We know that

these powers of Nature, which by themselves would produce such opposite effects, together balance one another ; and it is this *balance of power* which affords another proof that there is but one Creator and Ruler of the world.

I will try to explain what I mean by an example taken from the affairs of men. I dare say some of you read a newspaper ; and those who do not, hear now and then what is going on in the world. Now, you will almost always find a great fuss being made about some ambitious nation or another becoming too strong, or trying to become too strong, or endeavouring to master its weaker neighbour. When such things take place, you will generally find that the rulers of the other nations put their heads together and say that the thing ought not to be, lest it should disturb the " balance of power " ; in other words, lest the ambitious nation should become too powerful, and swallow up all the little nations. So, you see, the " balance of power " is maintained by one nation watching the other very closely, and keeping it in check.

Well, sometimes the ambitious nation says, " I *won't* be kept in check ; I *will* swallow up my weak neighbour." And perhaps he will try to make out that his weak neighbour is wicked and barbarous, and deserves to be swallowed up ; or perhaps he will try to show that his weak neighbour doesn't mind being swallowed up, and, indeed, rather likes it. Then there begins a terrible dispute, and perhaps the nations come to blows, and there is a long and frightful war. Generally it ends in changes which are scarcely improvements, and usually the " balance of power " is maintained ; but sometimes it has ended in the ambitious nation becoming more powerful, till it goes on, year after year, greedily adding fresh provinces to its empire. Such a state of things never lasts, but while it lasts it is very inconvenient and very burdensome.

Perhaps you now see how important this " balance of power " is, and how difficult it is to preserve it in the affairs of men.

But in Nature—that is, in the works of God—it is very different. There, the balance of power is quite as indispensable ; for, without it, we should now and then have all our houses blown down by a hurricane, all our fields burnt by the sun's heat, or all the inhabitants of the earth swept away by a deluge ; for, without speaking of the other forces of Nature, the winds, the sun, and the rain would be quite strong enough to produce such results, if they were not held in check.

Yet all the forces of Nature are so nicely balanced that, while each performs its work, it works without destroying. Now and then, indeed, there are slight, very slight, departures from the balance of power, but very soon it restores itself by some convulsion, affecting but a small portion of the earth, such as an earthquake, a whirlwind, or a thunderstorm. These are destructive sometimes, but they are no doubt for the general good, evil though they may at the time appear to be. We know and see the good of a thunderstorm ; perhaps we may some day, when we shall have grown more clever, see the good of an earthquake.

Be that as it may, the balance of power is the rule of Nature, and the exceptions above named, if carefully examined, will be seen to have for their object the enforcement of the rule.

Well, what do you think this proves ? I know what your answer will be. I am sure you will say that the forces of Nature cannot have separate and independent rulers, as the kingdoms of the earth have ; that, as all the forces of Nature pulling in different and sometimes opposite ways, and each performing different useful work, still balance one another, and balance one another *exactly*, there must be but One Creator who created these forces, but One who governs them.

And so you will believe in the Unity or oneness of God.

CHAPTER III

WHAT WE KNOW ABOUT GOD

IF you had a friend living a long way off, whom you had never seen, but who had always been very kind to you, frequently sending you presents, and paying you great attention in various ways, you would, I think, be very desirous of knowing all about this unseen friend.

You would try to find out what his likings and dislikings were, so that you might do something to please him. And if you had some idea that, one day or another, this unseen friend intended to send for you, and that if he then were pleased with you he would make you very happy, you would, I am sure, be most anxious to get all the information you could about this good friend.

You would inquire whether he received any news of your sayings and doings, and would endeavour to discover every peculiarity of his character. You would, moreover, try to find some one who had seen this friend, so that you might learn all about him ; but if you could not discover any person who had seen him, you would endeavour to find out his character in another way. You would think over all the presents he had sent you, and the manner in which they were sent, and the quantity in which they were supplied, and the purpose of each, and you would thereby be able to arrive at a pretty good guess of what your friend's character was like.

All this is supposing that you had never received from him any messages or letters, which would save you the trouble of guessing in the way I have described.

Now you and I have such a friend, and his name is GOD, and I have already shown you that we have only *one* such Friend. Neither you nor I have ever seen Him, but we receive presents from Him every day.

I dare say that you feel grateful to this good Friend, and would like to please Him. I dare say, too, that you have some sort of notion (which I hope will soon ripen into a belief) that He will one of these days send for you ; and you, therefore, would like to act in such a way that you will stand well in the opinion of this great Friend—the one and only God.

But before you can do this, you feel that you ought to know something about His power, His nature, His character, His likings and dislikings. This is what we mean when we talk of the *attributes of God*.

Well, let us see if we can find some of the information we want from the splendid gifts this great Friend has sent us. We shall afterwards see that He has sent us messages, in various ways, and that from them we can learn still more. But we will talk of the messages another time, and just now think only of the gifts.

God has given us the earth to live upon. What a magnificent present! Of how many thousands of presents does it consist! If we lived hundreds of years, we should never be able to count the treasures it contains, never grow tired of the beauties it exhibits. Well, I believe we shall conclude, after thinking a little about this splendid present, that He who gave it to us is good, kind, wise, and merciful. Let us try.

What a beautiful world it is! There is everything to charm the sight. The face of Nature is so fair that we never tire of it. The fields and the forests, the heavens and their hosts, the glorious sea—the grandest thing on earth—all delight our senses, whether we look broadly over the whole, or minutely into each little part.[1]

Think of the flowers, so sweet to the smell, so charming to the sight, filling our houses with fragrance and cheerfulness! Think of the food so bountifully supplied—necessaries of life, but yet so agreeable to the sense of taste as to render the satisfying of hunger one of the great pleasures of life! Think of the fresh air of Heaven, how balmy, how grateful to the senses, as we breathe it without an effort, or as its gentle breezes play upon our faces, enliven our limbs, and fan the flame of life! Think of the joys of the heart and of the soul, the emotions of love, of gratitude, of realised hope, and the proud sense of right in a conscience satisfied. It is a splendid place, this world of ours!

[1] Goethe beautifully describes the world as " the garment of God." *Cf.* Psalm civ. 1, 2.

WHAT WE KNOW ABOUT GOD

But I fancy you saying : " Pray stop ; do not go on so fast." I fancy you reminding me that you have heard of such things as disease, want, suffering in many frightful forms, hatred, crime— many, many shocking things that will hardly bear thinking about. I fancy you reminding me, too, that though the mountains look so beautiful, there are such things as volcanoes, pouring out devouring torrents of liquid fire ; that though the sea is so grand, so splendid a sight, there are such things as shipwrecks ; that though the birds sing so sweetly, and though their plumage is so lovely, there are such things as vultures and eagles who live only by the death of other animals.

Well, well ! You are quite right to remind me of all these things. We shall never get on if we shut our eyes to the truth.

Let me tell you, then, that there are many matters which we can never know during our life on earth, and among these there is none so impossible to know *for certain* as the reason for so much evil in the world. But a little thought will bring us to a conclusion probably not far from the truth.

Something within us tells us that there is a world beyond this ; that when we die, we shall live elsewhere in a happier and a better state. We are taught this at home and at school ; and to you and me, who have learnt this from other sources than our own thoughts and feelings, it may be difficult to think that this idea of a future state would come into our heads naturally, without any teaching. Nevertheless this would be the case.

The most savage nations, and those neglected members of the civilised races, who are perhaps more degraded than savages, have the notion of a future life implanted in their breasts, not merely as a hope, but as a conviction.

It would seem, moreover, that this world is a place of preparation for the future world; that here we have to make ourselves fit for the enjoyment of everlasting life, and that our enjoyment of the next world will depend on our conduct in this. This notion is perhaps as deeply implanted in the mind as is the main idea of a future state. The most savage nations think that their heroes who die in battle—according to their ideas, the most noble end—will have the rewards dearest to them in the world to come; and in civilised communities, even the most uneducated and neglected of human beings, who perhaps never think of a God ruling the world, yet have some vague idea that their crimes will be punished in a world beyond this.

You and I believe in a future state, in which we shall be rewarded or punished in accordance with our conduct in this world; and if we are asked why we believe it, we shall perhaps find no better nor more valid reason than the wonderful fact that *we are prepared to believe it without a reason*.[1] If this world be regarded as a mere place of preparation for the next world, there is not much difficulty in accounting for the presence of so much evil. Let us try to account for it by a familiar illustration.

[1] See p. 49 *seq*. below; and Part II. chap. xiii.

Suppose that, at school, you were not compelled to learn, but were allowed to do whatever you liked, so that if you felt inclined to talk, or to have a game, or to go out for a walk during school hours, you could do so, without your master finding fault with you ; would the master who so indulged you be really kind ?   Silly and thoughtless children might perhaps think he was ; but you know better. You know that you go to school for the purpose of learning those things which will be useful to you when you grow older. If you attend to your studies at school, you will get on in the world ; you will become clever and good, and people will respect and love you.

It is, therefore, the duty of your master to see that you do attend to your studies. The good master will always do this. Sometimes he will encourage you by fair words, by smiles, and by presenting you with prizes ; at other times, he may find it necessary to speak angrily to you, to frown at you, or perhaps even to punish you. Now, the sensible master, who occasionally frowns and punishes you, is your best friend ; while the foolish instructor, who always indulges your fancies and your frolics, is in fact your enemy.

I know it is difficult for you to see this at the time. While you are being punished, you feel angry with your teacher, and think him too harsh ; but the time will come when you will see things in their true light. When you have left school, you will feel thankful to him who checked your indolence by wholesome punishment, and will despise him who encouraged it by his indulgence.

Now, if you consider this life as a place of preparation for a happier and better life, you must regard the world as a school in which your soul is to be educated and trained, so as to fit it for a happy destiny in the next world. Thus it is that God acts towards us as a wise instructor. He calls into activity the noble impulses of our soul, and checks its evil tendencies. Sometimes He causes the light of His countenance to shine upon us, showering down blessings upon us, and prospering our undertakings ; at other times He finds it necessary to frown upon us, to disappoint our hopes, to afflict us with disease, loss of property, or other misfortunes. But all is done for our own eventual good. You may depend upon it, that God knows how to teach us the all-important lesson, how to prepare for the future life—that He knows when to encourage, and when to chasten. You may rest assured that it would not be for our advantage if we always had things as we would wish them to be.

As if to convince us of this, God has, from time to time, allowed a few individuals in high positions to enjoy almost unlimited power and wealth. History shows us that nearly in every such instance the individuals so gifted were spoiled by their good fortune. Nero, for example, was not an inhuman man before he became Emperor of Rome. It is stated that at the beginning of his reign he could with difficulty be induced to sign the death-warrants of murderers and other criminals. Yet, after he had enjoyed a few years of great power and prosperity, he caused his mother, his wife, and his tutor to be murdered in cold blood.

And Nero is not a solitary example of the evils resulting from unchequered good fortune. Even as children sometimes require to be checked and corrected, lest they become selfish and wilful, even so do men require trials and disappointments to recall them to a sense of duty and to improve their soul ; and God is far too wise and too good a teacher to withhold the needful correction. So you see how the seeming imperfection of our earthly existence conduces to our eventual happiness ; for by our very nature we require occasional sorrow and suffering.

But perhaps you may ask—Could not God, who created us, have so formed us as to have different natures ? Could He not have made us so naturally inclined to do good that we should not have needed correction ? I would answer, that we really know too little of God's plan to be competent to solve fully and with certainty such difficulties. We see but a very small portion of God's works ; we can have but a very faint idea of the working of the providential scheme. Man is but an atom on this earth, and the earth itself is but an atom of the whole of God's great universe. When we shall see the *whole*, when the future spiritual world, with all its hidden wonders, shall be revealed to us, then we shall doubtless see that God has ordained and arranged all things for the best, and that no other arrangement could ensure so much happiness to so many creatures.

Although the full solution of this great mystery —the mystery of the existence of evil—cannot be expected in this our little life, yet some faint glimpse of the truth may be further obtained by the help of an extension of our illustration.

Suppose that the schoolmaster offered prizes to those of his pupils who would answer a number of examination questions. Suppose that, contrary to the usual custom, he were to set very simple questions, and (to make it a very easy matter to answer them) allowed his scholars to refer to as many books as they pleased, and even to copy the answers from them. I know what you would say to this. You would object altogether to be examined on such terms. You would say : " I should not care for a prize so easily gained. The examination would not prove my merit at all. Any dunce could answer as well as I could in such circumstances. So I would rather be excused from being examined. If I gained the prize, I should not deserve it, and so would not value it."

Now suppose a contrary state of things. Suppose the schoolmaster were to give such questions as he thought his pupils ought to be able to answer, if they had worked hard and used their time well ; and suppose he left them entirely to their own resources, thinking that, with the knowledge he had conveyed to them, they ought to be well able to answer even the most difficult questions. What would you say then ?   You would say : " This is a very different affair. I shall be glad to be examined upon these terms. I know I shall have to work hard to deserve the prize ; but, if I work hard, I shall gain it. And when I shall have gained it, how glad I shall be ! Such a prize will be worth having."

Let us apply this illustration. Life is our school ; God our great Schoolmaster ; everlasting happiness the prize He offers to us, His pupils. If it required no exertion on our part to obtain this prize ; if life offered no difficulties and no temptations, so that we could hardly help doing good, where would be our merit ? Our happiness would be spoilt by the thought that it had not been earned by our exertions. Therefore God, in His goodness, has ordained it otherwise. Like the wise schoolmaster, He has made the examination hard, and consequently the prize worth having. He has placed difficulties and temptations in our way, that we might battle with them and obtain the victory. To some He has made life a struggle for existence ; but doubtless He has made them proportionately strong to enable them to carry on the struggle. Every one has his sorrows, his pains, his heartburnings, his temptations, and his difficulties. Even the most favoured are not free from them. Let us not cry over them. Let us rather remember that they are as the difficult examination questions.

And if we think how proud is our feeling of triumph when we have resisted a temptation, overcome a difficulty, struggled and conquered, perhaps we may therein catch a faint glimpse of our future prize—eternal happiness casting its beauteous shadow before.

Then if it be true—and who shall doubt it ?—that there is an eternal life, where eternal happiness is the prize of the good, there is no difficulty in accounting for the existence of evil in this world, and we see therein another and a signal mark of the goodness of our Creator. *The evil is there for man to conquer.*

And God has given him the power to conquer it. The passions are strong within us ; but the will is stronger, and can vanquish them. The voice of temptation is loud ; but the voice of conscience is louder, and can drown it. And so, too, in the world of matter. If the enemy be famine, man finds some mode of giving new fertility to the barren ground. If it be tempest, he has at hand the means of warding it off and protecting himself from its ravages. If it be the loss of worldly possessions, he has within himself the energy of character to take heart and to try to replace them with new. If it be disease, he finds remedies wherewith to baffle it, and even to prolong the span of life. If it be death, he has it in his power so to live as to make death itself the gate of eternal life —a passing evil for a lasting good.

Yes, there are evils in the world ; but they are the main-springs to our exertions, the incentives to our toil. They are the giants with whom we have to contend boldly, manfully, and honourably. To conquer them by honest strength of purpose, is the aim and end of the great battle of life.

Thus, then, we see how evil tends to our eternal welfare. It is mixed in small proportions with the good things of this earth, gently, wisely, and kindly ; not dealt out in quantities to crush mankind, but tempered with the good, so as to strengthen the immortal soul, and make it worthy of everlasting happiness. And as for those who seem by their undeserved inheritance of physical or moral evil unable to achieve happiness, we may rely on it that God will not only make allowances, but that in His own way and at His own good time will Himself do for these unhappy children of His what they have been unable to do for themselves.

If, then, we have to guess the disposition of our Great Friend—the One and Only God—from thinking about the gifts which He has presented to us —the earth and its contents, what shall be our guess ?

Shall we guess that the Being who has given us such a beautiful place to live in, endowed us with such powers of enjoying its beauties, mingled good and that which seems to us evil so wisely, so mercifully, and so kindly, ordained apparent evil as universal good, made us so marvellously, fashioned our body and mind so wonderfully, and adapted all things to our eternal welfare, is a Being immeasurably good, merciful, and wise ?

Shall we guess this of our great Friend ? If we do, we are not likely to guess wrong.[1]

---

[1] A portion of this chapter was written for the author by the late Rev. Barnett Abrahams.

CHAPTER IV

MORE ABOUT GOD

You are satisfied that the One and Only God, who created you, is good and merciful and wise. But I wish you to try to learn still more about Him.

1. GOD IS ETERNAL; that is, He always *did* exist and always *will* exist. How do we know this? We have already come to the conclusion that this beautiful world and all therein must have had one great Creator, who brought everything into being. Now, if this Great Creator did not always exist, there must have been some time when He was Himself created by some one else; but that would be nonsense, for when we speak of a Creator, we mean a being who was the first cause of everything. There could not have been a Creator prior to the first cause or Creator of All, and, as we cannot imagine a beginning to time, we cannot imagine a beginning to God. Hence we say, we believe that God has existed for ever.

But how can we tell that God always *will* exist? We can only judge of the future by the past, and we cannot conceive the possibility of a Creator who has always existed ever coming to an end. We cannot conceive it possible for Time and Creation to come to an end, and, while these exist, there must always be a Creator to rule and govern the world.

2. GOD IS IMMUTABLE ; that is, He never changes. How do we know this ? You might perhaps think, that because the works of the Creator exhibit constant change, the Creator Himself must be changeable. But I can show you that this would be a very false conclusion to arrive at.

It is quite true that we see change everywhere in Nature. Without it there would be no life. But that change is always produced *in precisely the same manner*, following always in the same order. The mode or manner of change is unchangeable.

Let us give one or two examples. If you take a pound of ice and pour boiling water upon it, the ice will change, it will melt ; but, however often you try the experiment, you will find that it will always require exactly the same quantity of boiling water to melt the pound of ice. Again, if you mix sand and potash in certain fixed proportions and put them in a furnace, they will produce the substance we call glass ; but, unless you keep to those fixed proportions, the glass will not be produced.

And as it is with small matters, so is it also with greater ones. The earth itself, and all the planets, revolve around the sun, each in a period peculiar to itself, a period which is always the same. We know exactly, by calculation, to a second, when an eclipse will take place, long before it occurs. We know exactly, to a second, when there will be new moon or full moon. Indeed, everything in Nature has always been found to be so regular that

people in olden times called any fixed order of
things, observed everywhere, "a law of Nature."
They ought to have called it a law of the Creator.

If the laws of the Creator are thus unchangeable,
what must the Creator be ? What must He be,
who made these laws, who rules His Creation by
the same fixed, everlasting rules, and who supplies
daily and hourly the power or force which keeps
creation in action ever in the same way ? Surely
He too must be free from all change—Immutable.

3. GOD IS INCORPOREAL ; that is, He does not
possess bodily form. If God is unchangeable, He
cannot be composed of matter, or have any bodily
form. For all things formed of matter, or having
bodily form, are liable to change. The hardest
rocks crumble to dust in course of time. Metals
rust away to powder. Everything natural or
formed of matter is changed by time. If then God
is unchangeable, He must also be incorporeal ; He
must be without bodily form.

You will perhaps ask, if God has no bodily form,
what is He like ? Now this is a question which
no mortal can possibly answer. For we cannot
form a perfect idea or give a correct description of
anything except by connecting with it some material
qualities, such as size, shape, hardness, weight,
and so on. And since God is incorporeal, and has
no such material qualities, no one can say what
He is like.

And if we picture to ourselves God, the Creator
and Ruler of the world, as some great giant with
enormous power, we shall be doing very much the

same as ignorant idolaters did, thousands of years ago, and we shall be committing a great error. We must not think of God in that way at all. When we think of our parents, and love them, we do not think so much of their looks or of their form, but of their goodness and kindness to us. Probably no one ever loved his mother any the less for her being ugly, or any the more for her being beautiful. And so we should think of God, not with regard to any bodily likeness, but with regard to His qualities. We should think of His goodness and kindness to us, shown in His providing for our daily wants ; of His wisdom and power, shown in the government of the world ; of His mercy and forbearance, shown in His permitting sinners to live that they may repent of their wickedness ; and if we think of all these qualities, we need no other picture of God.[1]

4. GOD IS OMNISCIENT AND OMNIPRESENT ; that is, He knows and sees everything that happens in the world that He has created. He, who creates and regulates all things, must surely have a perfect view and knowledge of all that goes on through His vast creation, and not only a knowledge, but, as there is design in all He has created, also a fore-knowledge, a knowledge of things before they take place, a foreknowledge of the result of His work.

For how could it be otherwise ? To regulate the works of the Creation and the course of events,

[1] " Assuredly there is no more lovely worship of God than that for which no image is required, but which springs up in our breast spontaneously, when Nature speaks to the Soul, and the Soul speaks to Nature face to face."—*Goethe*.

requires a knowledge of all things existing, and of every power, thought or instinct, moving or influencing them. Surely the great Creator must know everything which He has formed, and His power must be present everywhere among His works, though we see Him not ; for we discern His watchful care in all things. He who is the Creator of every cause, and who has ordained the law by which that cause should produce a certain fixed effect, must surely be aware of the effect ; for both effect and cause are of His creation. So God must know everything. He or His mighty power must pervade all space. How careful, then, should we be of our actions ! How careful even of our thoughts ! For they are ever open to the gaze of the God who made us.

5. GOD IS OMNIPOTENT ; that is, He is all-powerful. Let us first try to understand what this means. We mean that nothing that can be imagined possible to be done, is too great or too wonderful for the power of God to accomplish.

I use the words " possible to be done " not to put a limit or boundary to God's power, but to put a limit or boundary to our own belief ; for no one should ask you to believe a thing that is impossible. For example, we cannot believe it possible for anything to be wet and dry at the same time, hard and soft at the same moment, white and black at the same instant. We cannot believe it possible for two bodies to occupy the same space at the same time, or for the part of a thing to be greater than the whole. Such things you would

call *impossible ;* and if any one told you " You
only require Faith to enable you to believe those
things to be possible which seem to you physically
impossible," you would reply, " Faith cannot make
a man believe that to be possible which cannot be
even *understood* to be possible. I cannot believe
a thing which is inconsistent with all belief, and
which even contradicts itself. I set no bounds nor
limits to the power of God, but I cannot profess
to believe a thing which appears to me impossible,
because self-contradictory."

This would be a very proper answer for you to
make.

When, then, we say that we believe that God is
Omnipotent, or All-powerful, or Almighty, we mean
that nothing possible is too wonderful or too great
for Him to do. We see His mighty power wherever
we turn—in the giant mountains and in the vast
deep, in the peaceful valleys and in the flowing
streams, in the swift whirlwind and in the rolling
thunder, in the rustling breeze and in the gentle
dews. We see His power in the life which lives
and reproduces life, in the birds and beasts and
fishes, in the trees and shrubs and flowers, and in
ourselves, favoured above all beings. We see His
power in the earthquake and volcano ; in the
splendid sun, the gentle moon, and all the hosts
of heaven—countless beyond number, great beyond
measure, stretching through space beyond limit.

Looking at these His glorious works, and remembering, too, that He rules and regulates all
of them by His own Power and Will, who shall

say that there can be a limit to the power of God ?
He moves worlds, and keeps them ever moving.
Can we imagine anything requiring greater power ?
He gives life, and makes that life bring forth fresh
life, without end.   Can we imagine anything greater
than the power of the Great Being who works such
wonders ?   Surely not !   And therefore it is that
we say that God's power is immeasurably great ;
and that is what we mean by saying that God is
Omnipotent, All-powerful.

.   .   .   .   .   .

Thus we have learnt the attributes of the Creator
from His works.   We have examined the presents
He—our Great Friend—has sent us, and learnt
therefrom His character.   They show us that He
is One, that He is good, merciful, and wise, that
He lives for ever, that He never changes, that He
possesses no bodily form, that He knows and sees
everything, and that He is Almighty.

When we think of these attributes—all centred
in One Mighty Being, the Creator of the World—
and then think of ourselves, short-lived, weak,
ignorant, and imperfect, we wonder gratefully at
the goodness of the Eternal God, and feel that it
should be a pleasure and a duty to love, honour,
and reverence Him, and to strive to obey His Holy
Will, if we do but know it.

CHAPTER V

MAN AND HIS POSITION

If I ask you what you are, you will reply, " A human being " ; and as the words escape your lips, you will feel a certain sensation of pride in making this reply. You may, perhaps, remember that you are a very helpless creature ; very weak, very small ; oh, so small compared with the great earth—so ridiculously small compared with the mighty universe ; but the idea will still be upper-most in your mind, " I am superior to the hand-somest bird that soars through the skies ; I am nobler than the noblest beast that roams proudly through the forests."

If this idea rises in your mind, as I hope it will, you will be right to give play to it—right to en-courage it. But your pride must not be the pride of the rich man who looks down with disdain on persons of lowly station, exclaiming, " See how rich I am ! what a wonderful fellow I must be ! " It should be the pride of the rich man who wonders to himself, " How is it God has made me so rich ? Proud as I am of my riches, I should be prouder still, if I knew how to use those riches well. What shall I do to deserve such blessings ? "

Oh, how rich you are ! Let us count your riches.

The beasts of the field and the fowls of the air have
no recognisable speech. The wild beast roars ever
the same note; the birds sing ever the same tune.
Their enjoyments are few, because their wants are
so few. They live, they eat, they drink, they sleep,
they bring forth young, they die—that is the life-
history of every bird, beast, reptile, and fish. No
improvement, no progress. The bird builds its
nest to-day precisely as did its forefathers centuries
ago.

But with you, how different! Let us count your
riches. You have speech—the power of conveying
your thoughts, your feelings, and your wishes to
those around you. Your voice is unlike any other
voice in creation. What varieties of feeling it can
express! With it you may laugh, or you may
cry; with it you may express your admiration or
your disgust, your love, your pity, or your scorn.
The same words spoken in different tones will have
different meanings.

Then think of the music of the voice. The
cuckoo never tires of her two notes, and knows
no others; the nightingale, with a voice of wider
range, yet only knows one song. But man can
do much more than these. He can combine his
notes without limit, and make sweet music to
echo every thought; as many songs as thoughts
—without number.

Then reflect upon your face. You may be plain
or handsome, it matters not; there is that in
your face which is a treasure beyond price—the
power of expression. The voice utters words, but

it is the face which speaks. The voice of pity
is sweet ; but how much more eloquent the pitying look, the moist eye, the face suffused with
sympathy ! The voice of anger is terrible ; but
what its effect without the lowering brow, the
flaming eye, the pouting lips, the distended nostrils,
the fallen countenance ?

Then think of the noble form of man. He is the
only animal that stands naturally upright. Some
animals there are, indeed, which, from their habit
of climbing, assume something like the erect attitude ; but it is always forced and unnatural ; and
the creature seems to be glad to walk on all its
legs again. Those long fore-legs which, as they
swing gracelessly by the monkey's side, seem to try
to make us believe that they are arms, soon drop
listlessly to the ground. The legs will be legs.
The animal must walk bent to the earth. Even
the gorilla, that nearest approach to man, though
its strength is enormous, soon becomes fatigued
when it walks in an erect position. The beast
looks downwards, man upwards. There is something noble in the attitude of even the meanest
man.

But if man has cause to be proud of his superiority
over the brute creation, on account of his form, his
attitude, and other qualities of his body, he has still
greater cause for pride in the qualities of his mind ;
for they are qualities which he alone of all animals
possesses, and which are wholly absent in the brute
creation.

On man alone is bestowed the gift of Reason—

that power by which you can put facts together, and draw therefrom conclusions, or new facts arising from those with which you were previously acquainted. Some have maintained that the brute shares this gift with man, but only in a less degree, and that what we call instinct is but a low kind of reason. But it matters little by what name you call it. You know full well that the most sagacious brute never does anything which could indicate what you call close reasoning. Its senses are keen, and it readily distinguishes friend from foe ; its appetites are keen, and its senses guide the creature to the means of satisfying its cravings. It has its attachments and aversions, memory, hatred of a foe, and gratitude to a benefactor ; but in spite of its experience and memory, it shows no increase of intelligence after it has once reached maturity.

Man alone is an improving animal. You improve because you have the desire to improve, and Reason and Free-will afford you the means of improving. Man does not accept the position in which he is born as a fate. His Free-will gives him the power of rising superior to adverse circumstances. No man is ever truly contented. The striving for something higher is the blessed distinction of our race. Without it, you would settle down in life like the beasts of the forest, careless of the future, callous to improvement. The desire of improvement spurs you to healthy action, gives you a relish for the duties of life, and bids you try to leave the world better than you found it.

But that same desire of improvement does not end its mission when it has tended to the increase of knowledge, and the advancement of those arts which mark the distinction between civilised and barbaric life. The desire of improvement gives birth to that noblest of all desires—the hope of a future and better state.

And here again you feel the proud position of man. You feel that you have a Soul within you, a Spirit which can never perish, which must live, when your body will have decayed and crumbled into dust. You feel that it is this soul that sets in motion all your thoughts, your feelings, your reasoning, your judgment, and all the powers of your mind. You feel that it is this soul that bids you improve, that makes you dissatisfied even with the greatest worldly happiness, that tells you that the fulness of happiness is in a world beyond this.

If there were need to prove that this soul is immortal, you could not have a better proof than your own hopes—the hopes of all men. You would feel horrified if you were told that when your life here comes to an end, your soul would perish, and be annihilated. Your soul recoils from such an idea. Your fond hope, and the hope of every human being, is a happy immortality. And this universal hope is one of the best proofs of the immortality of the soul; for surely that God, whose greatest attribute is kindness, would not have breathed into you and every man so noble a hope, and so holy an aspiration, without giving you the means and power of realising them. Your

D

soul must be immortal, because an all-merciful
Creator has bid you hope for immortality.

If a further proof were wanted of the soul's
existence in a life hereafter, we might find one
in the history of every human being, however
lofty or however lowly his position.   Everything
in creation has an object and purpose.   If there
be no hereafter for man, what is the object, what
is the purpose of his life ?   Surely not the objects
and purposes he attains in this world.

Take, for example, the life of a poor labouring
man.   He works hard all the days of his life, and
all his wages are a morsel of bread.   He has
few enjoyments, few comforts ;   and the older
he gets, the more difficult he finds it to earn
a livelihood, the more burdensome his existence
becomes.

Perhaps he is more fortunate than such men
usually are.   Perhaps, as he grows old, his children
love, honour, and cherish him, and he thus has
few troubles to weigh down his hoary head.   But,
however fortunate the lot of such a man, as he
grows older, he will find in the world fewer and
fewer attractions.   Everything becomes irksome.
He used to like the music of children's voices ;
he cannot bear it now.   He used to like a nice
gossip with his neighbours ;   he does not care for
it now, for his tongue is sluggish and his memory
fails him.   He used to like to read what was going
on in the world ;   but now he can read no more :
his sight is too weak ;   and if any one reads to him,
he is nervous.   Ask him, " What would you like,

my good old man ? " and he will reply, " Nothing, thank you. Let me sit quietly in my old arm-chair, next a roaring fire. Let me sit there quietly, doing nothing ; only thinking."

Can this be the end for which this good old man has been labouring hard and working well all his life ?

Take another case. Take, for example, the life of a great statesman. He has worked very hard for the public good. Early and late he has laboured to improve the condition of his fellow-creatures. Suppose the most favourable state of things. His services have been successful, and have been fully valued. The nation honours him ; the great men of the earth court him ; and people say he is one of the greatest men of the age. And he has a loving family who almost adore him. As for riches, he has more than he can ever care to in-crease. What more can he have of the good things of this world ? And yet—and yet, though this great man has attained the summit of his worldly ambition, he is not happy. He is growing very old. He cannot help himself. He can scarcely walk. He goes to the Senate, the scene of his former triumphs, and people listen to a tremulous voice from lips which used to thunder forth fervid elo-quence ; and as they listen, fondly catching every syllable, mutter to themselves, " What a wonder-ful old man ! but how different from what he was ! " And then he knows himself how he has changed. He sees that the words of younger men have greater weight than his. So he enjoys the

world no more. Day by day he becomes weaker.
Even his high position weighs heavily upon him,
bringing him responsibilities which he is too weak
to bear. What can he do but follow the example
of the poor old labourer, and sit quietly by the
fireside, musing on the past ?

And can this be the end for which this great
and noble old man has been labouring hard and
working well all his life ? Impossible. There
must be a higher end in a world beyond this. There
must be an existence in a future state, where the
worker of good meets an eternal reward.

The two examples we have cited have been the
most favourable examples that could be named—
examples of men who, as far as their worldly hopes
could reach, have, each in his own sphere, had
those hopes amply fulfilled. But you must know
well that the majority of the human race are not
so fortunate. We are not all born to a happy
life, not all destined to be heroes. The great bulk
of the human race is made up of hard workers,
whose life is almost a struggle for existence, whose
happiness is chequered with many misfortunes, and
whose worldly hopes are seldom half fulfilled.
Surely, then, the aims and objects of their lives
are not to be found in this world.

And worldly happiness is, at best, but a very
partial kind of happiness. One man longs to attain
riches, and thinks he will have arrived at the
summit of happiness if he becomes a rich man.
He works hard, and becomes rich. And when
he is rich, do you think he has attained happi-

ness ? Another man longs for knowledge—a more worthy longing. He studies hard ; he travels ; he searches for truth everywhere, and becomes a very learned man ; and when he has acquired all this knowledge, what is his happiness ? He has the small gratification of feeling that he knows a little more than his fellow-creatures ; but he has learnt, among other things, the humiliating fact, that the more knowledge he has acquired, the more extensive has the field of knowledge become to him. The more he explores, the greater the extent of unexplored territory that rises before him.

And so with the object of every earthly hope, every earthly ambition that we foster in our heart. It looks beautiful, it seems perfect happiness at a distance. But when attained, there seems always something wanting to make the happiness complete. We always crave for something more.

What does all this show ? Does it not distinctly indicate that if happiness be the wages for toil, our wages are not paid in this world ? Does not the very fact that our powers of enjoying worldly pleasures diminish as we grow older plainly indicate that the great storehouse of happiness is in a future world ?

Yes. Wherever we look, we see facts which point clearly to the conclusion that this life is a preparation for another life ; that happiness may certainly be found on earth, but that perfect happiness cannot be attained in this life ; that we are constituted to improve, that we are placed here to improve ; that our improvement leads to our happiness ; that this world is a world of work, but that the real wages will be paid in a world beyond this.[1]

[1] Even John Stuart Mill, who is sceptical enough on the subject of Immortality on purely logical grounds, sums up his conclusions by admitting that the hope of a destiny after Death " is legitimate and philosophically defensible." Almost unconsciously he seems to admit that hope to be a necessary of life, without which all human effort would be " not worth while." He writes : " The beneficial effect of such a hope is far from trifling. It makes life and human nature a far greater thing to the feelings, and gives greater strength as well as greater solemnity to all the sentiments which are awakened in us, by our fellow-creatures and by mankind at large. It allays the sense of that irony of Nature, which is so painfully felt when we see the exertions and sacrifices of a life culminating in the formation of a wise and noble mind, only to disappear from the world when the time had just arrived at which the world seems about to begin reaping the benefit of it. The truth that life is short and art is long is from of old one of the most discouraging parts of our condition. This hope admits the possibility that the art employed in improving and beautifying the soul itself may avail for good in some other life, even when seemingly useless for this. But the benefit consists less in the presence of any specific hope than in the enlargement of the general scale of the feelings ; the loftier aspirations being no longer in the same degree checked and kept down by a sense of the insignificance of human life—by the disastrous feeling of ' not worth while.' "—*Three Essays on Religion* (by John Stuart Mill), p. 249.

CHAPTER VI

REWARD AND PUNISHMENT

THE real wages will be paid in the world beyond this. In the world to come, every man will receive the requital to which his actions in this world entitle him.

But you will say, "We know nothing of the next world. How can we talk about such matters?" To a certain extent you are right. No one has ever come back from that great unknown territory to tell us what is the reward of the pious, and what the punishment of the wicked.

And it is well that our knowledge upon this subject is wrapped in uncertainty. For if we knew exactly the nature and extent of the reward or punishment payable for each of our actions, there would be no such thing as pure motive, and consequently there would be no merit in doing right and avoiding wrong.

Men would balance and weigh their sacrifices and their restraints here against the happiness resulting therefrom in a future state, would probably find it worth their while to be good and moral, and would be so not because it was right, but because it was profitable. But would the happiness re-

sulting from such a commercial kind of virtue be
pure happiness ?   I think not.

Suppose you go to school with your work well
prepared, and that you have accomplished the task
set you by dint of great industry and perseverance ;
and suppose that your teacher is so pleased with
your work that he gives you a prize, which you
never had the least idea he would bestow, you
will feel delighted at receiving such a reward.
Your delight will be of the purest kind ; for you
will feel not only pleased at receiving the prize,
but you will feel proud at having received it as a
token of your industry, and not as a *payment* for
your industry. The knowledge which you will thus
have acquired will also give you an unusual degree
of satisfaction ; for you will feel that you have
acquired that knowledge for the love of knowledge,
and not for the sake of any benefit that you might
derive from it.

Next, suppose that your teacher set to his class
this very same difficult task, telling you and all
his pupils that whoever performed the task to his
satisfaction should receive a prize, I dare say you
would try to gain it, and I hope you would succeed.
But if you did, I am sure your pleasure would be
very different from what it was when you gained
the other prize, without it having been promised
to you. You would work for the prize, not for
the knowledge ; and when you took the prize, you
would feel as if you had taken a sort of bribe to
do something which was, after all, only right and
proper that you should have done without any

bribe. And, besides the happiness being less pure, the knowledge acquired would be less pure, and, probably, more easily lost.

And so it would be, if our great Master, our Creator, had announced to us the reward in store for us in a future life for every good action, and the punishment for every sin. The happiness derived from the reward would not be pure happiness. But, with the uncertainty of our knowledge as to the reward and punishment, virtue is truly its own reward on earth, and the happiness, be it great or small, which will be our prize in heaven will be a pure, a holy, an unsullied happiness. It will be unsullied by the sordid feeling that we had been bribed to do the right thing.

So you see that the uncertainty as to the nature and extent of reward and punishment in a future state is a positive advantage to us. But notwithstanding this uncertainty as to nature and extent, that such reward and punishment must exist is sufficiently clear. Let us reflect upon the subject, and see how it is that we must believe it.

In everyday life, we frequently see bad men prospering, and good men—honest, industrious, and religious men—whose labours end all in disappointment, who are stricken by poverty or disease, and who are ever bowed down under the weight of their misfortunes.

God is just ; and even though these cases may be exceptional, He cannot be unjust even in these exceptional cases. Now, if there were no punishment in a future life for the wicked man who prospers in this world, and no reward in a future life for the good man who is unfortunate in this world, would such a state of things be consistent with the perfect justice of God ? We know not fully the ways of God ; but we know for certain that He is just ; and justice requires that the wicked man who prospers here shall be punished hereafter, if not actively, at least by remorse, and that the good man who is unfortunate here should receive the reward of his good deeds in a future state.[1]

And even apart from these considerations, when we reflect upon the evident aim and object of our life we shall come to the same conclusion. If we believe in the immortality of the soul—and who can doubt it ?—we must believe that we are here in this world for some purpose connected with the everlasting state, which is to follow our present life. For what other purpose can this be than to improve the qualities of our soul, to prove our worthiness to receive heavenly happiness, and, above all, to enable us in part to *earn* that happiness by deserving it ? Just as the bread is sweetest for which we have to toil the hardest, just as the child is dearest for whom we have to suffer most anxiety, so is the happiness greatest for which we have to work the most.

[1] " If death only had been the end of all, the wicked would have had a good bargain in dying, for they would have been happily quit not only of their body, but of their own evil together with their souls " (Plato's *Phædo* (Jowett), p. 107). But there is a sense in which the future life is more *necessary* for the wicked than for the good, a life in which the wicked may be purified and brought near to the God who made them.

So we are here to earn the everlasting happiness, which will only be true happiness if we shall have fairly earned it by working for it and *deserving* it. We all have trials and temptations placed in our way ; and he deserves eternal reward the most who overcomes them. We all have passions and vices, and he earns best his title to everlasting reward who conquers them. We all have opportunities of doing good to our fellow-creatures, of improving our own minds, of contributing also, each in his own small way, to the improvement of the world. He who does this work well, deserves and earns the highest reward of immortal life.

But if, on the contrary, we submit to the dictates of our passions, if we encourage our vices, if we lead a selfish life, setting a bad example to those who are sure to copy us, if we abuse our opportunities, if we are dishonest to our neighbours, if we stifle the voice of conscience, if we transgress the laws of morality, if we forget all else in our love of wealth and worldly position, can we expect a reward in a future life from a just God ? Must we not rather expect a long term of remorse for spending a life ill, uselessly, mischievously, and wickedly, for neglecting golden opportunities, for abusing the wonderful powers with which we are endowed ?

We know not what may be the nature or degree of the reward or of the punishment. These are

> " Things which the invisible King,
>   Only omniscient, has suppressed in night."
> —*Milton*.

No man can, in the real sense, *earn* such a boon as immortal life; nor can any man *lose* it. But we are sure that in some way reward awaits the good, and at least absence of reward awaits the wicked. Every man is responsible for his deeds. According to his work, so will be his wages in the world to come.[1] The wicked are not in hopeless case, but the good are full of hope.

[1] The arguments in this and the preceding chapter will be found further developed in Part II. chap. xii.

PART II

REVEALED RELIGION

CHAPTER I

WHY RELIGION WAS REVEALED

ALL that we have shown so far about God and
His ways, we have learnt from looking into God's
works, within and without us—in other words,
from looking into Nature; and so the religion
we have at present learnt is known as Natural
Religion.

And I dare say you think that the conclusions
we have come to are also natural in another sense;
for they have nothing unnatural or unreasonable
about them; and you will be right in so considering them. Indeed, I should not be surprised
if you imagined, too, that what I have taught
you is so plain and so clear that it would be impossible for any men to come to any other conclusion about God and His ways than those which
we have arrived at.

I wish you were right in thinking so. I wish I
could tell you that all the world believes as you
believe, and that the "Natural Religion," which

you consider so very natural, was the religion of
the whole world.   I am sorry to say it is not.

Perhaps there might have been a time, when
the world was young, when all men's ideas about
religion were as pure and natural as your own.
Of this we cannot be sure ; for there is a great
uncertainty about all history, especially about the
early history of Man.   But this we know—that
before Man's world was very old there were all
sorts of religions, and that people were not satisfied with the simple and beautiful Natural Religion
—the religion taught by Nature—which declared
One only God to be the Creator of Heaven and
Earth.

How it all occurred no one can say with certainty.   But in course of time almost all men
worshipped idols, images of wood or metal or
stone, of their own making, or worshipped the
sun, or fire, or animals, instead of the Great and
Unseen God.

Perhaps it was because the Great God was unseen
that they at first made idols only to remind them
of Him.   Perhaps, when they at first worshipped
and bowed down to the sun, they thought they
were doing honour to God, its Creator.[1]   But, however that may be, in the course of time some
worshipped the sun as if it were their Creator,
and others bowed down to idols, the work of their
own hands, as if the idols had made them.   All

---

[1] The Parsees now worship God in this same manner, and
with the same idea.   The common notion that they are Sun-
worshippers is not true.

this is very curious—so curious that you will probably find it difficult to believe that people could have been so foolish ; but it is nevertheless true. You may see hundreds of those idols preserved in museums, some of wood, some of metal, and some of stone ; and there are learned people who could tell you much about each of those idols and the people who worshipped them ; and not the least wonderful fact about the matter is, that many of those who worshipped idols were very clever, and were only foolish in their religious belief and practices.

Now, if people simply believed in a foolish, unreasonable religion, and in other respects were good people, always doing right and acting justly, their foolish belief would, perhaps, do no great harm to any but themselves. But unfortunately it happened that idolatry, or the worship of idols, led to all sorts of wickedness.

I could not tell you a hundredth part of the dreadful sins that idolaters were guilty of ; but they often committed frightful crimes in the name of their religion, and did all sorts of wicked things, saying that their idols or gods bade them act thus. And, worst of all, they committed murder in the name of religion. The fire-worshippers, for example, used to sacrifice men and women and even children to their fire-god, burning them in fiery furnaces as offerings.[1] Captives of war, instead of being kindly treated or kept as slaves, were slain in like manner as offerings to the idols, and such

[1] Deut. xii. 31.

was sometimes the madness of idolaters that many
of them sacrificed their own lives or the lives of
their own dearest children to those idols they declared to be their gods. What folly to think that
this could please the Great Creator of Heaven and
Earth !

All this went on for very many years, for hundreds
of years. Religion ran wild in idolatry, and as the
religions of idolatry grew, all kinds of wickedness
grew, till at last the world became so wicked that
it could never have lasted in such a state.

But God ordained it otherwise. He could not
leave men to make their own religion, for the results had been too dreadful ; so God Himself had
to teach the religion that was true and good and
fit for mankind, not only to make known His own
existence, His own ways and works, but to make
known His Will, His Law, His code of right and
wrong. The making known or revealing to man
this knowledge is called *Revelation*.

CHAPTER II

REVELATION AND INSPIRATION

You will read in the Bible and in History how Religion was revealed.

It was not done in a moment. It was the slow work of many, many years. Perhaps that slow work is still proceeding, for God is always revealing Himself to us in many ways.

But, before I refer you to the Bible, I must say something about that wonderful Book. All who love it and estimate it at its true worth feel convinced that it *contains* the Word of God, and reveals to us His Will and purpose as no other book does.

You must bear in mind that this Bible, which we reverence so much, did not come into existence all at once, and did not drop from heaven as a beautifully printed and neatly bound volume, just as we see it now, but that it was composed by very many people at various times, extending over a period of at least eight hundred years; that much of its history—especially the earlier part— was at first not written at all, but was handed down from father to son for many generations by word of mouth, and that when at length it was written, it was committed to writing on bits of skin or on dried leaves of plants, some time after the events related were said to have taken place, and long after the words recorded were said to have been uttered.

Events and words handed down from mouth to mouth are called traditions, and we all know from experience how faulty such traditions may be, not from any wilful untruthfulness on the part of successive narrators, but from the errors that naturally creep into all stories and messages delivered by word of mouth.

We must always regard the Bible with the greatest reverence and love, for it is indeed our greatest treasure. But it is not our duty, because we reverence and love it, to treat it as an object of idolatry and adoration, as if every word in it were literally true, and as if every good character in it were so perfect as to be worthy of our imitation in every particular; for, indeed, the Bible itself does not overlook the failings of some of its greatest heroes.

But the Bible is, in all the most important points, a trustworthy guide to conduct, and it truly contains the Word of God; for it contains records of the most godly acts and thoughts of the most godly men, and these men were inspired by God to put those thoughts into noble words for the good of mankind.

And, truly, we may well ask ourselves how those words could have come without inspiration. Such noble thoughts and brilliant words as we find in the Pentateuch, in the Psalms, and in the

Prophets, spoken in barbarous times, thousands of years ago, by men who had not the education that we have, with scarcely a book to read, except the great book of Nature, could never have come into their minds unless inspired by God. And, indeed, their words and the form of their messages to us show that they themselves felt that God had breathed into their souls His Will and wishes, to be by them revealed to His World. Perhaps you will say—and rightly say—that such inspirations and revelations, so imparted to human minds, are as wonderful as any miracle described in any book.

I have said at the commencement of this chapter that God is always revealing Himself to us in many ways. The sun rises, and renews, day by day, the work of Creation, unfolding to our wondering gaze the beauties and bounties of Nature and the power and providence of God. To all of us who have eyes to see and hearts to understand, this is a Revelation. And so, too, in the spiritual world of Man, God reveals Himself continually, inspiring daily those of His servants who know Him best with new knowledge of Him and of His ways. The spirit of God breathes into the soul of man, and man to that extent partakes of God's essence ; that is, he obtains by God's grace an insight into His nature and demands. This is *Inspiration*. This is the mode and method whereby the Prophets of old learnt the Will of God as a new knowledge, and, with it, acquired the burning wish to impart it to their fellow-men as the gift of Heaven.

Such inspirations, varying, indeed, in nature,

degree, and importance, are within our own experience even in these our times. Those bright
ideas which are called original, coming into the
minds of men without apparent cause or origin,
are inspirations. The poet who dreams new and
brilliant thoughts, giving them to us in new and
starlike words, is inspired, and his inspiration comes
from a Source outside himself—from God. The
philanthropist, moved by the strong desire to work
the betterment of men's life and character, to
realise on earth some of the Divine ideals, derives
that loving impulse from a Source outside himself—from God. The inventor, who, struck with
a new idea that, brought into practice, makes the
world materially richer, can tell you nothing of
the birth and genesis of the idea. He is inspired,
and owes that new idea to a Source outside himself—to God. The philosopher, who, in his world
of imagination, builds up for us a new theory that,
applied to known facts, widens our range of
thought and knowledge, cannot trace the source
of his new idea. He too is inspired, and his
inspiration comes from God.

And so Revelation and Inspiration go on even
in these our times, whenever, indeed, the great
teachers of mankind—the poets, scientists, philosophers, and seers—inspired by the Immortal, All-
knowing God, have evolved new thoughts and
new or latent truths, which, like the Bible, will
be a precious heritage to us and to the world.

Who shall find words to say how precious a
heritage that Bible is ? It has given us our stan-

dard of Right and Justice. It has created for us a Law of Love and Mercy. It has taught us the language of Prayer. It has given us solace and hope in the centuries of our exile.

Now let us see what this Bible tells us of Revelation.

It tells us that God revealed Himself to Noah immediately after the flood, giving the world, through him, a few leading laws intended to prevent the repetition of those acts of violence which, before the flood, had disgraced the human race.[1]

The Bible tells us, further, that God revealed Himself to Abraham, the son of Terah, an idolater ; that He bade him leave his native land and travel in distant countries, and assured him that through him all the nations of the earth should be blessed. And, wherever he went, Abraham proclaimed the Name of the True God, and by his noble example of goodness, kindness, virtue, and unselfishness, he indicated to those with whom he came in touch that his religion must be the true one, and that his God must be the One and only True God.

You will read for yourselves in your Bible all the events of the life of Abraham, and you can also read many beautiful stories about him, translated from the Talmud ; and you will then not be surprised to hear that, according to tradition. Abraham made many converts to his belief.

Abraham had several sons, one of whom—Isaac —was alone considered worthy to succeed him in

---

[1] Gen. vi. 11.

his mission. He too travelled from place to place, and the Bible gives us in the details of his life pleasing glimpses of his character, telling us, too, that God renewed to him the covenant made with Abraham, and that he, like his father, " called upon the name of the Lord."

Of Isaac's two sons, the younger, Jacob, was considered, notwithstanding many faults, worthy to follow his father in his task of improving the world. He too became a wanderer, and probably he too made known the One True God, wherever he dwelt.

The Bible tells the eventful history of Jacob in terms so beautiful and so graphic that you will read it with the greatest interest. It truthfully tells of all his faults and failings. But in spite of these, it shows Jacob to have been a noble example of patient perseverance, and trustful confidence in the goodness and power of God. How he served faithfully for many long years as a humble shepherd ; how in time he was blessed with large possessions and a numerous family ; how he returned to his native land a wealthy prince ; how he lost his favourite son Joseph, and, after the lapse of long years, again found him, become, by a wonderful course of events, the greatest man in all Egypt, who had under God's wise providence saved that country from the effects of a terrible famine, and how he and all his children and grand-children—seventy souls—went down to Egypt and settled there : all this you will read for yourselves in the Bible, and you will find the history more stirring and marvellous than any tale you ever read.

Jacob died, and so too, after many years of prosperity, did his son Joseph, and all his other sons. While they lived they and their descendants were loved and respected by the Egyptians; but when they died, the great good which Joseph had worked for Egypt was soon forgotten. A new king arose who knew not Joseph, and all the Israelites, descendants of Jacob, were cruelly treated.

For they were too prosperous. They increased in numbers; and this increase alarmed the Egyptians,[1] who could feel no sympathy for a strange nation having a religion differing from their own. For the religion of the Egyptians was most peculiar. They worshipped living animals—birds, beasts, and reptiles. This is difficult to believe, but their own records establish the fact beyond a doubt; and those same records show, curiously enough, that while practising all the follies of idolatry, they were wiser in science and in the arts than any people of that age.

For a long time, the Israelites were oppressed by the Egyptians, used as slaves, persecuted, overworked, and tormented; but in spite of all this ill-treatment, they did not join in the idolatry of Egypt; they remained steadfast to their religion; and, when they suffered, they cried to the Lord God of their fathers, the One True God, whom they had been taught to regard as the sole Creator and Ruler of the Universe.

[1] Exod. i. 9, 10.

Their cry was heard. For Moses was sent to them to deliver them from the oppression of the Egyptians ; and it was the same Moses who was also to be the instrument of God's revelation to Israel, the man who was to make known God's law to His people, and through them to the whole of mankind.

The Bible tells you much about the early history of Moses : how he was, as an infant, preserved from drowning ; how he was brought up at the court of Pharaoh, the King of Egypt, by the king's own daughter ; how he went out among his suffering brethren and pitied them ; how he protected the weak against the strong ; how God inspired him with his life-mission, to be the herald of His Sacred Name, and the deliverer of his people ; and how He endowed him with the power of influencing his fellow Israelites, so that they came to regard him as the messenger of God and as their leader, endowed by God with power to lead them and to teach them.

You will read in the Bible how, in all things, Moses followed the inspiration of God, and how in all difficulties he appealed to the Divine Help ; how he communicated his message of deliverance to his brethren ; how he begged Pharaoh often, but in vain, to allow the Israelites to leave Egypt ; how the wicked king afflicted the Israelites more and more ; how Moses forewarned him of the anger of God, and how Pharaoh persisted in his wicked cruelty ; how ten terrible plagues were sent in succession to punish the king and his people, and how at length on the night of the tenth plague, which brought death to the first-born of Pharaoh and of all his subjects, the children of Israel were allowed by their panic-stricken oppressor to pass out from the cities of the Egyptians, to breathe for the first time the air of freedom.

The narrative proceeds to tell us how their oppressor soon relented, and, finding his victims vanished, how he pursued them with all his hosts of horsemen and foot-soldiers, overtaking them on the brink of the Red Sea ; [1] how behind them the Israelites beheld the teeming hosts of their cruel enemy ready to destroy them or lead them back into slavery, and before them the cruel sea ready to engulf them ; how, suddenly, the waters of the Gulf were driven by a high wind from their bed, permitting the Israelites to pass across on the sandy bed of the Bay, and to reach the opposite shore ; how the Egyptians followed in pursuit, and how, before they could reach the eastern shore, the wind dropped and the waters returned to their place, so that Pharaoh's mighty hosts perished in the rolling waves.

The Bible describes in graphic terms the effect of this unexpected deliverance on the minds of the rescued Israelites, and tells us that when " Israel saw the Egyptians dead upon the sea-shore . . . the people feared the Lord, and believed in the Lord and His servant Moses." The narrative then tells us how Moses led the Israelites from the banks of the Red Sea into the wilderness of Arabia ; how

[1] At the north-western gulf now known as the Gulf of Suez.

they were guided by a pillar of cloud by day, and by a pillar of fire by night; and how their daily wants were supplied by an unseen Hand without work or effort of their own; and how at length they came to the mountain of Sinai, with hearts full of gratitude to God for their marvellous escape from destruction and for their wonderful mainten-ance in the desert, ready and anxious to listen to all that Moses, the messenger of God, might tell them, and to obey His mandates with implicit faith.

The story proceeds to relate that at this point God called to Moses and bade him prepare the people for their mission. He was to tell them: " If ye will obey My voice, indeed, and keep My covenant, then ye shall be a peculiar treasure unto Me above all people, for all the earth is Mine. And ye shall be unto Me a kingdom of priests, and an holy nation. . . . And all the people answered together, and said : All that the Lord hath spoken we will do."

And then comes the climax of the narrative. It tells how, after three days' preparation, the people were summoned to assemble at the foot of Mount Sinai, which was blazing and smoking like a volcano; and that Moses, amid the sound of trumpets, ascended the mount, and there received from God the Words which he was to convey to the children of Israel—the Ten Commandments, of which the next chapter treats.

You must read for yourselves the narrative itself, which depicts a most majestic and awe-inspiring scene, and one which we, with our modern ideas

as to miracles, find hard to realise as fact. For
most intelligent men now find that miracle—the
deviation from the ordinary course of Nature—is
not only incredible, but rather derogatory to the
dignity of the Creator, who, under the light shed
by modern science, appears to rule His Universe
under the unswerving sway of Laws which never
change.[1] Yet there are many who, firm in the
old belief in the truth of every word of Scripture,
fully believe in the miraculous details of Revelation,
and of the long chain of miracles that led thereto,
as recorded in the Book of Exodus. Certain it is
that the good men who first related that miraculous
history to their children, and the equally good men
who set the history in written words, did believe in
their reality. To them it seemed reasonable that
the same God who made the world, and who has
boundless power, could, if He so willed it, for
some special purpose alter or suspend for a time
the established order of His Creation.

The story of Revelation as recorded in our Bible
is, therefore, one which, whatever may be your
opinion or mine, should be ever regarded with all
reverence and respect. It forms a noble setting for
an unique gem, and though, under the critical
touchstone of Truth, that setting may not be all
genuine ore, it owns a long history of trustful faith

[1] " We are wont, though not when at our best, to lament that
miracle is dead and prophecy silent. We ought rather to rejoice
that we too live in an age of revelation, when in the sublimest
majesty of self-manifestation, God is laying bare His ways to
the reverent scrutiny of man."—BEARD, *Hibbert Lectures*, xii.
(1883).

on the part of our forefathers, who honestly believed it all, and who were never harmed, but perhaps rather fortified, by that belief.

I have told you of the other, and more modern, view of Revelation as an effect of Inspiration into the souls of the best and wisest. That view is easier to accept, because, such inspirations coming within our modern experiences, it is far more credible, though it should be as great a subject of marvel as any miracle. There is, indeed, room in the world for both beliefs, for the minds of men are differently constituted, just as are their bodies; and while some are ready to accept any doctrine presented by authority, others accept only such as are consonant with reason and experience. Modern Judaism finds no merit in blind Faith, involving the abdication of Reason, and refuses to denounce the honest doubter as a heretic.

And, in truth, it matters little by what means Revelation came to us, whether by a Voice thundered from Sinai, or by a still small voice whispered into the ears of a Prophet, or by a voiceless inspiration into the soul of a Seer. The Revelation is ours, our heritage for ever. And we must ever cherish the " Law of Moses," the Prophets, and the Sacred Writings as containing treasures beyond price. For, however the truths they contain were revealed to us, our fathers lived under their guidance, believing them to be the revealed will of God. They not only lived, but died for them. Our Bible, therefore, comes to us not merely as containing the revealed will of our Creator, and sacred as such, but further

sanctified by the fervid obedience and willing sacrifice of our ancestors for many centuries.

And when we study the Bible, it should always
speak to us as containing the Word and Voice of
the Living God, summoning us to be a kingdom of
priests in His service—that is, devoted to Him and
to mankind. For all mankind are His children ;
and when we serve His children, we serve Him
best.

CHAPTER III

THE TEN COMMANDMENTS

1. I am the Lord thy God, who brought thee out of the land of Egypt, out of the house of bondage.

2. Thou shalt have no other gods before me. Thou shalt not make unto thee any graven image, nor any likeness of any thing that is in heaven above, or that is in the earth beneath, or that is in the water under the earth. Thou shalt not bow down thyself to them, nor serve them; for I the Lord thy God am a jealous God, visiting the iniquity of the fathers upon the children unto the third and fourth generation, to them that hate me: and shewing mercy unto the thousandth generation, to them that love me and keep my commandments.

3. Thou shalt not take the name of the Lord thy God in vain; for the Lord will not hold him guiltless that taketh his name in vain.

4. Remember the sabbath day to keep it holy. Six days shalt thou labour, and do all thy work: but the seventh day is a sabbath of the Lord thy God: thereon thou shalt not do any work, thou, nor thy son, nor thy daughter, thy man-servant, nor thy maid-servant, nor thy cattle, nor thy stranger that is within thy gates: for in six days the Lord made heaven and earth, the sea, and all that in them is, and rested on the seventh day: wherefore the Lord blessed the sabbath day, and hallowed it.

5. Honour thy father and thy mother; that thy days may be long upon the land which the Lord thy God giveth thee.

6. Thou shalt not murder.

7. Thou shalt not commit adultery.

8. Thou shalt not steal.

9. Thou shalt not bear false witness against thy neighbour

10. Thou shalt not covet thy neighbour's house, thou shalt not covet thy neighbour's wife, nor his man-servant, nor his maid-servant, nor his ox, nor his ass, nor any thing that is thy neighbour's.—Exod. xx.

When children are young, their wise parents do not teach them too many things as first, lest they might forget them ; but they tell them first the few things which are the most important, and as they get older, they go on teaching them more and more, little by little.

And Moses treated the children of Israel in the same wise way. He did not tell them all the Law at once, but began with the Ten Commandments, because, although the most important, they were quite easy and simple, and able to be understood and obeyed by every one. And that is the reason why I have quoted them in full.

The First Commandment

You will notice that the Commandments begin by telling the Israelites that the words come from the same God who had saved them from the Egyptians. They might have said that this was the God who had created them and all the world. But the people could not have understood that half so well as the great fact, which they themselves had so lately experienced—that He was the God who had saved them from slavery, and that He alone was to be the Lord their God.

The Second Commandment

In the Second Commandment you will find that the Israelites are told that they shall have no other

God but Him ; that they shall make no idols, nor
bow down to images.   And then they are told
something about God Himself ; that He is a just
God who punishes the wicked people and such of
their children as hate Him, and that He is also
a merciful God, who is good and kind to all who
love Him and obey His laws.

Now, if you are asked what is the chief difference
between Jews and other people, you might safely
say, that the Jews believe and obey all that is in
the Second Commandment, but that members of
most other faiths do not, although perhaps they
fancy they do.   For the followers of various other
religions believe that there is somebody besides God
who saves sinners from punishment.   But we are
told in this Second Commandment that God is the
only God, that there is none beside Him, that it
is He alone who visits or punishes iniquity and
sin, that we have to answer to Him for our actions,
good or bad, and that to Him alone we must look
for mercy.[1]

And so we have in these first two Commandments the main principles or chief points of our
belief—that the God who gave us the Law is the
One and only God, who will requite us according
to our works.[2]

[1] We find the same declaration in Deut. xxxii. 39 : " See now
that I, even I, am He, and there is no god with me : I kill, and
I make alive ; I wound, and I heal : neither is there any that
can deliver out of My hand."

[2] The Jewish Creed may be reduced to these three principles :
(1) THAT GOD IS ONE ; (2) THAT HE REVEALS HIS WILL TO
MAN ; (3) THAT HE WILL RECOMPENSE MEN ACCORDING TO THEIR
DESERTS, THOUGH HIS MERCY IS SHOWN UNTO ALL.

The Third Commandment

The Third Commandment forbids us to swear falsely; forbids us indeed to swear at all, unless it be necessary to do so in the interest of truth.

In courts of law people who give evidence, or tell all that they know of the matters inquired about, have to promise to speak the truth, and they call God to witness that every word they are about to speak is true. This is called swearing, or taking an oath. If, after taking the oath, they say anything untrue, they are guilty of perjury or false swearing.

People must never swear except when ordered to do so by law. If they swear without it being necessary, they take the name of God in vain; and God will consider them guilty.

An oath is a very sacred thing, and if you ever go into a court of law, you will see how important it is, where all sorts of weighty matters—often matters of life and death—are in question, that witnesses, or persons who give evidence, should speak the exact truth. And so, in this country, they have to promise to speak " the truth, the whole truth, and nothing but the truth," and it is customary then to kiss the Bible to show that they believe in the God of the Bible, and that they know and feel that He hears all that they say, and that they believe that He will not hold them guiltless if they say anything untrue, and so take His name in vain. I shall tell you more about this, when we come to the Ninth Commandment.

F

But taking the name of the Lord God in vain has yet another meaning. If we pray to God without thinking about what we are saying; or if we pray in a hurried, careless manner, only anxious to get through our prayers, or if we laugh or gossip in synagogue, we take God's name in vain.

Children, and indeed grown-up people too, often get into a bad and foolish habit of " saying their prayers " instead of praying. If you beg your parents to do you some favour, you will speak to them in an earnest, careful manner, and will not stare about you while you are addressing them. And if you caress them, and tell them how much you love them and how dutiful and obedient you will be to them, you will speak to them as if you meant it, and will not be thinking of something else while you are talking to them. But people who ask favours of God, and who address Him in words of praise and thanksgiving, often let their words fall from their lips without thinking of what they are saying, or of the meaning of the words they utter, but think meantime of all sorts of other things. This is *saying prayers*, not *praying*. This is taking God's name in vain. And we are told that He will not hold us guiltless, if we thus pray without turning our thoughts to Him.

The Fourth Commandment

The Fourth Commandment is a very long one ; but you will know almost all about it without my telling you.

You who have lessons all the week will no doubt

think this a very pleasant commandment, and one very easy to obey; and perhaps you will think that God need only have ordered the Israelites to rest on the seventh day without giving such a long commandment, and going into so many particulars.

You know how pleased you always are when the Sabbath comes, and what a treat it is to have no lessons to learn for a whole day, and how glad you are to see your parents with you all the Sabbath, doing all they can to make you happy; taking you with them to synagogue to hear the prayers and the singing; taking you with them afterwards for a nice walk and a pleasant talk, and not troubling you at all about lessons or books, except just a little piece of the Bible or a short Bible story, which you like too much to call a lesson, and which you would not miss for the world.

And I dare say you will wonder very much when I tell you that plenty of people break this law, and keep no Sabbath, but go on, by their own free will, week after week, working, and working, and working, without having any day of rest. And perhaps, when I tell you this, you will exclaim, " Poor people, how I do pity them ! " Well, there really may be some people who cannot avoid working on the Sabbath; there are, however, others who are not workers by necessity, but who think that if they stop working on Sabbath, they will lose the chance of gaining a little more, and they either forget or will not remember that they are disobeying God.

Now, in the Fourth Commandment we are told very plainly that we must and ought to be industrious, and do all our work on six days of the week ; but that the seventh is the Sabbath or day of rest, and that neither we nor our servants, nor even our cattle, should do thereon any sort of work.   In the version of the Ten Commandments found in the fifth chapter of Deuteronomy, we are exhorted to remember the terrible servitude that our ancestors suffered when they were slaves in Egypt, to be therefore kind to the servants, strangers, and cattle who work for us, and to let them enjoy the day of rest as we ourselves do.

If you will just think a little about the wonderful world and the creatures in it, I fancy it will strike you, as it has often struck me too, that the most wonderful thing in all God's creation is —Rest.

The world is so full of life and work and movement, that we are apt to forget how great a blessing and how great a wonder is *rest*.   You, young people, who revel in your sports, whose joyous spirits find their vent in merry laughter, while you run or leap or vault as if your legs were made of springs (as indeed they are to some extent), what would you be, I wonder, without rest ? How do you think you would get on, if, when tired out, you were to lie down and be unable to sleep, or if, when dreadfully fatigued, some cruel person were to come and tell you you must go on playing or running or jumping, whether you liked it or not ?   Do you think you would enjoy it, when tired out and ready for a nice refreshing sleep ? I think not.

And is it not wonderful how, without any trying, you go to sleep ? and how you wake up, feeling so fresh and vigorous and ready for fun, just as if you had never been fatigued in your life ? or how, after a long tiring walk, you sit down and rest, and then feel quite strong again and ready for another long walk ? Ah, rest is a wonderful thing —perhaps, next to work, the greatest blessing in the world—so you need not wonder that God should have blessed the Day of Rest and made it holy.

But if you, who only have to learn lessons or do needlework, and do no very hard work with your head or your hands, find rest so pleasant and so good for you, how must it be with grown-up people, who have to work hard for their living all the week ? How delighted they ought to be when Friday evening comes, and they feel that they need not, cannot, and dare not do any more work for a whole day ! Not only do they enjoy the rest for which they have worked so hard, but when the time comes for them to set to work again, they enjoy their work all the more, just as you feel all the more inclined for a good romp after you have awoke from a sound sleep. It is a splendid thing—this Sabbath—which God has given us as a holy day of rest, and you may feel quite sure that those who do not keep the Sabbath do not half enjoy their lives.

Now, most religions besides ours have a Sabbath ; although, as you know, some keep it on a different day ; but they do not keep the Sabbath as we do : and I dare say you will ask how we ought to keep it.

You might be inclined to say that, as it is a day of rest, people should lie in bed all Sabbath, and so have a long day of idleness. But if you look at the Fourth Commandment you will find that the seventh day is called the " Sabbath of the Lord thy God," also that God blessed the Sabbath day and hallowed it, or made it a holy day. Now, this shows that we ought to spend at least some part of the Sabbath in the service of God, in reflecting about Him and His wonderful works, in praising and thanking Him for His goodness, in thinking about our position as His creatures, and in trying to do acts of kindness to others. And this being a day on which we have no lessons or business to do, we have plenty of time to examine ourselves, and ask ourselves whether we have done right during the past week, and, if not, how we can do better next week.

But you must not for one moment imagine that God's Sabbath is to be, as some of our neighbours make it, a sad day, on which you may not laugh, or be merry, or read pleasant books. Judaism is a happy religion and a natural one, and you are meant to be happy and natural on the Sabbath day. When you have done the duties I have mentioned, you may amuse yourselves much as you like. Only there are things which you may not do, even though they be for enjoyment. I allude to burdensome work involving heavy exertion, and especially to labour of the same kind as that which is done on the working days, for the main idea is relaxation from ordinary duties. Nor may you use horses or cattle for work on the Sabbath, because God, mindful alike of all His creatures, and wishing that man should be merciful to the poor dumb beasts, commanded that they should also have a day of rest. But putting aside all these things, there are plenty of pleasures left to you for the Sabbath, and it must be not only a day of rest and quiet thought, but a day of joy and gladness.

The Fifth Commandment

I once heard a little girl say that God need not have troubled Himself to give the Fifth Commandment at all; and when I asked her why, she said she could not imagine any people who did not honour and love and obey their father and mother.

I wish this little girl was right. But unfortunately there are many children, and many grown-up people too, who are apt to disobey this simple commandment.

To honour one's parents means much more than merely paying them respect. It means that we must do willingly whatever they tell us, and even without asking why. It means that we must follow their good advice. It means that we must tend them lovingly when they grow old or ill or infirm, as lovingly as they tended us when we were young and helpless. It means that we must bear in mind their wishes when we are away from them, and even long after they are dead. It means that we must never do anything to dishonour their good name.

And we are told that if we obey this command, our days shall be long in the land that God giveth us.

The Sixth Commandment

"Thou shalt not murder" is one of the most important laws in the Bible. It was not a new law in the time of Moses. The same law was given to Noah when he and his family came out of the ark.

Obedience to this law makes the great difference between barbarous and civilised men. Among barbarians, life is never safe. One man hates another or envies his property, and he thinks nothing of killing him, if he be the stronger man. But an end to the reign of "might against right" came when it was declared, "Thou shalt not murder;" and even earlier still, when Noah was told, "Whoso sheddeth man's blood, by man shall his blood be shed." Human life was to be sacred, it being the great gift of God. We are to do all in our power to protect and save life. We may not stand by quietly and see a fellow-being perish if we can assist him. Our wise men remind us that as we are all descended from one man, Adam, he who saves a single life is as if he had created a world.[1] So when you read this commandment, you must not think that it does not apply to such

[1] *Sanhedrin,* iv. 5. Mahomet adopted this idea in these words : " Whoso kills a soul unless it be for another soul, or

as you, to whom the horrid thought of murdering a fellow-creature would never occur ; but you must remember, too, that it bids you assist your poor and suffering fellow-creatures, and do all that is in your power to help them to live.

You will find in the Mosaic Code very many other laws, having for their chief object the protection of human life ; such, for example, as the laws relating to dangerous animals,[1] the commandment to build battlements or parapets on the house-tops, lest persons might fall therefrom and be killed,[2] and the laws of the cities of refuge,[3] which were intended to shelter those who had by accident killed a fellow-creature.

The Seventh Commandment

This commandment forbids husbands and wives to be unfaithful, or untrue, or unkind to one another ; and the importance of this you will understand better as you advance in age.

The Eighth Commandment

This law is a very short one ; but it tells us a great deal in a few words. There are unfortunately a great number of people who steal rather than work for a living. If they are found out, they are sent to prison, or otherwise punished ; and you will probably be surprised to hear that there are people who have actually spent the greater

for violence in the land, it is as though he had killed men altogether, but whoso saves one, it is as though he saved men altogether " (*Sura,* v. 35).

[1] Exod. xxi. 28.　　[2] Deut. xxii. 8.　　[3] Deut. xix. 1–10.

part of their lives in prison, having been so often found guilty of theft. Perhaps they have been the children of bad, dishonest parents, and have seen all sorts of wickedness in their young days. Not that this excuses them; but it accounts for their wickedness, which to you would otherwise appear hardly comprehensible.

Now you, and children like you, who have been well and carefully brought up, would feel horrified at the idea of stealing even the most trifling article ; and I am sure, when you grow up, you will feel just as horrified at the notion of taking anything that belongs to any one else. But I ought to tell you that there is a good deal of stealing done in an indirect or roundabout way, but which is none the less a crime because the law cannot touch it so easily. I mean dishonest dealing and deceitful trading.

If a shopkeeper tells a customer a lie about some article he is selling, intending him to think it more valuable than it is ; or if a servant wastes his master's time or property ; or if a man borrows money which he knows he cannot repay ; or if he sells a faulty article, charging the price of a perfect one ; or if a tradesman sells short weight or adulterated goods ; or if he buys property which he knows, or suspects, has been stolen—all these are dishonest dealings, and are offences against the law, " Thou shalt not steal," quite as much as stealing a piece of money directly from a neighbour's pocket.

I told you that the *protection of human life* was one of the greatest marks of distinction between

savages and civilised men. The *protection of property* is another such mark of distinction. If property were not safe, no one would care to work
hard to make money or amass wealth ; and people
would only care to work enough for their use from
day to day, lest some one stronger than they should
come directly they had saved a little, and rob them
of all they had saved. Saving, or " thrift," as it
is called, is of great importance to the welfare of
the world ; for without thrift in good times, we
might starve when the bad times come. And
indeed this really happens in barbarous countries
even in our own days. Property not being safe
against thieves, the people do not care to save,
but eat and use all that they produce. When a
bad harvest comes, they have saved nothing, and
they starve to death. So you see the importance
of thrift ; and as thrift cannot exist unless property is safe, you see also the importance of the
law, " Thou shalt not steal."

Other parts of the Law of Moses contain commandments on the same subject, and give us particulars of the punishment of theft. In Leviticus,[1]
and Deuteronomy,[2] we are commanded to be just
in business matters, and to give full weight and
true measure. A thief, if the article stolen were
found with him, had to pay twice the value of
what he had taken ; and if he stole a living animal,
and slew it, he had to " restore five oxen for the
ox, and four sheep for the sheep." [3] If he had not

[1] Lev. xix. 35, 36.   [2] Deut. xxv. 13, 14, 15.
[3] Exod. xxii. 1, 9.

the means of paying, he was sold as a slave,[1] and this was the origin of what we now call " penal servitude," *i.e.* imprisonment for a certain term of years, with hard labour.[2]

The Ninth Commandment

You know already something about the Ninth Commandment—" Thou shalt not bear false witness against thy neighbour "—because, in telling you about the Third Commandment, I told you what a witness is, and what perjury, or false swearing, means.

The worst of all perjury is that in which a man bears false witness, or gives untrue evidence against his fellow-man.   It is a crime terrible

---

[1] Exod. xxii. 3.

[2] To the Israelites, the law " Thou shalt not steal " must have been truly needed after their long sojourn in Egypt.   For in Egypt, theft was not only unpunished, but was legally sanctioned within certain limits.   Diodorus Siculus tells us " It was ordained that those who practised the avocation of thief should inscribe their names with the president of the thieves. If they stole anything, they had at once to declare what they had done, and to show him their booty.   The robbed person was then required to send to the president of the thieves a written statement of all the things he had missed, and mention place, day, and hour of their disappearance.   In this way everything was easily found, and the robbed person received his lost property on paying a fourth of its value.   As it was impossible to prevent theft entirely, the law thus invented a means of getting back what was stolen in return for a certain redemption-money which was willingly paid."

Lane asserts that the Egyptian law has survived to modern times ; and Ebers tells us that it is " an institution which existed in Cairo not long since, and in which, as we know from the best sources, many still living Cairenes took part."

enough when his false evidence is likely to deprive another of his rights, or of his property ; but it is a thousand times worse when his false evidence is intended to deprive another of his character, or his liberty, or perhaps his life.

I have told you of the form of oath used in this country. When the Jews lived in their own country, in Palestine, and a witness gave evidence affecting the life of a prisoner, the Judges reminded the witness of the duty of speaking the exact truth, and told him that he who destroyed one single human life was as guilty as if he had destroyed a whole world.[1]

It is almost impossible to imagine any one guilty of so terrible a sin as bearing false witness against another ; and yet there have been many such cases, and not a few, too, in which people have even been condemned to death upon evidence falsely given.

In another part of the Law,[2] the punishment of the perjurer is ordained. He is to suffer the same punishment as the intended victim would have suffered, if the perjurer's evidence had held good : " If the witness be a false witness, and has testified falsely against his brother, then you shall do unto him as he had thought to have done unto his brother."

But, although you may find it difficult to imagine any one wicked enough to bear false witness against his neighbour in a court of justice, you will have less difficulty in imagining people wicked enough

[1] *Cf.* p. 88 above.   [2] Deut. xix. 18, 19.

to transgress this law in other places. Indeed, when you reflect a little, you will call to mind that bearing false witness against a neighbour is rather a common, everyday sin.

When you hear children speaking against one another, making much of their playmates' little faults, or taking away their schoolfellows' characters, although they are not perjurers, yet they bear false witness against their neighbours. As you grow older, you will find that nothing is more valuable to any one than a good *character*, or what is often called *reputation*. And yet nothing is so easily injured by a chance word, perhaps carelessly or thoughtlessly dropped. Gossips, who are too idle to work, are never too idle to talk, and they dearly love a little scandal about their neighbours. They mean it to be harmless enough, and have, perhaps, no notion of hurting any one ; but the harmless scandal, every time it is repeated, becomes greater and greater, exaggerated each time it is spoken, till at last it is by no means harmless ; for it destroys a good character.

It is always a safe rule never to speak ill of any one. People will often call you dull and stupid if you refuse to join them in talking scandal and laughing away the characters of their neighbours. But you must not mind that. The people who are really dull and stupid are those who have nothing sensible and amiable to talk about, and who talk scandal because there is nothing else in their silly heads.

The Tenth Commandment

A great deal might be written about the Tenth Commandment ; for covetousness is the root of almost every sin.

We are ordered not to covet anything that is our neighbour's ; and many people have thought this rather an unreasonable law, because they have not understood it properly. They say : Why should not a man be ambitious, and like to have things as good as his neighbour has ? If his neighbour has a nice house or a nice ox, why should it be a sin for him to say, " I wish that house were mine ! " or, " I wish that ox were mine ! " ?

Now, if he were to say, " I wish I had a house like his ! " or, " I wish I had an ox like his ! " he would be doing no great harm ; because, although it is always well to be happy with what one has, there is nothing to prevent a man working hard and earning money ; and, when he has earned enough, he may buy or build a house exactly like his neighbour's house ; and there are oxen enough in the world, so that he can buy quite as fine an ox as his neighbour has. The sin of coveting, then, consists not in your wishing for a *similar* article, but for the *same* article that your neighbour has. His house, for example, could not be yours unless you somehow dispossessed him of it, and in order to do this, you might be induced to do him some wrong.

If you read the history of King Ahab, you will

find that this was the sort of covetousness that led him and his wife to commit a terrible sin. He coveted the vineyard of Naboth ; and because Naboth would not sell it to him, the King's wife, Jezebel, procured some wicked men to give false evidence to the effect that Naboth had committed a fearful crime against God, and the poor man was stoned to death ; and then Ahab took possession of the vineyard he had so longed for.

Ahab and Jezebel were both very wicked : so you are, perhaps, not much surprised at their being covetous. But, when you read the Bible, you will find that even the great and good King David, in a moment of blind passion, committed a terrible sin, almost if not quite equal to murder, through coveting his neighbour's wife, and that he was fearfully punished in consequence.

So you see what covetousness may lead men to. Understand, there is no harm in being ambitious —that is, in wanting to improve our position, to grow greater, or richer, or more comfortable, and to have nice things about us. The harm is in letting the ambition become a passion, and letting the passion so get the better of us, that we do not mind what we do so long as we get what we want.

It is always best to be contented ; but if you are ambitious, there is one way of checking ambition so as to prevent it becoming a passion. While you are trying your best to grow rich, you should try at the same time—and still harder— to grow wiser, and more learned, and more pious ; and if your wisdom and knowledge and goodness grow as your riches grow, your riches will do you no harm. Then your ambition for wealth, position, or comfort will never lead you to covet anything that is your neighbour's. You will earn your money honourably, and perhaps become as well off as your neighbour, without wishing him or doing him any harm. You will spend your money well and wisely; for your great ambition will be to do to your fellow-creatures, who are less fortunate than you, all the good that is possible with the means with which God has blessed you.

But in all your efforts, you will never covet what is your neighbour's. Murder and war (war being, in fact, murder on the largest scale), theft and overreaching—and, indeed, almost every evil done by man—would vanish if people would only obey the Tenth Commandment.

CHAPTER IV

ABOUT THE LAW OF MOSES

You will read in the Bible that when the children of Israel heard the Ten Commandments, when they perceived " the thunderings and the lightnings and the noise of the trumpets and the mountains smoking," overcome by fear, they removed and stood afar off ; that they begged Moses to go near and listen to all that God had to order them, and promised him, that if he would tell them the commands of God, they would obey in all things.

And the Bible describes how " the people stood afar off ; " how " Moses drew near unto the thick darkness where God was," and how God said to him, " I will speak unto thee all the commandments and the statutes, and the judgments which thou shalt teach them." And thus it happens that the Law which God gave to our forefathers is called the " Law of Moses," or the " Mosaic Code," because the Bible tells us that, after the Ten Commandments had been given, God gave the other laws to Moses, who taught them to the people, through the chiefs of the tribes and the wise men, during the forty years' wanderings in the wilderness.

These laws are not stated to have been given to Moses all at once, but at different times, and as occasion required ; and when the forty years' wanderings were over, and Moses was about to die, he repeated in the Book called Deuteronomy (or the Second Law) the most important of them, and also added some which, for various reasons, had not been mentioned before. And, besides these, he gave to the Israelites a series of addresses and warnings full of sound advice, just such as a dying father might give to his beloved children.

It thus happens that the various laws are spread about the Books of Exodus, Leviticus, Numbers, and Deuteronomy, mixed up with the history of the wanderings, and with the events which appear to have given rise to many of those laws ; and, surely, no better way could have been found of teaching a people so many laws than by giving them a few at a time, and putting them in practice as they were given.

For you must remember that in those times— thousands of years before printing was invented— the Israelites could not each have, as we have, a neat little book containing all the laws of God ; so the laws had to be so taught as to be well kept in memory, and there is no better way of remembering things than by practising them.[1]

[1] It is right to add that many learned critics consider that the Mosaic Code was not all produced between the departure from Egypt and the entry into Palestine, but that it was the result of the labours of many legislators spread over many centuries, and codified only about the time of Ezra. With our view of Inspiration, as the basis of Revelation, it matters little whether there were many inspired legislators or only one— Moses. The Unity of Design that is seen throughout the Code shows its several laws to have been inspired by One Supreme Mind—the Mind of God.

You will find also some of the laws in the first Book—the Book of Genesis—laws which were given to the patriarchs Noah and Abraham, and these too are embodied with the laws given to the Israelites by Moses, and so the whole five books, Genesis, Exodus, Leviticus, Numbers, and Deuteronomy, are together called the *Torah* (תּוֹרָה), or Law ; not that these books are all law-books, for indeed they are history and law combined—the word *Torah* (תּוֹרָה) meaning much more than " law," for it means instruction,[1] or what we now call education.

So when you read the Pentateuch,[2] or Five Books of Moses, you must not be surprised to find that the laws are not arranged, like Acts of Parliament, in a Statute Book, one after the other, in what you would call systematic order ; and still, if you read carefully, you will find that there is, after all, a certain amount of system or regularity in their arrangement, and that though the history and the laws appear mixed up together, there is good reason for it, there being usually some connection between any one piece of the history and the series of laws which are next to it. You will also find that in Deuteronomy, the wording of some of the laws differs slightly from that of the other Books, as if to show us that we are not to slavishly follow the *words* of the Law, but to act upon their clear *intention* and *spirit*.

I do not propose to tell you all the laws of the

---

[1] The word *Torah* תּוֹרָה is derived from the verb יָרָה, one form of which means " to teach."

[2] Pentateuch—a Greek word which means Five Books.

Mosaic Code. If I did, I should perhaps tire you ;
for there are 613 laws, and you could not be expected to remember so many.

What I wish to do is, to tell you something about
the principal laws, just as I have already done as
regards the Ten Commandments, so that when you
read the Bible for yourselves, you will be able
better to understand their meaning.

But, before commencing, I ought to point out
one thing, which I have already hinted at, and
which you must always bear in mind, when you
read about the Law of Moses. It is this—that the
Israelites to whom the Law was given were meant
to be distinguished from all the rest of the world ;
they were meant, as I have already told you, to be
" a kingdom of priests, a holy nation." They were
to be a pattern of goodness and virtue for all the
nations of the earth, and it was with that intention
that God inspired Moses with His Law.

When you come to the end of Deuteronomy, you
will probably say, " Surely it was not intended that
all the world should obey all these laws ! " and you
would be right. But it was intended that the
Israelites to whom they were given should obey
them ; for Moses had told them that God had set
them apart to be a peculiar people, to be His own
chosen nation, so that all the world should look up
to them as examples. For this reason he told
them that they should be holy, since the Lord their
God was Holy. For this reason he told them to set
aside the evil customs they had learnt in Egypt,
and to follow only the customs which he taught

them ; not to adopt the laws of the nations among whom they were about to dwell, but to follow only the Law revealed to him by God, different from any law which up to that time had existed.

When you read ancient history, you will find how different this Law was. You will find that the laws and the customs which existed among the ancient pagan nations were terribly cruel, and in many respects terribly wicked. Those laws were the laws of "might against right." The slave, for example, had no rights—not even the right to live, if his master wished him to die. The creditor had full power over the life of his unfortunate debtor. The helpless had no protection for their lives ; for old people who were past work were put to death ; and little babies who were delicate at birth were exposed to cold and hunger, and thus neglected till they died. You will be shocked, indeed, when you learn how cruel were the nations of ancient times, and what wickedness was sanctioned by their laws.

So you see how necessary it was that, besides a model religion, there should be a code—a complete set of representative or typical laws—which should be followed by a model nation, and form, in outline at least, a pattern for other nations to copy, so far as it might apply to their special position and wants. True, the whole world was not meant to be a "kingdom of priests" like the Israelites ; so it was not expected that the whole world should follow all those special customs and observances, which were intended to make the Israelites, outwardly and inwardly, different from all other nations ; but the whole world could look up to the " kingdom of priests," and copy their charity, their brotherly love, their justice, their morality, and their steadfast faith ; and this was the meaning of the promise given to the Patriarchs that through their seed all the families of the earth would be blessed.

When you grow older, and read all about those two great religions,[1] which, in spite of their many imperfections, have sprung from our own Holy Faith, you will understand better how God's promise to Abraham has been fulfilled. And when you read history, you will understand, too, how it is that the Jews have, notwithstanding all their failings, yet deserved the name of the " kingdom of priests." For, dispersed among nations which have changed their religions and their morals according to the whim or fancy or fashion of the times, the Jews alone have remained the guardians of God's Holy Law, never allowing a word or a letter to be changed, and not simply guarding and preserving the Book as a volume of venerable antiquity, but keeping it as the ever-living Word of the Ever-living God, *keeping it by keeping its laws*,[2] observing the Law as did their forefathers for so many centuries—the Law of Moses.[3]

[1] Christianity and Islam.

[2] Excepting only such laws as were connected with the Temple service and sacrifices, or with the ancient Israelitish polity, and which the destruction of the Temple, and the dispersion of Israel, rendered either unnecessary or impossible of fulfilment.

[3] Mahomet called the Jews " the people of the Book," and his followers give them the same appellation to this day.

CHAPTER V

OBSERVANCES.—SACRIFICE AND PRAYER

You, children, who have good and affectionate parents, must often feel a great longing to *do* something to show how you love your parents. You are not satisfied to keep the emotion of love in your heart and mind—to keep it as a pleasant thing, only to be thought about. You feel that you must *tell* them how dearly you love them. You must embrace them, and make them feel that you return their love. And perhaps, at times, you will bring them from your own small possessions some trifling gift, a gift great in proportion to your little all, but yet an absurdly small trifle if they estimated it by its money-value.

We are all children of God,[1] and I hope we all love Him, and feel that we cannot do enough to show how we honour Him. But He, living for ever in the High Heavens, is so far above us, who dwell only a few short years upon this little earth of ours, that we know not how to approach Him to show our love. And yet we must do something to show it. We cannot rest satisfied with feeling that we love Him, or with thinking of His goodness. For as we are composed of soul and body, when the soul

---

[1] Deut. xiv. 1.

feels the emotion of love, the body must express that love ; and so we must *do* something to show God our love.

Even when the world was very young, men experienced this great want, and they did very much the same as little children do, who bring sweetmeats to their parents, thinking that what they themselves like best must be acceptable to their parents. And so we find that Cain and Abel brought to God offerings from their own substance—Cain from the fruit which he had tended, Abel from the firstlings of his flocks.[1] Soon afterwards, in the time of Seth, we find that " men began to call on the name of the Lord." [2] They found a vent for their gratitude in the language of prayer and praise. And thus both sacrifice and prayer existed very early in the history of the world.

These were the first " religious observances."

I have already told you [3] what these observances —sacrifice and prayer—led to. I have told you how, in course of time, the people became idolaters, and how they at last came to sacrifice men and women, and even their own little children, in the absurd belief that if they sacrificed that which was dearest to themselves, such sacrifices would be pleasing to their gods.

So one of the first things that had to be taught to the children of Israel was to give up the terrible practices of idolatry. To stop sacrifices altogether and all at once would not have been advisable— perhaps hardly possible ; for the desire to give

---

[1] Gen. iv. 3, 4.   [2] Gen. iv. 26.   [3] Part II., chap. i.

something to God could not be checked; so that
desire had to be made harmless and even useful;
and thus it seems God instituted the system of
sacrifices that we find in the Mosaic Code.   Thus it
was that in the first laws which, through Moses,
God gave the Israelites after the Ten Commandments, He forbade their making gods of silver and
gold, but explained to them how they might bring
sacrifices.[1] " You shall not make with Me gods of
silver, neither shall you make unto you gods of
gold.   An altar of earth thou shalt make unto
Me, and shalt sacrifice thereon thy burnt-offerings, and thy peace-offerings, thy sheep, and
thine oxen."

The Israelites were not upon any account to sacrifice human beings.   They might bring as offerings
beasts or birds; but these were to be of particular
kinds—clean animals without blemish.   Even then
the offerings had to be made in certain fixed and
particular ways, and those who brought the sacrifice might not offer it themselves.   It had to be
offered by a priest, one of the descendants of Aaron,
who were all considered holy servants of God.

Later on,[2] you will find that any animal required
for food by the Israelites during their abode in the
wilderness, had to be taken to the priest, slaughtered
by him, and the blood and fat offered as a sacrifice.
All this was to show how sacred a thing is life.   It
was to show that even the life of a brute was not
to be taken lightly, inconsiderately, or wantonly;
and thus the people would be led to think that if

[1] Exod. xx. 23, 24.   [2] Lev. xvii. 3, 4, 5.

the life of a beast be thus regarded, how sacred
must be the life of a human being!

You will read for yourselves in the Bible all about
the sacrifices, and you will doubtless be surprised
that the Mosaic Code contains such minute details
as to the manner in which the offerings were to be
made. You will find that the latter part of the
Book of Exodus is filled with particulars of the
manner in which the Tabernacle, the Ark, the
altars, and all the vessels of the Tabernacle were
to be made ; how Aaron and his sons were to be
set apart and consecrated as priests to minister to
God and offer up sacrifices ; and you will find a large
portion of the Book of Leviticus filled with particulars of the various sacrifices, and the manner in
which they were to be offered.

You will read about the burnt-offerings, the meal-
offerings, the peace-offerings, the sin-offerings, the
trespass-offerings, and the offerings of consecration.[1]
You will read also [2] about the daily offerings, the
offerings of the Sabbath, the Festivals, and the Day
of Atonement,[3] and you will be surprised, perhaps,
at so many small particulars being given as to each.

And, indeed, it is surprising till you see the
object. The object was to compel a fixed form of
sacrifice, to admit of no wild departure from a
certain routine, so that the Israelites might never
wander away to the wicked idolatries and human
sacrifices which they had been accustomed to see
in Egypt ; and yet the forms of sacrifice prescribed

---

[1] Lev. i. to viii.   [2] Num. xxviii. and xxix.
[3] Lev. xvi.

were sufficient to satisfy their religious feelings and cravings and wants, however fervid and zealous they might be.

See how this was accomplished.   Moses bids them make a beautiful Tabernacle, that God may dwell with them in spirit.   He invites them to bring free-will offerings of " gold, and silver, and brass ; and blue, and purple, and scarlet, and fine linen, and goats' hair, and rams' skins dyed red, and badgers' skins and acacia wood; oil for the light, spices for the anointing oil and for sweet incense ;   onyx stones, and stones to be set in the ephod and the breastplate." [1]

The gifts of the grateful people poured in ;   for they were delighted to offer tribute to the God who had saved them from slavery, and now intended to dwell in their midst.   The gifts poured in to such an extent that Moses had to restrain them.   " For the stuff they had was sufficient for all the work to make it, and too much." [2]

Then the work of constructing the Tabernacle is commenced.   Moses gives every particular and detail of how it is to be made, and how furnished ; and so it is prepared and fitted under the very eyes of the people, without mystery or concealment ; unlike the religious systems of other nations, in which the priests made a mystery of everything, lest the people should see the deceptions they practised.

Read carefully the account of the Tabernacle, and you will be struck with the idea that it must

[1] Exod. xxv. 3–7.   [2] Exod. xxxvi. 7.

have been very beautiful, but very simple, and you will also be struck with the idea that everything was so made that the worship therein was to be open and public to the whole assembly of Israelites. The priest was to be seen when he went into the sanctuary, and when he came out. There was no hidden mystery. The priest was one of themselves, one of the kingdom of priests. The priest was to minister to God, not as a mediator between God and His people, but solely as a servant of God, performing the service of God, according to fixed rules and ordinances.

When you read the laws relating to the sacrifices, and especially the laws of the sin-offering, the trespass-offering, and the offerings of the Day of Atonement, it will probably appear to you very strange that God should accept merely the blood of an animal as an atonement for men's sins ; and it certainly would be very curious, if it were true ; but it is not true. The common notion is that the sacrifice of the animal constituted the atonement, and that God accepted the life of the animal instead of the life of the man who had committed the sin. But this notion is altogether wrong. How such a strange idea came into people's heads you will one day understand, when you read about a religion [1] which is entirely based upon this mistaken idea of atonement by sacrifice. If you reflect a little, you will at once say that nothing could be more unreasonable than the idea that a man, who had committed some terrible sin, should receive the forgiveness of

[1] Christianity.

God by simply bringing to a priest an animal to be
slaughtered ; and when you read for yourselves in
your Bible the law of sacrifices, you will at once see
that there is nothing to warrant so absurd an idea.

> " For God is good, and does not thirst for blood ;
>   Who calls Him vengeful, but transfers the type
>   Of his own earthly nature into heaven
>   And stamps Him human." [1]

When you carefully read the fifth and sixth chapters of Leviticus, you will discover the spirit and
meaning of sacrifices. You will find that if a man
committed a sin against God, he had first to make
a confession of his sin, and afterwards to bring as an
offering a lamb or a kid ; and if he could not afford
a lamb or a kid, he might bring two turtle-doves
or two young pigeons ; and in case he could not
afford these little birds, he might bring as his
offering a tenth part of an ephah of fine flour, and
the priest burnt on the altar a handful of the flour.
In the last case—the sacrifice of the flour—there
was no life taken, so there was evidently no sacrifice
of blood. And thus you see the taking of life and
the sacrifice of blood were not essential to the
atonement. The really important part of the proceeding was the confession of the sin—the open
demonstration of the sinner's penitence.

Reading a little further, you will find that if a
man sinned against his neighbour by dealing falsely
with him, or by robbing him, or by deceiving him,
or by detaining lost property that he had found, or
by swearing to a neighbour's injury—then he had

[1] Goethe.

to bring as a trespass-offering a ram without blemish ; but, before bringing it, he had to make good to the neighbour he had injured all that he had wronged him of, and to give him in addition one-fifth part of the value.   In this case it is clear that the really important part of the transaction was not the offering, but the making good the injury.

If we wish further to see how small a value should be placed upon sacrifices, compared with the spirit in which the sacrifice was brought, we have only to refer to the prophets and sacred writings.

Samuel tells Saul, who, contrary to God's orders, had saved alive the sheep and oxen of the Amale-kites to sacrifice to the Lord at Gilgal, " Behold to obey is better than sacrifice, to hearken than the fat of rams." [1]

Isaiah exclaims thus : " To what purpose is the multitude of your sacrifices unto Me ? saith the Lord.   I am full of the burnt-offerings of rams, and the fat of fed beasts, and I delight not in the blood of bullocks, or of lambs, or of he-goats. . . . Wash you, make you clean ; put away the evil of your doings from before Mine eyes ; cease to do evil : learn to do well ; seek judgment, relieve the oppressed, judge the fatherless, plead for the widow." [2]

In like words God proclaims, through his prophet Jeremiah, that the aim of the Law was obedience and not sacrifice.   " I spake not unto your fathers nor commanded them in the day that I brought

---

[1] I Sam. xv. 22.   [2] Isa. i. 11, 16, 17.

them out of the land of Egypt, concerning burnt-offerings and sacrifices. But this thing commanded I them, saying, Obey My voice." [1]

The prophet Micah speaks in the same strain. He asks,[2] "Wherewith shall I come before the Lord, and bow myself before the High God ? Shall I come before Him with burnt-offerings, with calves of a year old ? Will the Lord be pleased with thousands of rams, or with ten thousands of rivers of oil ? Shall I give my first-born for my transgression, the fruit of my body for the sin of my soul ? He hath showed thee, O man, what is good ; and what does the Lord require of thee, but to do justly, and to love mercy, and to walk humbly with thy God ? "

Again, in the 50th Psalm, God declares, " I will take no bullock out of thy house, nor he-goats out of thy folds. For every beast of the forest is Mine, and the cattle upon a thousand hills. I know all the fowls of the mountains ; and the wild beasts of the field are Mine. If I were hungry, I would not tell thee ; for the world is Mine, and the fulness thereof. Shall I eat the flesh of bulls ? or drink the blood of goats ? Offer unto God thanksgiving, and pay thy vows unto the Most High."

In the twenty-first chapter of Proverbs it is declared, " To do justice and judgment is more acceptable to the Lord than sacrifice."

I have quoted these passages from the Bible to show that the performance of other duties, such as obedience to God, and works of honesty, justice,

---

[1] Jer. vii. 22, 23.   [2] Micah vi. 6, 7, 8.

and mercy were considered of greater importance than the bringing of sacrifice.

And I think you will now understand that, though these sacrifices occupy so large a portion of the Law of Moses, they were only temporary laws, their main intention being to fill up what would otherwise have been a great gap in the daily action of our ancestors' lives.[1] They had been accustomed to see around them sacrifices—wicked, sinful sacrifices—sacrifices to idols, even human sacrifices. They had to be weaned from such customs ; accordingly sacrifices, which should be not only harmless but beneficial, had to be ordained ; sacrifices, which would serve as an outlet for their gratitude, or as a proof of their penitence, or as a reminder of the everlasting presence of a watchful God, willing to receive the love and adoration of His creatures.

And so all the little details of the sacrifice were fully prescribed, so that nothing like idolatry should be practised. Nor were they to deceive themselves with the idea that they could sin, and atone by a sin-offering, and sin again, as often as they pleased ; getting absolution from the priest as often as they pleased, simply by bringing an offering, and so making wrong-doing a profitable business. No ; the offering had to be accompanied by an open confession, and by restitution, with one-fifth added as a penalty ; so that wrong-doing could not be made profitable or pleasant in its

[1] The view here given is that stated by Maimonides, *Moreh Nebuchim,* Book III. chap. 32.

H

results, if a man ever wished to be at peace with his Maker.

But the words which I have quoted from the Prophets will show you further that, though we have at present no sacrifices and no priests, there are other and far better means accessible to all men at all times of making themselves acceptable to God. By penitence, prayer, and praise ; by acting justly, mercifully, and charitably.

Of this last-named duty, acting justly, mercifully, and charitably—a duty which includes many hundred duties—I cannot speak here at length, but will treat of it in its proper place.[1] But the act of prayer and praise is an observance—was one of the first observances ; and as we are led to the subject by the words of the Psalmist, who bids us offer to God thanksgiving instead of sacrifices, it is right to tell you now something about prayer.

" What is the good of prayer ? " some of you may ask. Can we expect that the praises we offer to God are pleasant for Him to hear ? Can we hope or expect that He, who made all the world, listens to our puny voices and feeble words ? It seems at first hardly possible ; but we know that it is not only possible but certain ; for God Himself commands us, through His servant Moses, to pray to Him and to praise Him. He tells us : " When thou hast eaten and art satisfied, then thou shalt bless the Lord thy God for the good land which He hath given thee." [2] We are told also " to love the Lord your God, and to serve Him with all your

---

[1] Chaps. ix. and x.   [2] Deut. viii. 10.

heart and with all your soul." [1]   Also His servants
the priests are ordered to pray for the welfare of
the people in the well-known form of blessing : [2]
" The Lord bless thee and keep thee.   The Lord
make His face to shine upon thee, and be gracious
to thee.   The Lord life up His countenance upon
thee, and give thee peace."   And so in our prayer
and our praise we are to look to God as the source
of all blessing, to acknowledge Him as the Great
Power who supports, rules, and sustains us. *This
acknowledgment is the great principle of Religion.*

When, therefore, Ezra and the men of the Great
Assembly ordained, as tradition tells us, that we
should worship God three times a day,[3] and that we
should offer thanks to Him before and after every
meal, and utter a blessing on every suitable occasion, their object was a wise one.   They intended
that we should always have before us the thought
of an ever-present God, who sees our every act.
They intended that in every act of our lives we
should acknowledge the greatness and goodness and
providence of God, so that the thought that He is
always and everywhere at hand should keep us
from sinning, and so cause us to lead a good and
godly life.

But even if the Law of Moses and the ordinances

---

[1] Deut. xi. 13.   Upon this text our ancient teachers comment
thus, אֵיזוֹ הִיא עֲבוֹדָה שֶׁהִיא בַּלֵּב ? הֱוֵי אוֹמֵר זוֹ תְּפִלָּה:—" How can
we serve God with our heart ?   By devout prayer" (*Taanith*,
2, a).

[2] Num. vi. 24, 25, 26.

[3] Following the words, " Evening and morning and at noon
will I pray " (Ps. lv. 17).

of our wise men had been silent on the subject of
prayer, and had given us no hint of that great
duty, the dictates of our hearts would prompt us to
utter words of praise ; for gratitude must find vent
in open expression. If you have a favourite dog,
whom you feed and carefully tend, he will lick your
hand and dance around you in delight, and show
you his gratitude in many ways. If you have a
little bird to whom you daily give his dole of grain
and drink, he will warble out his notes of gratitude
every time he sees you. How, then, can man, who
alone has the gift of words, forbear to bring the
homage of his heart and the offering of his lips to
the Creator, who made him and supports him ?
That we should pray to God is a law of God, because it is a law of Nature engraved on our hearts,
a law which every man, woman, and child gladly
obeys. Perhaps God is pleased with our songs of
praise, just as you are pleased to hear the warblings
of the little bird you tend. " Behold, the song of
man is pleasing to Thee. Therefore will I praise
Thee, so long as the Divine Soul is within me." [1]

Foremost amongst the blessings derived from
prayer is the feeling that we are holding communion with our Supreme Creator, and that, by
the contemplation of His perfections, our hearts
become elevated, our moral tone improved, and our
impulses braced and strengthened for the performance of good and noble deeds.

The Psalmist, who taught all the world the language of prayer and praise, tells us, " It is good to

[1] *Prayer of Solomon Ibn Gabirol.*

sing praises unto our God ; for it is pleasant, and praise is comely." [1] And, lest we should think that the Great Creator of the universe would not concern Himself with the petty wants of us puny mortals, and would not hearken to our prayers, he tells us, " The Lord is nigh unto all them that call upon Him, to all that call upon Him in truth. He will fulfil the desire of them that fear Him ; He also will hear their cry, and will save them." [2]

The Prophets teem with similar declarations as to the power of prayer. " Before they call I will answer ; whilst they are yet speaking, I shall already have heard." [3] " Call unto Me and I will answer thee, and show thee great and mighty things." [4] " I called upon Thy name, O Lord, out of the low dungeon ; Thou hast heard my voice." [5]

> " More things are wrought by prayer
> Than this world dreams of.   Wherefore let thy voice
> Rise like a fountain . . . night and day.
> For what are men better than sheep or goats
> That nourish a blind life within the brain,
> If, knowing God, they lift not hands of prayer
> Both for themselves and those who call them friend ?
> For so the whole round earth is every way
> Bound by gold chains about the feet of God." [6]

Sceptics have often raised the objection, that we cannot hope to alter the pre-ordained design and intention of God by our puny prayers. But in truth the same objection might be raised against all other human exertion ; and a blind fatalism would result. And, after all, it may so happen

[1] Ps. cxlvii. 1.
[2] Ps. cxlv. 18, 19.
[3] Isa. lxv. 24.
[4] Jer. xxxiii. 3.
[5] Lam. iii. 55.
[6] Tennyson's *Passing of Arthur*.

that prayer is one of the means ordained by God to produce the legitimate ends we long for, and that God delights in granting such of our prayers as are worthy prayers, as a kind father delights in granting the reasonable wishes of his children. Certainly this is the case with all prayers which we sincerely offer for our own moral improvement. " There is an apparent connection, at least, between prayers for the greatest moral good and its attainment. Prayer for virtuous dispositions and conduct, for resignation, trust and tranquillity of mind, does certainly tend to procure them. The very posture of the mind in prayer tends to produce them." [1]

Now, perhaps you will think it rather strange that the Law of Moses, which tells us so many

[1] Sir J. B. Byles's " Foundations of Religion," p. 77.

We may also quote Johnson's paraphrase from the Tenth Satire of Juvenal :—

" Still raise for good the supplicating voice,
But leave to Heaven the measure and the choice ;
Safe in His hands, whose eye discerns afar
The secret ambush of a specious prayer.
Implore His aid, in His decisions rest,
Secure whate'er He gives, He gives the best.
But when a sense of Sacred Presence fires,
And strong devotion to the skies aspires,
Pour forth thy fervours for a healthful mind,
Obedient passions and a will resigned ;
For love, which scarce collective man can fill,
For patience, sovereign o'er transmuted ill,
For Faith, that, panting for a purer seat,
Counts Death kind Nature's signal for retreat—
These gifts for all the laws of heaven ordain,
These gifts He grants who grants the power to gain ;
With these celestial wisdom calms the mind
And makes the happiness she cannot find."

JOHNSON'S *Vanity of Human Wishes.*

things, does not tell us what prayers we should offer. It gives us full particulars and details of the sacrifices, but ordains very few forms of prayer. In the twenty-first chapter of Deuteronomy, you will find a special prayer to be said if a man be found slain, and his murderer cannot be discovered ; and, in the twenty-sixth chapter of the same book, you will find prescribed the prayers which were to be said on bringing the first-fruits, and on offering the tithes ; but these are rather confessions than prayers ; and in the sixth chapter of Numbers you will find the priest's prayer, of which I have already spoken. But besides these, there are really no forms of prayer specially ordained in the Law of Moses.

Why was this ? Because prayers were to be the natural outpouring of the heart.

> "Uttered not—yet comprehended
> Is the Spirit's voiceless prayer." [1]

In later times, forms of prayer were composed for common use, and certain Psalms were sung in the Temple by the Levites. Later still, when the Jews returned from the captivity, the prophets and scribes prescribed the Order of Service, consisting principally of the prayers and psalms then in common use ; and these you will find in your prayer-book, together with very many others of much later date, all in Hebrew, except a few which, having been composed in Babylon, during the dispersion, were written in the Aramaic or Chaldee dialect, then the mother-tongue of the exiled Jews.

[1] Longfellow's *Footsteps of Angels.*

You will readily understand why our prayer-book should be mainly in Hebrew. It is not only our own language, but the language of the Law and of the prophets; and it is the language of our ancestors' prayers during many generations. You would not be able to compose Hebrew prayers for yourselves; so it is fortunate that you have some ready prepared for you; and, though these are only *forms* of prayer, there is much in the reflection that they are the same that have been used by our people in their synagogues, and their homes, during many generations, and that they have served during so many ages to bring pious and holy thoughts into the minds and hearts of millions of our forefathers, and to comfort them in their sorrows.

But all these prayers are of no avail to you, unless, in praying, you think of their meaning, and unless you add to these set forms, composed by other people, prayers of your own, which need not be in Hebrew, and need not even be in words [1]—I mean, loving thoughts of God, grateful thoughts for all His kindness towards you; hopes that He will guide you and give you strength to do your duty and resist temptation; earnest longings that He will make you worthy of His goodness, and help you to improve day by day, and so enable you, small and humble though you be, to work His will on earth, and win a place in Heaven.

---

[1] "Every good and holy desire, though it lack the form, hath notwithstanding in itself the substance and the force of a prayer with Him, who regardeth the very moanings and sighs of the heart of man."—*Hooker*.

CHAPTER VI

FROM what I have told you, I think you must already understand that Religion consists of two parts—belief and observance ; belief being the act of the mind, observance the act of the body with the help of the mind ; and I think you understand, too, how the first religious observances—sacrifice and prayer—arose quite as a natural necessity, from men's anxiety to *do* something to show their gratitude to God and their dependence on Him.

Now, when a system of religion was ordained, it was necessary to fix particular periods and seasons when men should completely rest from their daily labours, and so withdraw themselves from the business of their lives as to enable them to turn their thoughts to God and to His service ; and it was for this reason that the Sabbath and Festivals were ordained.

And perhaps there was also another reason, namely, that men should not, in their great love of God and their strong wish to serve Him, neglect their worldly duties. And so the Lawgiver, in fixing those particular days for His service, wisely set *bounds* and *limits* to the religious fervour of men. We are not, like many of the devotees of

other religions, to spend our lives in penance and in
prayer ; we are meant to work, and religion is meant
to sanctify our work. And thus it is that we find
the Commandment of the Sabbath in almost every
case preceded by the words " six days shalt thou
labour." Work was to be the first of duties, and
a holy life was to be no excuse for a lazy life.[1]

THE SABBATH.—Of the Sabbath itself, I have
already spoken at some length when telling you
about the Fourth Commandment ; so I need not
say much here upon this subject. But I ought to
tell you, that it is the most important of all those
observances, which distinguish the Jews from the
other peoples of the earth. How important, you
will understand from the remarkable fact that the
Law of the Sabbath is so many times repeated in
the Books of Moses.[2] You must read for yourselves all the references given at the foot of this
page, and you will find that, though the wording
of the Commandment differs somewhat in different
places, the principle of the Sabbath is the same in
all—rest on the Sabbath-day for every one, for
yourselves, your household, your servants and your
cattle.

When you read the Bible for yourselves, you will
find how great a sin Sabbath-breaking was con-

[1] " The modern majesty consists in work. What a man can
do is his greatest ornament, and he always consults his dignity
by doing it."—*Carlyle*.

[2] Exod. xvi. 23 ; Exod. xx. 8, 9, 10, 11 ; Exod. xxiii. 12 ;
Exod. xxxi. 13–17 ; Exod. xxxiv. 21 ; Exod. xxxv. 2, 3 ;
Lev. xix. 3 ; Lev. xxiii. 3 ; Deut. v. 13–15.

sidered.   You will read how the prophets Jeremiah and Ezekiel [1] denounced the Sabbath-breakers; and you will find how the chief prophets, especially Isaiah,[2] promised the highest reward to those who keep the Sabbath holy.

We are told, " It is a *sign* between Me and you throughout your generations," and this continues to be true even to this day.   The Jew who, though he may incur great loss or inconvenience thereby, always keeps holy one day weekly as his Sabbath-day, shows himself to be a truly sincere Jew.   It is a " sign " between the Jew and his God.   It is a sign that the Israelite looks upon God as the Guardian of himself and of his race, the Source of all earthly blessings, the Sustainer of every living creature.

And so the Jew brings a sacrifice of one-seventh portion of his time to the observance of the Holy Sabbath, in the sure hope and confidence that the time so given to rest will not be lost.

THE FEAST OF PASSOVER.—Many of you may suppose that one day in seven ought to be quite enough to be set apart as holy, and you may perhaps wonder why, besides the Sabbath, so many other holy days were ordained.   I will try to tell you why.

All nations have certain days in the year which they celebrate as anniversaries.   Just as you celebrate every year the anniversary of your birth, many nations celebrate, as each year comes round,

---

[1] Jer. xvii. 27 ; Ezek. xx. 12–21.   [2] Isa. lvi. 2.

the events which they call to mind with pride or
pleasure. But these events are not always such as
are worthy of being remembered, and these anniversaries are not usually celebrated in the most sensible
manner.

When you read ancient history, you will learn
what shocking sports, what cruelties and what
wickedness were practised on some of the anniversaries in Greece and Rome. Even in civilised
Europe, people now celebrate the anniversaries of
victories and other historical events by the absurd
practice of firing guns ; and even in this country,
the great winter anniversary, which is half national
and half religious, is celebrated amongst many
classes as a period of gluttony and excessive indulgence in strong drinks, certainly not in a mode
worthy of human beings.

It was to be different with the Israelites. Their
early history was full of events fitting to be remembered ; and the commemorations were to be
worthy of the events. The escape from the slavery
of Egypt, the giving of the Law, the wonderful
travels in the wilderness—these were events which
were worth remembering, and they were to be com-
memorated, not by cruel sports, not by races, not
by gluttonous feasts, but by joyful thanksgiving, by
intelligent enjoyments, and by charitable deeds.

We shall see, in detail, how this was ordained
in the Mosaic Law, and shall commence with the
Feast of Passover.

I can almost fancy some of my readers making
up their minds to skip the next few pages, feeling

sure that I can tell them nothing about this festival that they do not know already. And it is quite likely that they are right, and that the only good I can hope to do will be to set them thinking a little, not only about the observances themselves, but about the reason why. For, in these days, the " reason why " is all-important. And so it ought to be ; for what is Religion without reason ?

Now, if I ask you why you keep the Passover, you will tell me at once that you keep it to remind you of the great deliverance of our fathers from the bondage of Egypt. You will be quite right in so answering ; but you will not have told me nearly all in those few words.

We, who live in this happy land, free to worship God according to our conscience, free to do as we please, to go where we please, to work as we please, can hardly imagine what it was to live as did our forefathers in Egypt, under the rule of the wicked Pharaohs. To be slaves ; to be obliged to work not for ourselves but for others ; to have nothing of our own ; to be beaten by cruel taskmasters, who give impossible tasks, so that the worker cannot escape punishment ; to work in fear and dread, without hope and without the comforts and joys of home—this was the state of the poor Israelites. And, worse than all, the lives of their offspring were not safe ; for the cruel King, at one time, doomed all the male children to destruction. Such was the state of bondage from which, by the mercy of God, our ancestors were delivered.

But why should we, year after year, and after so

many centuries, call to mind, by the observance of Passover, these terrible trials of our forefathers ? To show our gratitude to God, is doubtless one reason. But there is yet another reason—to declare to the world the right of man to be free. Passover is the Festival of Freedom. We read the history of our ancestors in Egypt, and relate their wonderful deliverance and the fall of the mighty tyranny which had oppressed them ; and we thereby declare that God ordained Man to be free—free in body, and free in mind, and we offer a warning to slave-owners, to tyrants, and to oppressors, that God will break their power.

For you, living in this free and happy land, must not suppose that, all the world over, people are now free and happy as you are. You must know that slavery still exists in many parts of Africa, though England has long been working there for the suppression of the slave-trade. You must know, too, that there are many countries where Jews are still oppressed, their lives and their property in constant danger ; and other countries where our people cannot meet for public worship, and can hardly permit it to be known that they are Jews.

Pharaoh's hosts were drowned in the Red Sea ; but in every age there have been other Pharaohs who have sprung up in his place, tyrants who have enslaved at times the bodies, at times the souls of their subjects.

When you read History, you will find that the power of the tyrant has always been, in the end, broken. Tyranny after tyranny has collapsed, power after power has perished, nation after nation has disappeared; but one people alone has remained alive through all these thousands of years —scattered about the world, but yet alive and full of life—the Jews; and these, year after year, celebrate with joy and gladness and gratitude the great Festival of Freedom.

You know well, all of you, how the festival is celebrated; how, before the festival begins, the home is cleared of leaven, so that no particle of it remains; how the סֵדֶר (*Seder*) night is observed, every household joining in solemn prayer and praise, reading the narrative of the Exodus,[1] seated around the table whereon are spread the memorial of the Paschal Lamb,[2] the unleavened bread and the bitter herbs;[3] how at that table all sit as equals, parents and children, master and servant, host and guest; how, for a week, unleavened bread is eaten,[4] and no leaven is allowed in our homes; how we meet in the Synagogue to praise God for His mercies; and how, on the seventh day of the Festival, we there read the narrative of the wonderful passage of the Red Sea, and sing the Song of Moses in the words stated to

---

[1] As commanded in Exod. xiii. 8.

[2] See Exod. xii. 11. It is worthy of remark that, even now, the Samaritans, who live in Nablous (in Palestine), celebrate the Passover by actually slaying and roasting the paschal lamb, and eating it with all the ceremonial details ordained in the twelfth chapter of Exodus. A highly interesting account of this observance may be found in Dean Stanley's *History of the Jewish Church*, Appendix to Vol. I.

[3] Exod. xii. 8.   [4] Lev. xxiii. 6.

have been used by our forefathers, when they had
just escaped from the ruthless sword of Pharaoh.

When you thus keep Passover, how happy, how
joyous, how grateful must you be !—how thankful
you must feel that your lot has fallen on better
days, and that you are free and happy !

How proud you must be that you are Jews and
Jewesses, declaring before the world the greatness,
and goodness, and glory of God, in that you, the
survivors of long centuries of persecution, are the
living witnesses of His greatness, and goodness, and
glory ! For every Passover, year after year, for
hundreds of years, have those same words of
prayer and praise been sung, which you sing ; those
same customs been observed which you observe ;
thus joining the past with the present, and making
you feel, in the words of the *Hagadah*, as if you
yourselves had just come out of Egypt, the objects
of God's special mercy and special providence !

THE FEAST OF WEEKS.—Why is that pleasant
festival of early summer called the Feast of Weeks ?

You know the beautiful custom, *the counting of
the Omer*, which is observed on forty-nine evenings,
commencing on the second evening of Passover.
This custom is ordained in the Law of Moses,[1] and
you can read for yourselves all the particulars in
the words of the Bible. Its object is to impress
upon us all a due estimate of the value of time, that
precious possession of which not one of us, old or
young, can tell whether we have much or little ;

---

[1] Lev. xxiii. 15, 16 ; Deut. xvi. 9.

and to remind us, at a season when time is of the highest value to the worker, that we are answerable to God for the use or abuse of our time.

You will find in the Bible that on the second day of Passover, when the sickle was first put to the corn, and the wheat harvest began, the Israelites were to bring as an offering " a sheaf (*Omer*) of the first-fruits of the harvest ; " that, for seven weeks after-wards the days were to be counted, and that on the fiftieth day, when the seven weeks were over, the Feast of Weeks was to be kept ; there was to be a " holy convocation," and it was to be observed " with a tribute of a free-will offering." [1] The " first of the first-fruits " was to be brought to the House of the Lord ; [2] and so this festival is not only called חַג הַשָּׁבֻעֹת, " the Feast of Weeks," but יוֹם הַבִּכּוּרִים, " the Day of First-fruits."

In Palestine the summer is much earlier than here. The barley was ripe at the Passover season, and the corn was all reaped when the Feast of Weeks had arrived. On this festival the first-fruit offering was brought into the Temple, consisting of " two wave loaves of two tenth parts baken with leaven." [3]

After this festival the first-fruits were brought by each Israelite to the Temple.

How the first-fruits were brought, and what prayer was said when they were brought, you will find in the twenty-sixth chapter of Deuteronomy.[4] It is a remarkable prayer, one of the few set forms

---

[1] Deut. xvi. 10.   [2] Exod. xxxiv. 26.
[3] Lev. xxiii. 17.   [4] Deut. xxvi. 2–10.

I

of prayer ordained by the command of God, and it is, perhaps, rather a declaration than a prayer ;—a declaration of the early history of our race, a narrative of the wonderful redemption from Egypt, and a confession that all our possessions come from God ; for it concludes with the words, " And now, behold, I have brought the first-fruits of the land which Thou, O Lord, hast given me."

These last words, again, involve that great principle of our religion—the recognition of God in every act of our life, in every good thing that we receive, in every happiness that we enjoy.

The prosperous farmer, fresh from his harvest-field, might feel puffed up with a sense of his importance, might grow too proud of his possessions, and might think that it is to his own industry and talent that all his wealth is due.   But the Day of the First-fruits draws near.   He obeys the Divine command and brings his offering to the Holy place. He joins the procession which, as the Mishna tells us, came from every city and village of Palestine, bringing to the Temple of Jerusalem the choicest first-fruits, decked with the finest flowers, amid the sound of music and the voice of song, echoing the words, " O come, let us go up to Zion, to the Lord our God." [1]   No matter how rich he may be, he himself must carry on his shoulder his own first-fruit, and, standing before the priest, he recites the ordained prayer, and finishes with the words, " And now, behold, I have brought the first-fruits of the land which Thou, O Lord, hast given me ! "   The

[1] *Bikkurim,* III.

pride half rising in the heart, the boast half rising to the lips of the successful farmer, would be suppressed at the humble confession of his lowly origin, and at the prayer which acknowledges God as the Source of all good.

To us, who have lost our Sanctuary, and who live in a climate where the wheat-harvest is gathered several months later than in Palestine, the Feast of Weeks, held in May or June, can present only a shadow of its former beauty ; and instead of bringing, like our ancestors, our first-fruits, we are forced to content ourselves with adorning our Synagogues with choice flowers as a memorial of Nature's productiveness and God's loving bounty.

But, from another point of view, the Feast of Weeks is as much to us as ever it was to our forefathers. It is, according to tradition, the anniversary of the giving of the Law, the bestowal of the greatest gift that our people ever received.

Of Revelation I have already treated at some length, so I need not here do more than impress upon you the importance of the Festival which calls it to our remembrance. Your hearts must be full of gratitude to the Great God, who chose us from all peoples to receive His Holy Law, and who has kept us alive amid constant dangers and persecutions to be the custodians of His Word for the good of the whole world.

THE FEAST OF TABERNACLES.—We are commanded in the Holy Law to dwell in booths for seven days, commencing on the fifteenth day of the

seventh month, to remind us that God caused the
children of Israel to dwell in booths when He led
them out of the land of Egypt.[1]   These seven days
are the Feast of Tabernacles,[2] and the eighth day
was ordained to be kept as a " solemn assembly."

We are commanded, too, to take on the first day
of the festival " the fruit of a goodly tree,[3] the
branches of palm-trees, the boughs of thick-leaved
trees,[4] and willows of the brook, and to rejoice
before the Lord seven days."

You will find it interesting to read in the Book
of Nehemiah [5] how, after a long interval of neglect,
the Feast was observed by our ancestors under
Ezra the scribe ; how they published and proclaimed in all their cities and in Jerusalem saying :
" Go forth unto the mount and fetch olive-branches,
and pine-branches, and myrtle-branches, and palm-
branches, and branches of thick trees to make
booths, as it is written," and how the people went
forth and brought them, and made themselves
booths every one upon the roof of his house, and
in the courts, and in the Court of the House of
God.

In this climate it happens, unfortunately, that
the season when the Festival falls is usually a

[1] Lev. xxiii. 34, 39-43.

[2] The word " tabernacles " in the name of this festival must
not be confounded with the term " tabernacle " as applied to
the " tabernacle of the wilderness," which was quite a different
structure.   To avoid confusion the Feast of Tabernacles should,
perhaps, be called the " Feast of Booths."

[3] According to tradition, the citron.

[4] According to tradition, the myrtle.

[5] Neh. viii. 15.

rainy and inclement time of the year ; and thus the command to dwell in booths or temporary huts is not so generally observed by our people as it might be. But there are yet many zealous Jews in this country who, in spite of the great inconvenience, yet make an effort to observe the command as ordained, and who erect tabernacles wherein they eat their meals and spend a portion of their time during the Festival.

Perhaps there are few of you, my young readers, who have never seen such a Tabernacle, with its shifting roof and its ceiling of evergreens ; and some of you may probably have lively recollections of many happy hours spent in such a frail and slight abode. Those who can afford it decorate their Tabernacles with lamps and pictures and flowers and fruits, making their little temporary home truly a thing of beauty. The Law of Moses does not tell us how to make a סֻכָּה (*Succah*) or booth ; but, according to tradition, the main characteristic of the *Succah* is the roof, which is usually formed of green leaves arranged in such a manner that the sky may be seen between the leaves, so as to indicate the temporary character of the structure as distinguished from the permanent ceiling of an ordinary habitation.

This slight and temporary home is not only to remind us of the wanderings of our ancestors in the wilderness, but also to bring to our minds thoughts of gratitude towards the God who loads us with His bounty. At the feast of ingathering, when we might perhaps be filled with pride at our worldly success, we are told to leave our warm, substantial homes, and to take up our abode in the frail booth, roofed like the hut of a wanderer.

Looking at this leafy roof, we see the sky, and call to mind the Heavenly Hand that made and fashioned us, and gave us all we have : we see the starry hosts of heaven, and understand our own nothingness ; and the frail covering, which scarcely keeps out rain and wind, makes us think of those poor distressed creatures who would have no roof to shelter them, but for our timely aid.

The beautiful trophies of nature, too, which we are commanded to take during the Festival, are meant to lead us to like thoughts of duty, and humble gratitude. The palm, emblem of upright-ness ; [1] the citron and myrtle, emblem of that charity that spreads its fragrance far and wide, giving much and yet losing nothing ; and the willow, emblem of true humility—these choice gifts of nature we are to gather, and, looking at them, learn from them a holy lesson.

And in all our rejoicings we are to be mindful of others besides ourselves. Not only " shalt thou rejoice," says the Bible ; but " thy man-servant, and thy maid-servant, and the Levite, the stranger, and the fatherless, and the widow, that are within thy gates," [2] are to share the bounties of nature, and to take part in the joys of the happy harvest-home.

The eighth day of solemn assembly, which follows the Feast of Tabernacles, has no defined object stated in the Bible, but it would seem to have been

[1] Ps. xcii. 12.   [2] Deut. xvi. 14.

intended to inspire us with gratitude at our having been permitted to celebrate the solemn series of holy days of the month of Tishri.

It is the custom of the Synagogue to signalise the close of these holy days by a festivity, thoroughly characteristic of our religion, known as *Simchath Torah* (שִׂמְחַת תּוֹרָה), " the rejoicing in the Law." You are aware that on every Sabbath during the year a section of the Holy Law is publicly read in our places of worship,[1] in such manner that the entire Pentateuch may be completed in one year, and that the last section (comprising the last two chapters of Deuteronomy) may be read on this Festival.

Directly the Pentateuch is thus completed, it is again commenced, the first chapter of Genesis and part of the second being read with great solemnity. On this occasion the synagogue is made to wear its most festive aspect ; the sacred scrolls of the Law, decked in gorgeous vestments, are carried in procession round the holy edifice, while hymns of praise and thanksgiving, attuned to joyous music, testify our gratitude to God for His goodness in having permitted us again to complete the perusal of that Law which is our greatest treasure.

[1] A portion of the prophets is also read after the *Sedrah*, or lesson from the Pentateuch. This is called *Haphtarah*, literally " conclusion." In the fourteenth century Abudarham explained the custom as follows : During times of persecution, the public reading of the Law was prohibited under pain of death. Our people, thus debarred from reading the weekly portions from the Pentateuch, read, as a substitute, lessons from the prophets which contained some reference or resemblance to the respective portions from the Law they were compelled to suppress.

CHAPTER VII

OBSERVANCES.—THE NEW YEAR'S DAY AND DAY OF ATONEMENT

At the commencement of the last chapter I told you that it was an essential part of the system of our Holy Religion to set aside certain days upon which we should turn our thoughts to God, and that this was one reason why the Sabbath and Festivals were ordained. But besides these, the Law ordained for a like purpose two other Holy days—the Day of Memorial (or New Year's Day) and the Day of Atonement—to remind us of our position, to recall us to our duties, if we have forgotten them, and to enable us to remove from our souls the burden of sin.

"Now what does all this mean?" some of you young folks will ask; for probably most of you will be ignorant of what I mean by the "burden of sin."

You young people, who, in your several pursuits and studies, have little worlds of your own, though I trust you may know little or nothing about great sins, will no doubt remember that there have been times when you have done wrong. I hope not often, but I doubt not it has sometimes happened so with all of you. And, perhaps, some of you may have known children who very often do wrong, and who seem to get worse and worse, the older they grow, till something shocking occurs to them—some illness, perhaps, or some misfortune—which sets them thinking about their wrong-doing, and makes them resolve to do better in future.

Now, just as there are sometimes wayward, disobedient children, there are sometimes wicked men and women, who seem to forget God and His laws, and who keep on sinning daily more and more. The souls of such people are burdened with sin.

But though, happily, there are not many of these downright wicked people, there are yet a very great number of people in the world who now and then do wrong, who forget or neglect to do some duty, or who do something that is forbidden, and who, without being very wicked, are yet far from perfect. Indeed, no mortal is perfect. Every one has his faults—most of us very many faults—and these faults would become, as we grow in years, sins— perhaps even great crimes—if we did not from time to time check them, and make up our mind to put a stop to them.

Now, the Lawgiver ordained [1] the New Year's Festival to be a Day of Memorial, or Day of Remembrance ; that is to say, a day on which we are to call to mind everything we have done during the past year, and pass judgment on our work. And, as God has placed within every one of us a con-

[1] " In the seventh month, in the first day of the month, shall be a solemn rest unto you, a memorial of blowing of trumpets, an holy convocation. Ye shall do no servile work " (Lev. xxiii. 24, 25).

science, the Law ordained that on that day the
שׁוֹפָר (ram's-horn) should be sounded to awaken
that conscience, so that all of us may on that day
consider our acts, examine our own conduct, and
judge ourselves truthfully, even as God judges us.

This duty—the duty of self-examination and self-
judgment—is one of the greatest of the duties we
owe to ourselves ; and it is right that we should
perform this duty not merely once a year, on the
Day of Memorial, but every night when we retire
to rest.   The Psalmist tells us, " Stand in awe, and
sin not ;   commune with your heart upon your
bed," [1] in the silence of night.   And I have already
told you that self-examination is one of the duties
of the Sabbath-day.

Some of you will no doubt fancy such frequent
self-examination quite unnecessary, and may think
it likely to make you too serious, and rather
miserable.   But this is a mistake.   Every morning,
and perhaps twice or thrice in the day, you look at
yourselves in the glass, to see if you are clean and
tidy, and when you are satisfied with your appear-
ance, the sight does not make you miserable or
serious—perhaps quite the reverse.   And so, if the
examination of your acts and thoughts, and the
judgment of your conscience be satisfactory, and
you feel you are good and clean and spotless in
the sight of God and your conscience, the result
is increased happiness.

But as we are apt to forget this great duty of
self-examination, the Day of Memorial has been

[1] Ps. iv. 4.

ordained, so that, at least once a year, we should be judged by Himself and our conscience, and so be prepared for the great Day of Atonement, which is to follow nine days after. Therefore, when in the synagogue you hear the *Shophar* (שׁוֹפָר), the ram's-horn, sounding in plaintive and tremulous notes, remember that it sounds an alarm. It is meant to arouse you from your fancied security, to awake your slumbering conscience, to remind you of your position. Year by year, you are expected to improve, not alone in education and worldly knowledge, but in heart and mind and soul. Every year as you grow older, and draw nearer to that day which will be the close of your life here and the opening of your new life in the world to come, you are expected to become purer and nobler in spirit ; every year to have fewer faults and greater virtues ; every year to grow more godly ; and as each Day of Memorial comes round, you have to satisfy yourself that this improvement is taking place in your soul, in that part of you which is immortal.[1]

But if not, what then ? If, when the trumpet sounds, and you review your ways and works, and examine your heart and soul, you find all vain and unprofitable—duties neglected, bad passions encouraged, vices increased, days wasted—what then ? Shall you, in despair, go deeper and deeper into wickedness ? Shall you waste your time in useless

[1] Socrates said : " I believe we cannot live better than in seeking to become better, nor more agreeably than by having a clear conscience."

tears ? No. God has opened to you the door of escape from evil, has given you the power of repentance and the chance of forgiveness and reconciliation, by ordaining for that purpose His great Day of Atonement. " For on that day shall atonement be made for you to cleanse you, that you may be clean from all your sins before the Lord." [1]

The Day of Atonement ! What thoughts crowd into the mind at the mention of that day ! It is the holiest day of the year, the day which we give entirely to God and to the purifying of our soul by repentance. During that day, no thought of the world or of its profits and pleasures may enter our minds. We are to spend the whole day in meditation and prayer. We are to afflict ourselves ; and tradition has ordained that part of that affliction shall consist in abstaining from food and drink from sunset to sunset. For one whole day we are to forget our body, and to think only of our soul— that " living soul " which God planted within us, when He breathed into our nostrils the breath of life.[2]

You, young people, who would not on any account be seen with soiled hands or dirty faces, and who take just pride in your neat and cleanly dress, may well ask yourselves what is the use of being clean in the sight of man, if your soul is unclean in the sight of God ? And just as you feel how refreshing it is to take a bath, to cleanse your body from impurity, so must you feel how refreshing it is to take means for purifying your soul, and

[1] Lev. xvi. 30.   [2] Gen. ii. 7.

causing your transgressions to pass away year by
year, so that, at least once a year, " you may be
clean from all your sins before the Lord."

And truly it is a great privilege, that God should
have given us the great Day of Atonement, to
remove from the soul the burden of sin, so that
every year we may, as it were, begin a new life with
a clean and spotless soul and a light and joyful
heart.

Now, how is this accomplished ? I have told
you about the sacrifices, and especially about the
sin-offerings ; so you know what was their meaning and what their intention. But now we have
no temple and no priests, no altar and no sacrifices.
How, then, can we celebrate the Day of Atonement
so as to receive pardon for our sins ?

The Bible tells us how this may be done. By
confession, by penitence, by prayer, and by good
deeds. If you read the ordinance of the sacrifices
of the Day of Atonement, as found in the 16th
chapter of Leviticus, you will see [1] that confession
was a very material part of the Atonement-service.
The high-priest was to confess over the scape-goat
" all the iniquities of the children of Israel and all
their transgressions in all their sins." In your
prayer-book you will find the form of public confession of sins (וִדּוּי), which probably includes every
possible kind of transgression, and indeed many of
which you probably do not even understand the
meaning. But although it is right that every Jew,
worshipping in public, should join with his fellow-

[1] Lev. xvi. 21.

worshippers in one general form of confession, yet
this is not the confession which can satisfy us as
individuals. Each one of us must make a confession of his own special sins, not to a priest, as
is the custom with members of other faiths, but to
God and to ourselves.

Confession is the first step towards amendment.
We must feel and own that we are wrong, before
we are likely to cease our wrong-doing. And the
confession must be accompanied by a firm resolu-
tion never to repeat the wrong, and, so far as may
be possible, to repair its effects.

Penitence, then, does not consist (as many think
it does) of mere sorrowful prayers for forgiveness,
nor of mere empty confession. There must be
active penitence, reparation for the past, and resolu-
tion for the future.[1]   If we have injured or offended
our neighbour, the injury or offence must be made
good, before we can hope for forgiveness ;[2] and if
the wrong has been the neglect of a duty, we must
do our best, by our future efforts, to remedy the
effects of our neglect. This is the true penitence
of the Day of Atonement. It is little better than
a superstition — indeed, it is a superstition — to
suppose that our iniquities are removed by a
miracle, as the result of our prayers and our fasting.

[1] Among the ancient Egyptians, regret, without amendment,
was accounted one of the forty-two deadly sins.

[2] The Talmud tells us עֲבֵירוֹת שֶׁבֵּין אָדָם לַמָּקוֹם יוֹם הַכִּפּוּרִים
מְכַפֵּר עֲבֵירוֹת שֶׁבֵּין אָדָם לַחֲבֵירוֹ אֵין יוֹם הַכִּפּוּרִים מְכַפֵּר עַד שֶׁיְּרַצֶּה
אֶת חֲבֵירוֹ : "The Day of Atonement expiates sins between man
and his Maker; but for sins between man and man the condition
precedent to atonement is the redress of the injury" (*Yoma*, 85, *b*).

The prayers and the fasting are but empty forms, without the active practical penitence, of which I have spoken. The prayers and the fasting are aids to true penitence, for they bring the penitent to a proper frame of mind. But they are incomplete, taken by themselves.[1]

Indeed, one cannot imagine a great and kind and merciful God taking delight in our torturing ourselves by hunger, or in our crying aloud to Him for forgiveness, unless these be a means to an end, the end being *our improvement*. If you would learn the thoughts of God upon this subject, as expressed by the mouth of His prophets, you should read the fifty-eighth chapter of Isaiah,[2] and the seventh chapter of Zechariah. From the first of these I will quote a few verses, for nothing could be more forcible, and nothing can indicate better how futile are all religious observances—even the great fast of Atonement—unless accompanied by practical contrition, practical well-doing, and the practical virtues of Justice and Mercy.

" Ye shall not fast as ye do this day, to make your voice to be heard on high."

" Is such the fast that I have chosen ? the day for a man to afflict his soul ? is it to bow down his head as a rush, and to spread sackcloth and ashes under him ? Wilt thou call this a fast and an acceptable day unto the Lord ? "

[1] Our sages point out that when the Bible describes the penitence of the people of Nineveh (Jonah iii. 10), we are not told that God saw their fasting and their sackcloth, but that " God saw their works, that they turned from their evil way."

[2] The *Haphtarah* for the morning of the Day of Atonement.

"Is not this the fast that I have chosen? to loose the bonds of wickedness, to undo the bands of the yoke, and to let the oppressed go free, and that ye break every yoke?"

"Is it not to deal thy bread to the hungry, and that thou bring the poor that are cast out into thy house? when thou seest the naked that thou cover him, and that thou hide not thyself from thine own flesh?

"Then shall thy light break forth as the morning, and thine health shall spring forth speedily; and thy righteousness shall go before thee; the glory of the Lord shall be thy rearward."

"Then shalt thou call and the Lord shall answer; thou shalt cry, and He shall say, Here I am." [1]

So if you observe the fast as Isaiah bids you observe it, the Day of Atonement will be to you a true blessing. Year by year each Day of Atonement will find you purer in heart and soul. Year by year, your penitence, prayer, and good deeds will have wrought for you the true atonement, will have brought you the approbation of your conscience—the Divine Spirit within you—and with it the grace and forgiveness of your loving and merciful Creator.

[1] Isa. lviii. 4–9.

CHAPTER VIII

OBSERVANCES.—OUTWARD DISTINCTIONS

THE Bible tells us that when God made a covenant with Abraham, promising him that he should be the " father of many nations," that his descendants should be a great people who should possess all Canaan, and that He would be their God, He established the rite of circumcision, which was to be " a token of the covenant," [1] an outward sign and bodily distinction between Abraham's descendants and the rest of the world.

This rite was again enjoined by Moses,[2] and has been observed by all Israelites down to the present time. But you can hardly understand its true meaning and significance till you grow older.

There are other laws of the Pentateuch, which may also be called laws of outward distinctions — the law of מְזוּזָה, *Mezuzah*, the law of תְּפִלִּין, *Tephillin*, and the law of צִיצָת, *Tsitsith*. All these were to be signs of our allegiance to God, signs that we differ from all nations of the earth.

I will talk of the *Mezuzah* first.

Among the ancients, it was usual to set up images of their gods at the doors of their houses, so as

---

[1] Gen. xvii. 11.   [2] Lev. xii. 3.

to remind them of their duties every time they
entered or left their homes. Some of the colossal
idols, taken from the entrances of Egyptian palaces,
you may see in the British Museum. Of idolatry
and its frightful effects, I have already spoken ; so
you need not be surprised when I tell you that, in
the Law of Moses, everything was ordained so as
to root out idolatry.

You will find in the sixth chapter of Deuteronomy, from the fourth to the ninth verse, the שְׁמַע
(*Shemang*), those well-known words, which form the
declaration of the Israelite's faith : "Hear, O Israel,
The Lord our God, the Lord is One. And thou
shalt love the Lord thy God with all thine heart,
and with all thy soul; and with all thy might.
And these words, which I command thee this day,
shall be upon thine heart. And thou shalt teach
them diligently unto thy children, and shalt talk
of them when thou sittest in thine house, and
when thou walkest by the way, and when thou
liest down, and when thou risest up. And thou
shalt bind them for a sign upon thine hand, and
they shall be as frontlets between thine eyes. And
thou shalt write them upon the door-posts of thy
house, and upon thy gates."

These simple words, declaring our allegiance to
the One and only God, were to be written on the
door-posts of our habitations. And now, after
the lapse of many ages, this Commandment is
observed as follows. Upon a strip of parchment
are written the Declaration of Faith, the *Shemang*
above quoted (Deut. vi. 4–9), together with a por-

tion of the eleventh chapter of Deuteronomy (verses 13–21), in which the same Commandment is repeated and the doctrine of reward and punishment declared. The parchment is folded and enclosed in a case of glass, wood, or metal, the word שַׁדַּי *Shaddai* (Almighty) being alone visible on the outside ; and this enclosed parchment forms the *Mezuzah*.

It is still the custom with more observant Jews to put the *Mezuzah* on their door-posts, and, in many continental and Eastern towns, it is found *outside* the street-doors, as if to declare to the world, " This is the house of an Israelite." Judaism has rightly been called the religion of everyday life. It is intended to permeate our life, to become part and parcel of our existence, so that at every act of our lives we may keep in mind the idea of an ever-present, ever-watchful God, who sees us everywhere, and from whom we can conceal neither our acts nor our thoughts.[1] The sages tell us, " The consciousness of God's presence is the great teaching of our Religion." [2] And so the *Mezuzah*, which we cannot help seeing daily and many times in the day, cannot fail to remind us of the God whose Name, " Almighty," is inscribed thereon, and of our allegiance to that God, as expressed in the words written within the *Mezuzah*.

Next, the *Tephillin*, or phylacteries.

All of you must have seen, and many of you

---

[1] God asks through the prophet Jeremiah אִם יִסָּתֵר אִישׁ בַּמִּסְתָּרִים וַאֲנִי לֹא אֶרְאֶנּוּ " Can any hide himself in secret places, that I shall not see him ? " (Jer. xxiii. 24).

[2] שִׁוִּיתִי ה" לְנֶגְדִּי תָמִיד זוּ כְּלָל גָּדוֹל בַּתּוֹרָה:

must have used, the little square cases of leather, enclosing folds of parchment, on which are written certain passages from the Law, one case being attached to the left arm by a long thong of leather, the other to the forehead, just between the eyes, with a leather fillet or circlet, and long thongs of leather hanging therefrom. These constitute the *Tephillin*, and they are both worn during the time of Morning Prayer, except on Sabbaths and festivals.

The passages written on both the parchments are the two sections already referred to, as written in the *Mezuzah*—viz. the Declaration of Faith (Deut. vi. 4–9), and the promise of reward and punishment (Deut. xi. 13–21) ; and, further, the narrative of the wonderful redemption from Egypt and the sanctification of the first-born (Exod. xiii. 1–16). In these passages the command is four times repeated, that these words shall be bound as a sign upon our hands, and as frontlets, or as a memorial, between our eyes.

Now, what is the meaning, and what the teaching, of the *Tephillin ?* I will try to explain.

In olden times, and indeed in days not far distant, it was a custom among most nations to wear amulets or charms. These were of different sorts and kinds ; but they were usually little idols or images in human form, or sometimes (as among the Egyptians) representations of animals that were held sacred. These amulets or charms were worn upon the body, and were supposed to protect the wearer from evil.

You will be astonished at the absurdity of such a

practice. But you will be still more surprised to know that even now the same custom prevails among many barbarous nations of Asia, Africa, and America, among the half-civilised tribes of Russia, and even in Spain, Italy, and other countries, among people who claim to be educated and enlightened.[1] In Russia and Italy the priests are probably to blame for this ; for they traffic in such charms, bestowing upon them their blessing, without which they are supposed to be of no effect. What a horrid idea ! What a wretched superstition ! To suppose that men and women can be protected from evil, not by the Almighty Hand that made them, but by a puny little object fashioned by one man and blessed by another man !

That the wearing of such charms is a form of idolatry, I need not tell you ; for everything which derogates from our exclusive allegiance to the One and only God is idolatry. I have already related by what stringent laws the Israelites were guarded, and for what reason they were so guarded, against any and every form of idolatry, or against any custom that would lead thereto.

Now, when the *Tephillin* were ordained, God told the children of Israel, through His servant Moses, that if they would wear a charm upon their hands or upon their heads to protect them from evil, the words which He commanded them should be that charm. The constant remembrance of His law was the only charm which could protect them from

[1] The Italians wear a charm to guard themselves against the imagined mischievous effects of the *jettatura* or evil eye.

evil. This would be a charm different from that
worn by idolatrous nations. Not a lifeless image
of man or beast, but God's living word was to be
their protection. That word declared the Unity of
God, the doctrine of reward and punishment, and
the fact of the Divine redemption and revelation,
which together constitute the chief articles of our
faith. These were the words which were to be our
protection through life ; they were to encircle our
brain, the seat of understanding, and be ever
present in our mind ; they were to be bound upon
the left arm, near the heart, to remind us that we
must curb every unholy desire, repress every
impure thought, and that we must be filled with
the love of God ; they were to encircle our hands,
and bind those hands to be righteous and godly
in their work.

Of the *Tsitsith* or Fringes I need not say much ;
for their teaching is very similar to that of the
Mezuzah and *Tephillin*. In Num. xv. 37–41,
you will find that the Israelites were ordered to
wear fringes on the borders of their garments. In
Deut. xxii. 12, we find that these fringes were
to be on the outer garment, so as to be a dis-
tinctive mark before the world. These fringes are
still used on the *Arba Kanfoth*, and also on the
Talith, which every male Israelite is accustomed to
wear in synagogue. They are made of wool
or silk, and are twisted in a peculiar fashion with
a large number of threads. These threads are
meant to be typical of the many commandments
which form the Holy Law. And the text above

quoted tells us that the reason why the fringe is worn is that we may " look upon it, and remember all the commandments of the Lord and do them."

It was a custom among many ancient nations, before the invention of the art of writing, to use coloured threads for the purpose of reminding them of the chief events of their history. Thus, the ancient Mexicans and Peruvians used the so-called *quipus*—cords composed of threads of different colours, tightly twisted together, from which were suspended a number of smaller threads, which formed a fringe ; and these were used to record certain important events and facts in their history. It is difficult for us, with our widely different systems, to understand how this was done ; but probably the mental faculty, which we style the association of ideas, enabled them to associate certain numbers, colours, and patterns of threads with certain dates and events.

The *Tsitsith* or fringes fulfil a function somewhat similar to that of the *quipus*. If we bear in mind that these symbols have been instituted as memorials of God's commands, they will, every time we look upon them, arouse in our minds pious reflections, and stimulate us to godly actions.

In olden times, a peculiar blue thread formed part of the fringes ; but the special dye, produced from a worm—the *techeleth*—which was used for this purpose, is no longer procurable. This blue tint was intended to remind the Israelites of the blue vault of heaven, and of Him who is there enthroned, ever watchful of their every act and word and thought—for His eye is upon us continually; there is not a word on our tongue, but the Lord knoweth it entirely; not a thought in our heart, but it is laid open before Him.[1]

[1] See also "Sabbath Readings," No. 51, "The Fringes;" No. 29, "Tephillin;" No. 75, "Mezuzoth."

CHAPTER IX

SOCIAL DUTIES

THE Bible records that after God had given the
Ten Commandments, He ordered Moses to deliver
a series of " Judgments," [1] which were to form the
basis or foundation of the moral and social laws of
the Israelites ; that is to say, the laws which were
to regulate their manners and their dealings with
one another. It would have been easy to have said
in a few words, " Be just and kind to each other ; "
for this would have included almost everything.
But it would not have been sufficiently practical ;
so it was necessary to go into detail.

Laws relating to Servitude

The first series of these judgments referred to
slavery, or more properly to servitude. Now, you
might suppose that one of the first laws that would
have been given to a nation just released from
slavery would have been a law for putting an end
to all sorts of bondage ; and many writers who
have looked only on the surface of the Bible, have
regarded the Mosaic Law as cruel, because they
allege that it countenanced slavery. But it will be
seen that, far from countenancing, it almost entirely

[1] Exod. xxi., xxii., xxiii.

153

prohibits slavery—that is, slavery in the sense in
which we understand it. The Code ordains that
" he that stealeth a man and selleth him, or if he
be found in his hand, he shall surely be put to
death." [1] So slavery, such as we understand it,
such as existed until the middle of the last century
in some parts of America, and such as still exists
in certain parts of Asia and Africa, never could
have existed ; for it was an act punishable by
death to steal a human being.

Still, there was a mild kind of slavery permitted ;
but it was so hemmed in by laws for the protection
of the slave, that the words " servitude " and
" servant " should be used to designate this condition of semi-bondage rather than the words
" slavery " and " slave." [2] If you carefully read
Exod. xxi. and Deut. xv. 12–17, you will understand the nature of these protective laws. Only
under three conditions could such servitude exist.
First, foreigners who were taken prisoners of war
could be bought and sold as bondsmen. Secondly,
Hebrews who had been found guilty of certain
crimes were sentenced to penal servitude,[3] and
were liable to be sold as slaves, but for no longer
than six years, unless they, of their own accord,
renewed their servitude.[4] " In the seventh year he
shall go out free for nothing." [5] Thirdly, Hebrews,
who had become so poor that they could not sup-

[1] Exod. xxi. 16.
[2] In the Hebrew Bible, the word used—עֶבֶד—means equally
" slave " and " servant."
[3] Exod. xxii. 3.   [4] Exod. xxi. 5, 6.   [5] Exod. xxi. 2.

port themselves or their families, might sell themselves [1] into servitude ; but their servitude would also expire at the end of the sixth year, unless voluntarily renewed.

No unkindness of any sort was permitted towards servants or slaves. A runaway slave might not be captured and restored to his master.[2] If a master struck his servant or slave, and injured him, however slightly, he was obliged to let him go free ; [3] you may, therefore, be sure that no Israelite would risk the loss of his servant by striking him. And when the time of servitude was over, the Hebrew slave or servant did not go out into the wide world empty. He was to have enough to enable him to re-commence his life of freedom. " Thou shalt furnish him liberally out of thy flock and out of thy floor,[4] and out of thy wine-press ; of that wherewith the Lord thy God hath blessed thee, thou shalt give unto him : and thou shalt remember that thou wast a bondman in the land of Egypt, and the Lord thy God redeemed thee, therefore I command thee this thing to-day." [5]

Now you understand why the laws of slavery or servitude were the first of the judgments given to the Israelites. Moses tells them, You have yourselves been bondmen ; remember, when you become masters, not to be tyrants, like the Egyptians, but to be kind and merciful to those who have to serve you.

[1] Lev. xxv. 39.   [2] Deut. xxiii. 15, 16.   [3] Exod. xxi. 26, 27.
[4] Threshing-floor or granary.
[5] Deut. xv. 14, 15.

Protection of Life and Limb

In treating of the Sixth Commandment—" Thou shalt not murder "—I have already told you something about the care shown by the Mosaic Code in protecting human life.   But, before you will fully understand this, you must read for yourselves the laws relating to personal injury, as detailed in Exod. xxi. and xxii., and in other parts of the Pentateuch.

If a man killed another intentionally, " with guile," it was wilful murder, and he was surely to be put to death.[1]   But if a man killed another by accident,[2] then he was to be exiled to one of the cities of refuge, where his life was to be safe from the " avenger of blood," and he was to remain there till the death of the high-priest.   This exile must have been a terrible punishment for carelessness, and must have prevented many of those accidental deaths, which now too commonly occur from negligence and want of thought.

But the establishment of " cities of refuge " constituted a further protection to human life, in so far as it abolished the right of the " avenger of blood " in cases of accidental killing.   In olden times, and even in modern times among barbarous nations, it was the custom for the nearest relative of a person killed, either intentionally or by accident, to be " the avenger of blood," and to slay him who had caused his relative's death.   The

---

[1] Exod. xxi. 12, 14 ; Num. xxxv. 16, 18 ; Deut. xix. 11, 12.
[2] Exod. xxi. 13 ; Num. xxxv. 11, 12 ; Deut. xix. 4.

humane Mosaic Code permitted this revenge to be carried out only when the death was the result of a wilful act, clearly proved ; and the avenger of blood was not allowed to follow to the city of refuge, and to slay, the man who had been guilty of manslaughter, or accidental killing.

Even the life of the murderer was not to be sacrificed without an absolutely certain proof of his guilt. He could be put to death only on the evidence of at least two witnesses,[1] and these were bound to be eye-witnesses, not merely witnesses bringing circumstantial evidence, or facts tending to criminate the accused, but actual eye-witnesses of the crime.

Other crimes besides murder were punishable by death, such as blasphemy (or speaking disrespect-fully of God), worshipping strange gods, Sabbath-breaking, striking a parent, cursing a parent, man-stealing, and practising witchcraft ; but the punishment of death was so hemmed in by laws of evidence, all in favour of the accused, especially by the law requiring two eye-witnesses of the guilt, that an execution was, at least in the days of the Second Temple, a very rare occurrence,[2] and the death-punishment might rather be regarded as a preventive—a terror to evil-doers—than a social revenge.

The laws relating to personal injuries, not involving death, have frequently been criticised as barbarously severe. The words used in the Bible

---

[1] Num. xxxv. 30 ; Deut. xvii. 6.
[2] The Talmud says, not once in seventy years (*Maccoth, 7, a*).

are,[1] " Eye for eye ; tooth for tooth ; hand for
hand ; foot for foot. Burning for burning ; wound
for wound ; stripe for stripe." If the injury was
intentional, the injured party might claim an actual
infliction of similar injury : " As he hath done, so
shall it be done to him." [2]   The same law is repeated in Deuteronomy,[3] in connection with the
law for the punishment of false witnesses.

It will be readily understood that this law must
have been a terror to evil-doers, and must have
prevented many an act of violence. At first sight,
it seems terribly vindictive, and appears to foster
the passion for revenge so natural to injured
humanity. But in reality it is conceived in a true
spirit of mercy, regard being had to the condition
of society in olden times. In an age when strong
passions and lawlessness prevailed, no better means
could have been adopted than this for curbing the
spirit of " might against right," and for protecting
the weak against the strong.

Within recent times, the British legislature has
adopted the principle of this law, by inflicting
flogging upon that class of thieves known as
" garotters "—thieves who accompany their theft
with acts of violence or assault. The principle
might well be carried further. The dastardly
assaults on women and children, so common among
the lower classes, would soon vanish if the bully
who commits such crimes were led to regard the
contingency that " as he hath done, so shall it be
done to him."

[1] Exod. xxi. 24, 25.   [2] Lev. xxiv. 19, 20.   [3] Deut. xix. 21.

Far from fostering a vindictive and unforgiving spirit, as many have declared, the law has quite the contrary tendency. In a primitive state of society, it frequently occurred that the man who had suffered an injury would himself, or through his relatives, inflict the like injury upon the offender. A sort of lynch-law prevailed, such as even now prevails in some parts of Italy, Corsica, and Sicily, where the principle of personal revenge known as " *la vendetta* " exists—a sort of deadly family feud, transmitted from generation to generation, in consequence of some injury done to a remote ancestor centuries ago. The Mosaic law stepped in between the injured party and the offender, and declared that the offence must first be proved according to strict rules of evidence, and, if proved, must be regarded as an offence against society, which no longer the individual but the strong arm of the law must avenge. It was to be no longer a case of private revenge, which might overstep the bounds of justice, and mete out a punishment disproportionate to the offence. It was to be a case of calm, deliberate decision by the judges, according to strict rules of evidence, and the punishment was to be no greater than the offence.

It is a matter of absolute certainty that the law of " eye for eye " was never enforced to the letter. The difficulty of awarding a punishment exactly similar to the injury is obvious, especially in cases where an internal injury had been inflicted. It is therefore probable that the law was intended rather as a threat to prevent crimes of violence, and was interpreted in later Jewish legislation as indicating the debt due by the perpetrator to his victim. The law, in its textual form, only referred to cases of personal injury intentionally inflicted. For the infliction of accidental injury, or even of injuries resulting from a fair fight, the offender was to pay compensation, the amount being determined by the judges. We find [1] that if two men fight, and one injures the other, " and he die not, but keepeth his bed, if he rise again, and walk abroad upon his staff, then shall he that smote him be quit ; only he shall pay for the loss of his time, and shall cause him to be thoroughly healed."

The like principle of compensation is enforced in the cases of injuries resulting from negligence. If an ox, known to have been mischievous, gored a man to death, the ox was destroyed, the owner was considered responsible, and deserving of the punishment of death : but he was allowed in this case to do what was not permitted in other capital offences—to " give for the ransom of his life whatsoever is laid upon him ; " [2] that is, the judge awarded compensation to the family of the victim, in lieu of inflicting the punishment of death on the careless owner of the ox.[3]

If an ox injured a servant, the owner of the ox

[1] Exod. xxi. 18, 19.
[2] Exod. xxi. 29, 30, 31.
[3] This is not in opposition to the principle enjoined in Num. xxxv. 31, not to take redemption or ransom ; for that law refers to cases of wilful homicide, not to cases of accidental homicide, or to manslaughter caused by culpable heedlessness.

was bound to pay compensation to the master for the loss of service, and the ox was to be killed. It must be understood that in all these precepts the ox is to be regarded only as a representative animal, being the beast most likely to inflict injury ; and that similar laws were applicable to injuries resulting from the attacks of other animals.

The law of battlements is another representative law, having for its object the protection of human life from possible danger. It is enacted [1] that " when thou buildest a new house, then thou shalt make a battlement for thy roof, that thou bring not blood upon thy house, if any man fall from thence." No modern code contains laws guarding more jealously the interest of human life and limb. The law just referred to doubtless had greater significance in oriental countries, where most of the roofs are flat, and where people walk about on the housetops. But the law equally applies to other places besides roofs, such as unfenced cliffs and open wells or excavations, and indicates that any source of possible danger to life must be carefully and religiously avoided.

It may be interesting, in connection with this subject, to call attention to the law prescribed in case of the finding of the body of a person slain by an unknown hand.[2] The solemn procedure was one calculated to ensure the discovery of the murderer, if the discovery were at all possible. No one can read this precept without feeling the strong probability that it gave rise to the institution of

[1] Deut. xxii. 8.   [2] Deut. xxi. 1–9.

L

coroner's jury, one of the oldest legal institutions
of this country.

Rights of Property

In treating of the Eighth Commandment, I told
you that the protection of property was one of the
marks of distinction between savages and civilised
men, and I gave you a few examples of the laws of
the Mosaic Code for the prevention of dishonesty
and for the protection of property. I propose now
to tell you a little more about the same subject.

It was declared unlawful to remove any boundary
mark,[1] defining the ancient limits of land ; for the
removal of such land-mark might rob a neighbour
of part of his possessions.

It was declared unlawful to appropriate any lost
property ; and the finder was bound to search out
the owner, and restore the property to him.[2]

The master might not keep back the wages of
his servant, but was bound to pay him promptly.[3]

Any injury done by leaving an open pit unpro-
tected had to be paid for by the careless owner of
the pit.[4]

If one ox killed another, the owners of the two
oxen were to share the dead and living animals ; [5]
but if the assailing ox was known to have been
previously mischievous, and the owner had not tied
him up, he had to pay ox for ox, but the dead
animal became his property.[6]

Compensation was to be made for any injury, to

[1] Deut. xix. 14.   [2] Deut. xxii. 1–3.   [3] Lev. xix. 13.
[4] Exod. xxi. 34.   [5] Exod. xxi. 35.   [6] Exod. xxi. 35, 36.

a field or to a vineyard, caused by straying cattle ;
and in case of the accidental burning of standing
crops, the person who kindled the fire had to make
restitution.[1]

If an animal or other property deposited with
any one was lost or stolen, damaged or destroyed,
and the delinquent could not be discovered, he who
had taken charge of the property had to be put on
trial ; and if he satisfied the Judges by a statement
on oath that he had not himself been the cause of
the loss, theft, or damage, he was absolved.[2]   But
he had to make good the loss, if the animal or
property had been lent to him, the actual owner
not being present.

The rights of property might not be unduly or
harshly enforced against the very poor, or against
the hungry wayfarer.   Those who had occasion to
work in, or were passing through, a vineyard, might
eat some of the grapes, but might not carry any
away with them.   And a man passing through a
cornfield might pluck a few ears of corn with his
hand, and eat them ; but he was not allowed to cut
any with his sickle, and to remove them in bulk.[3]

Rights of Poverty

That poverty should have any rights is a pro-
position that would startle many economists even of
the present day.   These would probably admit the
pauper no right but that of a home in a workhouse,
or a pauper's grave.   But in Palestine there were

[1] Exod. xxii. 5, 6.   Exod. xxii. 7, 9.
[3] Deut. xxiii. 24, 25.

no workhouses ; for the Poor-law of the Mosaic
Code gave the poor certain rights, whereby they
might sustain life, and even recover their lost
position.

Charity has always been looked upon by the
Jews as a cardinal virtue. Even people not of our
faith and race have always regarded the charity
of the Jews as their greatest merit ; and the care
they have bestowed upon their poor has ever
evoked the wonder and admiration of the Gentile
world.

However, the charity of our people has probably
not been due to mere sentiment, but rather to a
habit—the result of the action of *our* poor-laws—
the result, too, of the fact that the poor, in accordance with those laws, occupy a recognised position
amongst us. A noble virtue, the effect of noble
sentiment, is a subject for just pride ; but when it
is the effect of long-established practice and habit,
from generation to generation, becoming part and
parcel of a people's instinct and character, it is a
subject for deep gratitude to the Great God, who
inspired His servant Moses to give us a Law of
Mercy, and to show us how to make Mercy the
habit of our life.

That Code tells us : " The poor shall never cease
out of the land ; therefore, I command thee, saying,
Thou shalt open thine hand wide unto thy brother,
to thy poor and to thy needy in thy land." [1]

These words left much to the liberality of the
individual ; but there were certain rights which the

[1] Deut. xv. 11.

poor possessed independently of such liberality.
The gleanings of the field were not to be gathered
by the farmer, nor was he permitted to reap the
corn standing in the corners of the fields. These
were to be left for the widow, the fatherless, and
the stranger. So, too, the forgotten sheaf, the
gleanings of the oliveyard and vineyard, and their
second crop were to be left for the poor and the
stranger.[1] We are enjoined to lend money to the
poor,[2] a loan being less humiliating and less
pauperising than a gift; and a loan to any of our
own people must invariably be without interest.[3]
"Thou shalt not give him thy money upon interest,[4] nor lend him thy victuals for increase."
Interest was allowed to be charged to an alien
settler, if the money was borrowed for trading
purposes; but it was not allowed to be charged
at all if the debt was incurred by one who had
fallen into poverty, or who required help for his
subsistence.[5]

At the end of every seven years, every debt was
released. "Every creditor that lendeth aught unto
his neighbour shall release it; he shall not exact
it of his neighbour or of his brother, because
the Lord's release hath been proclaimed. Of a
foreigner thou mayest exact it again."[6] But even
against the foreigner no act of oppression was
allowed. "Thou shalt neither vex a stranger nor

---

[1] Lev. xix. 9, 10 ; Lev. xxiii. 22 ; Deut. xxiv. 19, 20, 21.
[2] Deut. xv. 8.   [3] Lev. xxv. 36, 37.
[4] נֶשֶׁךְ mistranslated " usury " in the Authorised Version.
[5] Lev. xxv. 35.   [6] Deut. xv. 2, 3.

oppress him, for ye were strangers in the land of Egypt." [1] Nor was the thought of the year of release, and the possible loss of the money, to weigh with the lender. "Beware that there be not a wicked thought in thy heart, saying, The seventh year, the year of release is at hand, and thine eye be evil against thy poor brother, and thou givest him nought ; and he cry unto the Lord against thee, and it be sin unto thee. Thou shalt surely give him, and thine heart shall not be grieved, when thou givest unto him." [2]

Again it is said, "Thou shalt not harden thine heart, nor shut thine hand from thy poor brother." [3] Nor was the lender, who took security for a loan, to retain the article pledged, if it was an article of necessity : "If thou at all take thy neighbour's raiment to pledge, thou shall deliver it unto him by that the sun goeth down. For that is his only covering, it is his raiment for his skin : wherein shall he sleep ? " [4] A widow's raiment might not be taken in pledge,[5] nor might any implement of daily labour be accepted as a security.[6]

But the greatest of the rights of poverty was enforced by the law of Tithe. Besides the tithe of all produce which was annually given to the Levites, the Israelite was obliged to bring every third year the tenth part of his increase for the use of the poor. "At the end of three years, thou shalt bring forth all the tithe of thine increase in the

[1] Exod. xxii. 21.   [2] Deut. xv. 9, 10.
[3] Deut. xv. 7.   [4] Exod. xxii. 26, 27.
[5] Deut. xxiv. 17.   [6] Deut. xxiv. 6.

same year, and shalt lay it up within thy gates :
And the Levite (because he hath no part or inheritance with thee), and the stranger, and the
fatherless, and the widow, which are within thy
gates, shall come and shall eat and be satisfied ;
that the Lord thy God may bless thee in all the
work of thy hand which thou doest." [1]   In every
city, storehouses were established for the reception
of the tithe, and from this reserve the necessitous
were enabled to draw when misfortune befell them.
In the twenty-sixth chapter of Deuteronomy [2] you
may read the prayer which had to be recited when
each individual brought his tithe.   It began with a
solemn declaration that he had truly given the full
tenth of his profit, withholding nothing, and forgetting nothing ; and it terminated by imploring
the blessing of Heaven on those who had so obeyed
the Divine command.   You may read in the Books
of Chronicles and Nehemiah,[3] how truly and plenti-
fully the tithes were brought, and you will then
readily understand how the tithe liberally supplied
the wants of the poor.[4]

But even these were not the only rights of
poverty. The year of release was also the sabbatical year, the year in which the land rested.
Although during the sabbatical year the farmer
was not doomed to idleness (for he could dig water-
tanks, erect farm buildings, construct terraces for
his vineyards, repair his hedges and boundary

---

[1] Deut. xiv. 28, 29.   [2] Deut. xxvi. 13, 14, 15.
[3] 2 Chron. xxxi. 5, 6, 12 ; Neh. xiii. 12.
[4] See also Appendix III., " The Tithe."

walls), the land had to rest, so as to recruit its exhausted strength. No seed was then sown, no vineyard pruned, and no fruit gathered by the owner, the produce of the sixth year being always stored for the consumption of three years.[1] But though the land was wholly, and the farmer was partially, to rest on the seventh year, the crops still grew, the fruits still ripened. All these crops and fruits belonged to the poor,[2] and this beneficent arrangement probably enabled them to clear themselves of debt by payment, when their sense of honour would not permit the year of release to wipe off their obligation to their creditors.

Thus did our Sacred Code aim at the alleviation of the evils of poverty ; but by the laws which it instituted for the holding of land, it did more ; it aimed at the prevention of permanent poverty or hereditary pauperism.

The Land Laws

Every fiftieth year, the year of Jubilee, all land that had been sold reverted to the original owner, or to his family. So it was possible to the family of the poor man, who had been compelled to sell his possessions, to become again possessed of worldly means ; and thus the institution of the Jubilee, at a time when, apart from flocks and herds, land was the chief item of wealth, prevented that cardinal evil of civilised life, the concentration of wealth in the few, to the detriment of the many—a circum-

[1] Lev. xxv. 21.　　　　[2] Exod. xxiii. 11.

stance that gives rise to those terrible contrasts of modern society, excessive wealth and excessive poverty.

Except houses in walled cities, which could be sold as a perpetual possession, no landed property could be sold as perpetual freehold,[1] " for the land is Mine," saith the Lord. You will find in the Book of Joshua, how, when the Israelites had arrived in the Promised Land and conquered it, the country was divided by lot among the various tribes, and each man had his share. Thus at the outset every one possessed his parcel of land. Now, if a man became poor and sold his land, he or his relatives might, if they had the means, at any time repurchase it, paying for it according to the number of years that had to run to the Jubilee.[2] Even a house in a walled city, which might be sold for ever, could be repurchased at the same price by the original owner at any time within a year of the sale.[3] But, however poor he and his descendants might be, in the year of the Jubilee the land must revert to them, and so their poverty would not be a lasting poverty.

All these laws tended to check the greed for acquiring more and more land, seemingly one of the appetites of man, which, if inordinately indulged, must tend to the prejudice of his fellow-creatures.

Connected with the land laws may be mentioned the laws of inheritance. You will find these fully set forth in the twenty-seventh chapter of Numbers.

[1] Lev. xxv. 23, 29, 30.   [2] Lev. xxv. 25–27.
[3] Lev. xxv. 29.

They are particularly interesting; for one cannot help feeling that these laws of inheritance must have given rise to the Statute of Distributions, which regulates in this country the inheritance of the personal property of those who die without having made a will.

Laws of Government

I have already pointed out to you that, in its general laws, the Mosaic Code deals mainly with principles, and that when it descends to details, those details may be considered as representative examples of the application of those principles. This was necessary for a code which was to be permanent in outline, and whose principles consequently had to be applied to every age, clime, polity, and circumstance.

In the Mosaic laws relating to government, this is clearly seen. They are merely outline laws, which can be applied equally to a monarchy, a republic, or an oligarchy.

No special form of government is prescribed in the Law. But it was ordained, that *if* the Israelites were to elect a king, he must be one of themselves and not a stranger; that the king so chosen must not accumulate great wealth or worldly possessions, but that his chief duty was to keep intact the words of the Law. To this end he was bound to write, or to have written for himself, a copy of the Law, which was to be his text-book " all the days of his life." [1]

---

[1] Deut. xvii. 18, 19.

But though these laws were made for the guidance of the future kings of Israel and Judah, Monarchy was not enjoined as a necessary form of government. Provision was made for the Republic which was to succeed the rule of Moses [1]—the Republic over which Joshua was to preside as ruler, general, and judge ; and the people were ordered to hearken to his words and obey his mandates. In this commandment, the test of the true prophet is given, and the nation is warned against the false prophets who might " speak in the name of gods other " than the one true God.

Social order is the great object of all good government. Hence the law, " Judges and officers shalt thou make thee in all thy gates which the Lord thy God giveth thee according to thy tribes, and they shall judge the people with just judgment." [2]

How the judges and officers were first appointed, you will find described in the eighteenth chapter of Exodus. The law had not yet been given, and Moses was sole judge of Israel. Jethro his father-in-law found him engaged in judicial work from morning till evening, and remonstrated with him, saying, " Why sittest thou thyself alone, and all the people stand by thee from morning unto even ? " To which Moses, knowing himself to be inspired, modestly replied : " Because the people come unto me to inquire of God. When they have a matter, they come unto me ; and I judge between one and another, and I do make them know the statutes of God, and His laws." Thereupon Jethro

[1] Deut. xviii. 15.   [2] Deut. xvi. 18.

tells him that he will wear himself out with all this toil, and advises him to "provide out of all the people able men such as fear God, men of truth, hating covetousness, and place such over them to be rulers of thousands, rulers of hundreds, rulers of fifties, and rulers of tens, and let them judge the people at all seasons." The advice was followed, and we find that "the hard cases they brought unto Moses, but every small matter they judged themselves."

The charge to the judges so appointed we find in Deut. i. 16, 17 : "Hear the causes between your brethren, and judge righteously between every man and his brother, and the stranger that is with him. Ye shall not respect persons in judgment, but ye shall hear the small as well as the great ; ye shall not be afraid of the face of man, for the judgment is God's."

The judges were to discharge their duties with perfect justice, without fear, or favour, or chance of corruption : "Thou shalt not wrest judgment ; thou shalt not respect persons, neither take a gift ; for a gift doth blind the eyes of the wise, and pervert the words of the righteous." [1] In Leviticus we read : "Ye shall do no unrighteousness in judgment ; thou shalt not respect the person of the poor, nor honour the person of the mighty ; but in righteousness thou shalt judge thy neighbour." [2]

You have already seen that all difficult legal questions were referred to Moses, and you will read in the Pentateuch many examples of reference to

[1] Deut. xvi. 19.   [2] Lev. xix. 15.

him, such as the case of the blasphemer,[1] the
punishment of the Sabbath-breaker,[2] and the inheritance of the daughters of Zelophehad.[3]   But it
was necessary to make provision for a Supreme
Court of reference for future times ; and hence the
following law : " If there arise a matter too hard
for thee in judgment, between blood and blood,
between plea and plea, and between stroke and
stroke, being matters of controversy within thy
gates, then shalt thou arise and get thee up unto
the place which the Lord thy God shall choose.
And thou shalt come to the priests, the Levites,
and unto the judge that shall be in those days, and
inquire, and they shall show thee the sentence of
judgment.   And thou shalt do according to the
sentence which they shall show thee from that place
which the Lord shall choose." [4]   It is said that this
Law was the origin of the Sanhedrin or Supreme
Court of seventy-one members.[5]   You may read
in Chronicles [6] how Jehoshaphat, King of Judah,
appointed in Jerusalem such a supreme tribunal,
having previously placed local judges [7] in every
walled city of Judah.   You will read how he
charged the judges with the words, " Take heed
what ye do ; for ye judge not for man, but for the
Lord, who is with you in judgment."

[1] Lev. xxiv. 11.   [2] Num. xv. 33.
[3] Num. xxvii. 2.   [4] Deut. xvii. 8, 9, 10.
[5] See Appendix IV.   [6] 2 Chron. xix. 8–11.
[7] The local courts consisted of three judges for the trial of
civil suits, and twenty-three judges for the trial of criminal
suits. The decision of a majority decided ; but though a majority
of one was sufficient to acquit a prisoner, a majority of at least
two was necessary to convict him. (*Sanhedrin*, chap. i.)

The Court was to be formed of the priests, the Levites, and the judges, the best and most learned "that shall be in those days," and its judgment was to be final and conclusive.

It was a wise provision to establish Courts of this kind to pronounce judgment on matters of difficulty not specially provided for by the Mosaic Code ; for no code, however perfect, could intelligibly provide laws for every possible future change, circumstance, and contingency ; and as times and circumstances change, and human knowledge progresses, the details of the observance of those laws must be adjusted by competent and recognised authorities to suit the requirements of those times and circumstances, and the altered condition of human knowledge.[1]   And yet they must be so adjusted that the principle of the Law shall not be violated in practice, for " thou shalt not add thereto nor diminish from it." [2]   Hence the Israelites were bidden to refer to the living fountain of living knowledge, to the best contemporaneous opinion, " to the priests, the Levites, and unto the judge that shall be *in those days*."

Education

In these early days of compulsory education, when the lowest classes of society are only just

[1] " As to changes, great or small, Nature teaches us that nothing can live which cannot grow and change, and history confirms her lesson, that nothing is so fatal to institutions as a faith in their finality."—*Max Müller*.

[2] Deut. xii. 32.

emerging from the darkness of ignorance, and the " religious difficulty " has not yet disappeared, it is refreshing to turn back to the Mosaic Code, and see what provision was there made for the instruction of the young, and especially for their religious education.

The Levites were the appointed instructors of the people : " They shall teach Jacob Thy judgments, and Israel Thy law." [1] From the age of twenty-five to fifty, they performed the service of God in the Tabernacle or Temple, and after the age of fifty " they ceased waiting upon the service," but " ministered with their brethren in the Tent of Meeting to keep the charge." [2]

But though the Levites were thus ordained to be the ministers of religion and the public teachers, the Holy Law established a principle of religious instruction, which was to be by far the most important part of education—the instruction of children by their parents. The laws of God were not to be taught solely by public teachers. " Thou shalt teach them diligently to thy children, and shalt talk of them when thou sittest in thine house, and when thou walkest by the way." [3] It was to be the province of parents to instil religion into their own children, not only for the sake of the children, but for their own sakes. Moses tells the people,[4] " Only take heed to thyself, and keep thy soul diligently, lest thou forget the things which thine eyes have seen, and lest they depart from thy

[1] Deut. xxxiii. 10. [2] Num. viii. 24–26.
[3] Deut. vi. 7. [4] Deut. iv. 9.

heart all the days of thy life ; but teach them thy children, and thy children's children." To teach religion to our children is to keep religion alive, both in ourselves and in them. What teaching can be so forcible as a parent's teaching ? and what lesson can be so impressive as the lesson given by a father to his children, while walking abroad with them, discoursing of the wonders of Nature and the will of Nature's God ?

And so, when God gave, through His servant Moses, ordinances for the guidance of His chosen race, " He established a testimony in Jacob, and appointed a law in Israel, which He commanded our fathers, that they should make them known to their children ; That the generation to come might know them, even the children which should be born, who should arise and declare them to their children ; That they might set their hope in God, and not forget the works of God, but keep His commandments." [1]

History shows that many branches of knowledge have been lost, and many arts and sciences utterly forgotten, because parents have neglected the natural duty of teaching their own children. This happened with the ancient Egyptians, greatest of all nations of antiquity in the arts of construction, in science and in philosophy ; their knowledge became lost to the world, because instruction was in the hands of a privileged and dominant class— the priests—who used their position for their own aggrandisement, keeping their knowledge to them-

[1] Ps. lxxviii. 5, 6, 7.

selves, and leaving the multitude in ignorance and superstition. So with the ancient Chinese, conspicuous among Eastern nations for the cultivation of science and literature (traces of which have surprised advanced minds of modern times) : nearly all their knowledge was lost to the world in the like manner. But our Code maintains knowledge to be the heritage of the whole human race, and not the monopoly of priest or Levite. It declares that there are to be no priestly mysteries or secrets ; that education is a public right of the whole nation as well as a private duty of parent to child ; that all revealed knowledge is public property ; that though " the secret things belong to the Lord our God, those things which are revealed belong unto us and to our children for ever." [1]

Religious Toleration

We are told, " Thou shalt not vex a stranger nor oppress him, for ye were strangers in the land of Egypt." [2] Even the Egyptians, by whom the Israelites had been so unmercifully treated, were to be requited with charitable forbearance : " Thou shalt not abhor an Egyptian, because thou wast a stranger in his land." [3] The law knew no difference between Jew and Gentile. " If a stranger sojourn with you in your land, ye shall not vex him. But the stranger that dwelleth with you shall be unto you as one born among you, and thou shalt love him as thyself, for ye were strangers

[1] Deut. xxix. 29. [2] Exod. xxii. 21. [3] Deut. xxiii. 7.

M

in the land of Egypt." [1]   " One law shall be to
him that is home-born, and unto the stranger that
sojourneth among you." [2]

A stranger was permitted to join in the Divine
service of the Tabernacle and Temple, and was
even allowed to bring an offering to the altar of
God.   " If a stranger sojourn with you, or whoso-
ever be among you in your generations, and will
offer an offering made by fire of a sweet savour
unto the Lord ; as ye do, so shall he do. . . . One
ordinance shall be both for you and also for the
stranger that sojourneth with you, an ordinance
for ever in your generations, as ye are, so shall
be the stranger before the Lord." [3]   No lesson of
religious toleration could be enforced in stronger
terms than these.   The Bible practically tells us,
If God can thus tolerate those who believe not in
the true religion, why should not we ?   " He loveth
the stranger in giving him food and raiment ; love
ye therefore the stranger." [4]

There is, however, a kind of spurious tolerance
which is not the result of true philosophy or true
liberality, but rather the effect of religious indifference.   It is common enough to hear persons, in-
different to religion, say that one religion is as good
as another.   Against such indifference the Bible
warns us.[5]   There may be no lax attachment to
our religion.   There must be full and complete
loyalty to the One and only true God.

That such loyalty need not detract from our

[1] Lev. xix. 33, 34.   [2] Exod. xii. 49.   [3] Num. xv. 14, 15.
[4] Deut. x. 18, 19.   [5] Deut. xiii. 6.

tolerance of the religion of others, may be best proved by reference to a prayer—perhaps the most remarkable in the whole Bible—the prayer of King Solomon at the dedication of the Temple. He craves the blessing of Heaven on the building he had raised to the glory of God, and begs that the prayers and supplications, that he and his people may there offer, may be favourably answered ; and then he craves the same blessing for those who were not of his own faith : " Moreover concerning the stranger that is not of Thy people Israel, but is come from a far country for Thy great name's sake, and Thy mighty hand and Thy stretched-out arm ; if they come and pray in this house ; Then hear Thou from heaven, even from Thy dwelling-place, and do according to all that the stranger calleth to Thee for." [1] We know from the Talmudical and other accounts of the Temple (and these accounts are supported by the results of recent investigations) that this prayer was not, as some might suppose, the mere individual expression of the liberality of a wisely liberal king. For it has been found that, surrounding the *chel*, or raised platform on which the Temple was erected, and lying between the outer portico and the Temple proper, there was a great corridor thirty cubits (forty-five feet) wide, which was known as the " court of Gentiles," destined for the worship of strangers, and that this court, which formed an inner belt encircling the Temple, was many times larger than the " court of the men of Israel." [2]

[1] 2 Chron. vi. 32, 33.   [2] Fergusson's " Temples of the Jews."

The prayer of King Solomon, in its application
to the Gentile world, was therefore no dead letter.
The liberal spirit which pervades this noble prayer
is the spirit of our holy law. If that spirit had
permeated the two creeds which have sprung from
our religion, then history would not have had to
record, as it unfortunately does, so many stories of
persecution, so many reigns of terror, so many
orgies of fire and sword.

In the nineteenth century, for the first time in
the history of the world, a few Gentile nations
declared the same principle of religious toleration,
propounded in our Code thousands of years ago.
In some countries it has been proclaimed by the
civil powers, the spiritual powers still denying the
principle. Many of the clergy of religions other
than our own, doubtless actuated by sincere though
mistaken motives, still condemn to perdition all
who refuse to believe as they do. The Jew, living
among people many of whom would hold a close
monopoly of God and of eternal happiness, represents to-day the true spirit of religious charity and
tolerance, proclaiming, as did the Psalmist, that
God is not a sectarian God, but that " the Lord is
good to all, and His tender mercies are over all His
works." [1] The Jew, acting in the spirit of the
noblest commandments of the Mosaic Code, proclaims all men equal in the sight of God, and
repudiates even the possibility that perdition and
everlasting torment can follow religious error,
honestly believed.

[1] Ps. cxlv. 9.

The Jew hopes and believes that the day will come when all the world will recognise the One true God.   Till then, there may be many religions ; there can be but one morality ; and so our sages, in the true spirit of toleration, have declared that " the righteous of every faith have their share in the world to come." [1]

---

[1] Maimonides, *Hilchoth Teshubah*.   Comp. *Sanhedrin*, 105 *a*.

CHAPTER X

MORAL DUTIES

THE laws to which I have referred in the last chapter, I have described under the head of " social duties," because they are the laws which tend to keep society together, and they constitute, in fact, a sort of public law. The laws of which I propose next to treat are also in a great measure social, seeing that they affect every individual, and that society is made up of individuals ; but I prefer to set them by themselves, because they relate to private virtue rather than to public law, and also because they appeal to every human being, regardless of race or creed.

It has been truly said that men cannot be made virtuous by Act of Parliament. The restraints of law may prevent men from being criminal, but will not make them virtuous. One constantly meets men who are seemingly good citizens, and who yet are bad, immoral, and irreligious men. But such a contradiction the Mosaic Code does not recognise. " Thou shalt be perfect with the Lord thy God," [1] perfect before God as before the world. It is not sufficient to do one's duty to the country in which we live, to obey its laws, to be patriotic, and to pay

[1] Deut. xviii. 13.

our dues to the State. No one can be a truly good citizen without being a virtuous man.

You know already that there are, unfortunately, a great number of religions in the world besides your own holy faith. Considering the terrible wars, strifes, and persecutions that have resulted, and still result, from differences of religious belief, staining with blood nearly every page of history, it seems a sad thing that there should ever have been a multitude of religions; and one must sincerely long for the time when, in the fulness of God's wisdom, He may bring the whole world to adopt that one great and sacred belief, which you proudly regard as your own.

But terrible as have been the consequences of these religious differences, there remains one consoling fact that, with very few exceptions, all religions are agreed upon the laws of morality, and the principles of right and wrong.[1] Indeed, curiously enough, many savage nations, with but little religious sentiment, and no defined ideas about the nature of God, have yet in their rude literature

---

[1] "Morality is the one thing eminently serious and true, and by itself it suffices to give meaning and direction to life. Impenetrable veils hide from us the secret of this world, whose reality is at once irresistible and oppressive. . . . But there is one foundation which no doubt can shake, and in which man will ever find a firm ground amidst his uncertainties; good is good, and evil is evil. No system is necessary to enable us to love the one and hate the other; and it is in this sense that faith and love, possessing no seeming connection with the intellect, are the true base of moral certainty, and the only means possessed by man of understanding in some slight measure the problem of his origin and destiny."—RENAN.

recorded laws of morality not differing greatly from our own, though these laws may, perhaps, have been but lightly regarded by them.

Love of God

First among the moral duties which belong to every religion is the duty to love, fear, and honour God. It seems so simple a matter to love the Great Being to whom we owe our existence, our food, our clothing, our strength, our faculties, and all we possess, that obedience to this law should be as natural as obedience to the appetites of hunger and thirst. But our faith, whatever may be the case with other creeds, does not permit us to indulge in a piety that costs us nothing, and that is a mere obedience to a natural instinct; for we are told not merely to love God, but to love Him " with all thine heart, with all thy soul, and with all thy might." [1]

What does this qualification signify? The history of Judaism, with its large army of worthies who have suffered persecution for their faith and yet steadfastly adhered to it, and the long array of martyrs who have sacrificed their lives for the sake of their religion, will afford the best interpretation of these words. With all our heart, the centre of our emotions; with all our soul, the fountain of our thought, our reason, and our faith; with all our bodily powers, with every nerve and every muscle that makes us beings of action—we are to show our love and adoration of the God who made

[1] Deut. vi. 5.

us, and are to be prepared to sacrifice everything
for the love of Him.

But you may reply that this is a vague gener-
ality ; " to sacrifice everything " is a pretty phrase.
True, we Jews in this country are no longer called
upon to bear the crown of martyrdom, to die for
our faith ; how, then, can we show our love to the
God of Heaven and Earth ? The Bible tells us
how to do this : " To keep the commandments of
the Lord, and His statutes, which I command thee
this day, for thy good." [1] We have to keep the
Law not only for God's glory or His pleasure, but
for *our* good. Our good and our happiness are the
benign objects of God in giving us the Law. How
can the obedience of a small nation in one of His
little planets profit Him, the Creator of the mighty
universe ? " Behold the heaven, and the heaven of
heavens belongeth to the Lord thy God, the earth
also and all that therein is. Only the Lord had a
delight in thy fathers to love them, and He chose
their seed after them, even you, above all peoples,
as it is this day." [2]

Thus, love of God means obedience to His will ;
and obedience to His will brings, as its results and
reward, our happiness.

And here it may be well to make a digression
to indicate one great point of difference between
Judaism and many other religions. Although our
religion undoubtedly requires of us many sacrifices
and deprivations, yet Judaism is essentially a
happy religion. It is not a religion of long faces,

[1] Deut. x. 13.   [2] Deut. x. 14, 15.

many fasts, much self-mortification, and everlasting
seriousness. The Sabbath of the intelligent Jew is
a rational, not a puritanical Sabbath. Light and
gladness (אוֹרָה וְשִׂמְחָה) are the outward characteristics of our sacred festivals. We are not to show
our love to God by making ourselves miserable :
though we are called a "kingdom of priests," we
are not to be a nation of monks and nuns. The
Nazirite was esteemed a sinner for his asceticism,
and had to bring a sin-offering.[1]

We are not to "groan away our lives in a busy
contemplation of our sins."[2]   Although several
fast-days were instituted in the course of time, to
commemorate sad events that had befallen our
nation, on one day only in the year does the Law
bid us afflict our souls. We are to "serve the
Lord with gladness, enter His presence with singing."[3]   Our religion and our happiness are to go
hand in hand. Our love of God and obedience to
His laws are to make us happy.

But though the love of God is a duty enjoined
by every religion, there is something special about
that duty as enjoined upon the Jew. For his belief
in the Unity of God compels him to give undivided
homage to the Deity he adores. Other creeds have
their secondary deities, or demi-gods, or mediators ;
but the God of the Jew is the One sole God, the
One Creator of the universe, who works by His
own great power, and who, nevertheless, may be
approached in prayer and supplication by the

---

[1] Num. vi. 14.
[2] *Sabbath Readings :* "Sunny Aspects of Religion."   [3] Ps. c. 2.

humblest of His creatures, *without any mediator*.
And in these words does He declare His sole and
sovereign power : " See now that I, even I, am
He, and there is no God with Me ; I kill, and I
make alive ; I wound, and I heal ; neither is there
any that can deliver out of My hand." [1]

Herein lies the great comfort of our sacred
religion ; and this constitutes another source of
happiness for the Jew.   Other faiths have regarded
their God as a Deity who will not forgive without
the mediation of a being, half-God, half-man ; or
of a priest, who represents himself as the accredited
agent of this mediator.   Our religion represents
God, as He represents Himself, as a " God, merciful
and gracious, long-suffering, and abundant in goodness and truth, Keeping mercy for thousands, forgiving iniquity, transgression, and sin," [2] so that we
need no secondary deity to crave pardon on our be-
half.   The priests of other faiths, anxious to establish their position as mediators, by playing upon the
fears of their credulous flocks, and wishing to make
a profit out of the too susceptible consciences of
their congregations, have invented the terrible idea
of hell, with the devil as its presiding deity ; and
this hell they represent as a place of eternal torment
for the souls of the wicked and the unbeliever.

Our religion knows no such sacrilegious ideas.   It
cannot contemplate the possibility that the same
loving God, who claims our love, and whose universe teems with proofs of His kindness, can be a
vindictive God, capable of giving *eternal* punish-

[1] Deut. xxxii. 39.   [2] Exod. xxxiv. 6, 7.

ment to a human soul. It cannot conceive that
the same God, who inspired into our code a true
message of love, in which we are enjoined to be
kind to our neighbours, our dependants, and even
to the helpless brutes, could think of inflicting
everlasting torture on the souls of those whom He
created with faults and failings ; nor can it admit
the possibility that the Almighty God of good
would permit the existence of a devil, or god of
evil, side by side with Himself, to counteract His
goodness and to check His mercy. "There is no
God with Me," is the Divine declaration.[1]

But you will ask, "How about reward and
punishment in the future state ?" We are taught
to believe this doctrine, and we are told that God
"will not wholly clear the guilty ;"[2] but the idea
that the loving God should inflict on a soul eternal
punishment, or eternal perdition, is too revolting to
be even contemplated. It would be blasphemy to
believe it. We are told to fear God, to fear His
displeasure, not as we would fear a tyrant king, but
as we would fear to incur the displeasure of a

[1] "And to declare that we have such a loving Father, whose
mercy is over *all* his works and whose will and law is so lovely
and lovable, that it is sweeter than honey, and more precious
than gold, to those who can taste and see that the Lord is Good
—this surely is a most pleasant and glorious good message and
spell to bring to men—as distinguished from the evil message
and accursed spell that Satan has brought to the nations of the
world instead of it, that they have no Father, but only ' a
consuming fire ' ready to devour them, unless they are delivered
from the raging flame by some scheme of pardon for all. . . ."
—JOHN RUSKIN'S *Letters to the Clergy* (v.).

[2] Exod. xxxiv. 7.

parent, or the forfeiture of his love. When, in His Sacred Book, He speaks of punishing us, it is in the language of a wise father to an erring child. He does not threaten us with eternal, or even with long, punishment. " For a small moment have I forsaken thee, but with great mercies will I gather thee. In a little wrath I hid My face from thee for a moment ; but with everlasting kindness will I have mercy on thee, saith the Lord, thy Redeemer." [1]

This, then, is the God we are told to love with all the emotions of our heart, with all the faith of our soul, with all the might of our body ; and therefore, when He bids us love Him, He permits us not to couple with His worship any other god. Our forefathers were, therefore, ordered not only not to worship any other gods, but not even to mention their names. They were to overthrow their altars, to break down their pillars, burn their groves, and hew down their graven images.[2] Their love and worship of God was to be whole and un-divided ; they were to have no secondary gods, no intercessors, no mediators.

And when idolatry was ordered to be rooted out, another arch-enemy of religion had also to be destroyed—superstition, the offspring of idolatry. Hence there were laws for the prevention of those superstitious practices which had been carried out by the priests of idolatrous nations, who recognised powers other than the Great Power who rules the universe. So we find the command against Moloch-worship, divination, witchcraft, the observing of

---

[1] Isa. liv. 7, 8.   [2] Deut. xii. 3.

times, and the other so-called black arts, by means
of which the priests of ancient religions were wont
to gain ascendancy over the vulgar and the ignorant, by playing upon their fears and exciting
their morbid imaginations.

Even in these our times, superstition is not quite
dead ; for, besides those who cling to the superstitions of other religions, there are people who,
under the mistaken title of spiritualist mediums,
pretend to possess occult supernatural powers. But
the Jew laughs at such superstitions. Believing in
One only God, the First Cause, Sole Ruler of the
Universe, he knows and recognises no other Power
as divine ; and all the wonders he sees, whether he
understands their action or not, are wonders of
Nature, the work of Nature's One sole God, whom
he loves and adores with all his heart and soul and
might, and who requites that love and adoration
with a mercy enduring for ever.

On the duty of prayer as an outward mode of
exhibiting our love of God, I need not here dilate,
having treated of that subject elsewhere.[1] It is
sufficient to add, that prayer must ever be the
spontaneous homage of the heart ; not an irksome
duty, like a tax unwillingly paid. It must be the
voluntary outpouring of the heart, not alone in the
set phrases of the prayer-book, but in the unspoken
language of our soul. " The Highest," says Goethe,
" cannot be spoken of in words."

For as, in the highest form of love, at the supreme
moments of life, soul speaks to soul without word or

[1] Page 114.

sound or utterance, so can man, abstracting himself from his surroundings, at all times hold silent communion with his Maker ; he can raise his soul upon the wings of wordless prayer, and render silent praise to the One and only God.[1] Surely this is the meaning of the Psalmist when he exclaims, " Unto thee, O Lord, do I lift up my soul." [2]

Respect for Parents and for the Aged

In treating of the Fifth Commandment, I have already told you something about the duties we owe to our parents. But it is not only in the Decalogue that those duties are enforced. In the 19th chapter of Leviticus, from which so many ordinances have been quoted, we find, " Ye shall fear every man his mother and his father." [3] In the 21st chapter of Exodus,[4] death is ordained as the punishment of the child who strikes or who curses a parent ; and among the terrible imprecations that were pronounced on Mount Gerizim as a warning to the Israelites, we find, " Cursed be he that setteth light by his father or his mother." [5]

First and foremost among the duties that we owe

---

[1] " To Thee, even silence is praise " (Ps. lxv. 2). — The ancient Egyptians, long before the time of Moses, worshipped one chief god, Amun-Ra, whose name they were not allowed to pronounce, and they always worshipped him in silence. This sentiment was well appreciated by Goethe, who remarks : " People treat the Divine Name as if that Incomprehensible and Most High Being, who is even beyond the reach of thought, were only their equal. If they were truly impressed by His Greatness, they would be dumb, and, through veneration, be unwilling to name Him."

[2] Ps. xxv. 1. [3] Lev. xix. 3.
[4] Exod. xxi. 15, 17. [5] Deut. xxvii. 16.

to our fellow-creatures are those that we owe to
our parents. These duties are impressed upon us
strongly by nature ; for without being taught them,
every right-minded child fulfils them by intuition.
The Bible, therefore, justly treats the wicked,
irreverent son as an unnatural monster not worthy
to live. The bad son is certain to be a bad man,
and a bad citizen, in every relation of domestic and
social life. He is a social pest, and is consequently
worthy of death. In the twenty-first chapter of
Deuteronomy, you will read about the punishment
incurred by the stubborn and rebellious son. The
men of his city were to stone him to death.
Throughout the Bible, and in our later records,
there is no mention of the infliction of capital punishment on a son for an offence against his parents ; so
we may hope that there was never cause for such
punishment, and that the law, severe as it seems,
was rather declared as a terror and a warning to
those who might be apt to disregard the duties
they owed to their parents.

Closely connected with the laws as to filial duties
is that which ordains respect to the aged—" Thou
shalt rise up before the hoary head, and honour
the face of the old man, and fear thy God." [1] For,
one aspect of this law, as well as that relating to
assaults on parents, must not be forgotten. It was
a custom among many barbarous nations to slay
old people who were overwhelmed with the in-
firmities of age ; and this act of murder was even
committed by sons on their parents.

[1] Lev. xix. 32.

Although such a custom is shocking to contemplate, it is perhaps no worse than might be expected from nations with whom brute force and physical strength were the only qualities that were valued. The Mosaic Code puts old age on a different basis. The aged are not to be regarded as mere encumbrances, burdening the world with their weaknesses. They are not to be cast aside when their work is over, and their power of work is spent. They are to be treated reverently and respectfully; for though their strength of body may have departed, they have acquired knowledge and accumulated experience as useful to the world as physical prowess. And this is the meaning of the proverbs: "The hoary head is a crown of glory, if it be found in the way of righteousness." [1] "The glory of young men is their strength, and the beauty of old men is the grey head." [2]

"Thou shalt love thy neighbour as thyself"

The duty involved in this law [3] is one that is included in almost every code of morality and in almost every religious system. There is a well-worn tale told of two learned and rival doctors of the Talmud, Hillel and Shammai, which bears upon this commandment, and indicates the importance attached to it by Judaism. A scoffing heathen applied to Shammai, requesting him to teach him the laws of Judaism in the short space of time that he could stand on one foot. Shammai, in anger, sent the scoffer away. Thus repulsed, he went to

[1] Prov. xvi. 31.   [2] Prov. xx. 29.   [3] Lev. xix. 18.

Hillel, and made the same request of him. And Hillel replied, " Do thou not unto another what thou wouldst not have another do unto thee. This is the whole law ; the rest is mere commentary."

The precept, " Thou shalt love thy neighbour as thyself," truly embraces every other law of morality. It is a protest against selfishness—the origin of every vice, and itself the greatest vice. If you love your neighbour as yourself, you will be just to him, you will not wrong him in any way, you will not hate, despise, or dishonour him ; you will help him in misfortune, and you will judge him charitably.

But perhaps you may think this law to love one's neighbour as one's self is a little unreasonable—nay, impossible. You may ask, How can any one love his neighbour as dearly as he loves himself ? Perhaps you love yourself very dearly, and think a great deal of yourself, your hopes, your aims, and your ambitions. It is quite natural that you should. Self-love is deeply implanted in every human heart. How, then, can you be expected to love your neighbour as yourself ?

In this way. Your own happiness and welfare depend on the happiness and welfare of others. No king was ever happy whose subjects were unhappy. No head of a household can be happy if his family and servants are in a constant state of discord. No employer can be happy if his workpeople are dis-contented, sullen in their demeanour, and per-petually at war with him. Thus the happiness of every individual depends on the happiness of those with whom he comes in daily contact. If, therefore, you truly love yourself, and prize your happiness, love your neighbour as much, and prize his happiness. The machinery of the social world can only be kept in action, free from friction and disturbance, by recognising the fact that no one can possibly be truly, permanently, and honourably happy at the expense of his fellow-creatures. Wealth, with its unequal distribution, will always create different social grades, and on some the burden of work will ever fall more hardly than on others. It does not follow that this heavy burden of work entails unhappiness. On the contrary, those who have to work too hard are not more unhappy than those who lead a lazy, unprofitable life. Still, poverty has its undoubted evils; and it is the duty of the rich to soften down the asperities and hardships that afflict the poor.

Our duties to the poor have already been frequently referred to in this book, but they should again come under our consideration when we regard the precept to "love thy neighbour as thyself." For philanthropy—the love of one's fellow-creatures —has always been, with our people, not a mere pious sentiment, but a practical virtue that forms part of our lives. Hence our synagogues have always been centres of benevolent work, so that our lip-worship, our heart-worship, and our hand-worship (or charity) have always existed side by side, and we show our love to our poor neighbour not merely by pitying him and saying, " Poor fellow ! " but by relieving his pressing wants, and striving to improve his position permanently.

Many rich people, unfortunately for themselves and the world, neglect their duty to the poor, the chief offenders being usually young people who have inherited the wealth of others, and not gained riches by any effort of their own. These, unable or unwilling to spend their money usefully and rationally, often lose their fortunes by their own imprudence. We must charitably pity such people, however well they may deserve their fate; for they have missed a great chance of happiness for themselves and others.

Our sages tell us that "Charity is the salt of wealth," מֶלַח מָמוֹן צְדָקָה. It acts, like salt, as a preservative. No man who gives wisely in charity is likely to dissipate his fortune by gambling or other acts of imprudence, for he, in the bestowal of charity, has learnt the true value of money. And, in another sense, charity is the salt of wealth; for, as salt gives flavour and relish to our food, so does charity give zest and enjoyment to the possession of money; for, to the right-minded man, there is no purer pleasure than to give to those who need his aid, and no higher delight than to witness the good results of his liberality.

Nor is it only by money gifts that we can show our love to our neighbour. We cannot all afford to give money. But there are kindly acts and words that are even more precious than coin; and these can be given by rich and poor alike. Our rabbis recognised this distinction between alms-giving (צְדָקָה) and charity in the sense of acts of kindness (גְּמִלוּת חֲסָדִים). "Alms," they said, "can

only be given to the poor.   Acts of kindness
can be given to poor and rich."   The former is
chiefly offered in money, the latter in loving personal service.   Such services can be bestowed—
indeed, best bestowed—by the young, who are quick
in sympathy and generous in thought.   So you
must never let a day pass without being able, at
its close, to call to mind some kind and gentle act
or word of yours that has brought on that day a
gleam of happiness to at least one relative or friend
or neighbour ; and so in your daily life you will
show you love your neighbour as yourself, and will,
in that unselfish love, be happy.

Unfortunately, in our artificial state of society,
the relations of employer and employed are far
from satisfactory, both frequently forgetting the
command, " Thou shalt love thy neighbour as
thyself."   The master is frequently too exacting to
his servant, the servant too careless of the employer's interests ; and hence arise those unhappy
relations between employer and employed, which
have so often culminated in ruinous trade-disputes,
outrages, and strikes.   A selfish policy never thrives.
There are in this country industries which have
been established and prospered, mainly because
masters and men have treated one another as
fellow-workers with a common interest, each loving
his neighbour as himself, seeking his welfare, and
looking for happiness in the happiness of his fellows.
But there are other industries which have failed
and disappeared, because masters and men have
tried to make as much as possible out of each

other, regardless of all considerations but their own selfish aims.

Nor is it only in the conflict between labour and capital that this primary law of morality is so often forgotten. The disputes between individuals which find their way into the law-courts, and the disputes between nations which give rise to sanguinary wars, all have their origin in the neglect of this same law. The principles of right and wrong are sufficiently clear, so that no man need wrong his neighbour in ignorance. If he loved his neighbour as himself, he would not wrong him, and would no more think of damaging the interests of his neighbour than of endangering his own.

But as regards nations, the law has greater force. War, that dread curse, which has converted many of the fairest gardens of the earth into huge ceme-teries ; which has changed friends into fiends, human beings into brutes, and aroused passions which only the chill hand of death could subdue— war would have no existence if every nation, instead of envying, despising, or hating, would love its neighbour as itself. Patriotism becomes the worst of vices when, forgetful of that duty, a nation wages a war of aggression against a neighbour whose land it covets.

War is, in sober truth, a hideous thing ; and so men strive to clothe its hideousness in decent garb. They hide the blood beneath the crimson uniform, and stifle the groans of wounded men with music jubilant and gay. They drown the sobs and sighs of orphans and of widows with songs of victory, and call the murderous work of battle a work of glory.

But if the truth be told, whispered, or thought, war is at best but wholesale homicide, the aggressors but wholesale murderers ; aggressive war, at best, but wholesale robbery ; the nation longing for its neighbour's lands but wholesale plunderers and thieves.

And of the wars waged or pretended to be waged for a principle of honour, none would exist if honour meant but honesty, and glory meant God's glory and not man's. His glory is to " make the whole world kin," to make this world a world of peace and happiness, to make man's life " like days of heaven upon earth." Therefore He gave to man this law of love—" to love his neighbour as himself "—to widen the sphere of human sympathies, to bridge the rivers, seas, and oceans with one broad span of wide philanthropy, to make the earth one nation, and all mankind fellow-citizens.

Honesty and Truth

The duty of truthful, honest dealing has been already enforced in treating of the Third and Eighth Commandments. The command is again repeated in Leviticus, " Ye shall not steal, neither deal falsely, neither lie one to another." [1]   " Thou shalt not defraud thy neighbour." [2]   " Just balances, just weights, a just ephah, a just hin, shall ye have." [3]

The arm of the law, in all civilised countries,

[1] Lev. xix. 11.   [2] Lev. xix. 13.   [3] Lev. xix. 36.

protects the weak against the strong, and prevents direct robbery by the highwayman.   But there is an indirect robbery which too often evades the law, and is unfortunately very prevalent in most commercial countries.   To deal falsely, to misrepresent wares and merchandise to be what they are not, to lie to a purchaser as to the value or cost of a commodity, to give short weight, to accept illegal commissions or bribes, are all forms of commercial immorality which sap the foundations of society, and yet by some are regarded almost as matters of course and mere incidents of business.   The evils engendered by such loose principles of dealing are incalculable.   General distrust and suspicion take the place of confidence.   The purchaser is bound to waste his time in a vigilant examination of what he buys, lest he may be defrauded ; and, notwithstanding his vigilance, he may yet be cheated. Goods have to be weighed and measured, over and over again, lest, at some point of transfer or transit, something may have been abstracted.   Nor must it be imagined that acts of dishonesty exist only among small traders.   Recent experience has shown that merchants of the highest reputation have been guilty of gigantic frauds ; and when those frauds were discovered, their plea was simply that they were quite the usual thing, and that most people did as they did.

Distrust, suspicion, and loss of time are not the only evils resulting from commercial dishonesty. Dishonesty breeds dishonesty.   The honest trader finds that he cannot compete successfully with the

dishonest one, and becomes dishonest like his
neighbour ; and so the standard of morality becomes generally degraded. Many think this condition of things harmless, because every man of the
world is prepared for it, and believes nothing but
the evidence of his senses. But, practically, the
results are very serious, and, most serious of all,
not to the intended victim, but to the dishonest
trader himself. His notion of honour becomes
vitiated and blunted. He acquires loose ideas
regarding honesty and truth.

But Moses has declared that " all that do such
things and all that do unrighteously are an abomi-
nation unto the Lord thy God ; " [1] and it is surely
not difficult to imagine that He, who is the Essence
of Truth and Justice, must abominate those who
steal, or deal falsely with, or lie one to another.

Truth is the basis of all morality. " A righteous
man hateth lying," says the Book of Proverbs.[2]
He who adheres to truth will be righteous in all
things. Nor must the truthfulness consist merely
in abstaining from a direct lie.   Equivocation,
flattery, misrepresentation, and duplicity are all
forms of lying as hateful as the bold and direct lie,
perhaps more so. " Deliver my soul from lying
lips and a deceitful tongue," is the prayer of the
Psalmist.[3] " Guard my tongue from evil, and my
lips from uttering deceit," is our own thrice-repeated
daily prayer. Truth is the guardian of the soul. If
it retain truth, it will retain innocence ; and contact
with the world will leave it unharmed and unstained.

[1] Deut. xxv. 16.   [2] Prov. xiii. 5.   [3] Ps. cxx. 2.

" Who," asks the Psalmist, " shall ascend unto
the mountain of the Lord ? or who shall stand in
His holy place ? He that hath clean hands, and
a pure heart ; who hath not lifted up his soul unto
vanity, nor sworn deceitfully ; He shall receive a
blessing from the Lord, and righteousness from the
God of his salvation." [1]

Avoidance of Slander and False Report

When treating of the Third and Ninth Commandments, I told you something about the frightful sin
of speaking falsely of others. Our concern is now
with a group of laws all closely connected with the
law against false evidence.

" Thou shalt not raise a false report," [2] applies
not alone to individuals, but to things and circumstances. Great injury may be done by publishing
false reports or rumours, though they be not intended to injure any individual. The law just
quoted is directed against exaggeration, misrepresentation of facts, and misstatement of events. In
modern times press-writers have been the greatest
offenders against this law, and have been too often
responsible for the promotion of international
hatreds by false and garbled reports, which, being
sensational, are eagerly read, and are believed by a
too credulous public.

The love of the marvellous is strongly implanted
in the human mind. It is curious to notice how
easily people believe what they are told, regardless

[1] Ps. xxiv. 3–5.   [2] Exod. xxiii. 1.

of the goodness or badness of the authority ; and the more marvellous a tale is, the more ready people are to believe it.[1] " It does no one any harm," is the common reply to the censure of such false reports. But to the nation or the community maligned it does much harm by keeping alive those ancient prejudices which, without those false reports, would long since have come to an end.

History has been frequently falsified, whole nations libelled, religion perverted, by the raising of false reports. "Speak ye every man the truth with his neighbour," says the prophet Zechariah.[2] The lies that have been told in the name of religion have been truly frightful in number and magnitude and results. It is not too much to say that the true interests of religion have, in all ages, greatly suffered through the raising of false reports of miracles by the over-zealous priests of many religions. The priest bids the layman believe all he tells him with complete and unquestioning faith. The intelligent layman cannot believe what seems to him nonsense ; and from being asked to believe too much, ends in believing nothing. " Truth, above everything," should be the motto of priest, preacher, and teacher. " As for truth, it endureth and is always strong ; it liveth and conquereth for evermore." [3] It is common enough to hear men in authority say this or that is dangerous doctrine. No doctrine can be dangerous if it be true. The

[1] Bacon says : " Talkers and futile persons are commonly vain and credulous withal ; for he that talketh what he knoweth will also talk what he knoweth not."

[2] Zech. viii. 16.   [3] 1 Esdras iv. 38.

interests of religion are always identical with the
interests of truth. The great God of Truth does
not want a lie to be told in His service.   He
declares, "The prophet which shall presume to
speak a word in My name, which I have not commanded him to speak . . . shall die." [1]

The law, "Thou shalt not curse the deaf, nor
put a stumbling-block before the blind," [2] may be
considered to belong to the same group as the law
last referred to ; for no one can imagine it possible
that any human being could be so diabolically
wicked as actually to curse a deaf man, or actually
to put an obstacle in the path of a blind man.
"Cursing the deaf" must assuredly mean, speaking slander of those who, being absent, are deaf
to what we say of them ; and putting a stumbling-
block before the blind must mean, laying a trap
for the unwary, who are blindly ignorant of what
is being done to their prejudice.

"Thou shalt not go up and down as a tale-
bearer among thy people," [3] is another and more
direct law against slander. No matter if even the
tale be true, and though your neighbour be worthy
of blame, you are not to be a tale-bearer. However blameworthy he may be, the fact is no excuse
for your hating him. "Thou shalt not hate thy
brother in thy heart ; thou shalt in any wise
rebuke thy neighbour, and not suffer sin to rest
upon him." [4] This law represents the true principle of religious charity, and is at the same time

[1] Deut. xviii. 20.   [2] Lev. xix. 14.
[3] Lev. xix. 16.   [4] Lev. xix. 17.

a caution to those self-righteous people, who take delight in reviling their less religious, or perhaps less outwardly observant neighbours. Such people, who are "righteous overmuch," as Ecclesiastes calls them, are directed to show their piety, not by looking down with supercilious glance upon their less pious neighbours, but by remonstrating with them privately, and by gently winning them over to the path of virtue.

The Duty of Purity

I have already quoted at the commencement of this chapter the Commandment, "Thou shalt be perfect with the Lord thy God," [1] and though there are very many ordinances which relate to the subject of moral purity, this one comprehends all the rest. For it enjoins us to be modest, chaste, and pure ; it bids husband and wife to be faithful to each other ; it bids us to be decent in our conduct, demeanour, and conversation, and even in our thoughts, and so to "be perfect with the Lord."

It is just in such points as these that the virtue of the Jewish race has always been pre-eminent ; for the true Jew ever remembers that an All-seeing Eye is watching him, and carefully noting his every deed, word, and thought.

The Duty of Forgiveness

Most difficult of all private duties is the duty of forgiveness ; for forgiveness is not always within our control. Still, we are commanded : "Thou

[1] Deut. xviii. 13.

shalt not avenge nor bear any grudge against the children of thy people, but thou shalt love thy neighbour as thyself : I am the Lord ; "[1] and a little consideration will show that forgiveness of an enemy is a duty that we owe equally to God, to ourselves, and to our fellow-creature.

To God, because He who is Omnipotent can avenge our cause if He will ; and if we ourselves retaliate, we seem to doubt His justice, His power, or His will to defend us. "Say not thou, I will recompense evil, but wait on the Lord, and He shall save thee."[2] To ourselves it is a duty to forgive ; for the sooner an injury is forgotten, the better for our own peace of mind ; moreover, by forgiving others, we make ourselves worthy of forgiveness by the Almighty. "To the merciful, God will show Himself merciful."[3] To our enemy it is also a duty ; for we give him the opportunity of making us amends, and so enable him to blot out his sin against us ; for, enemy though he be, he is our neighbour, and we have been taught, "Thou shalt love thy neighbour as thyself."

> "Be noble, and the nobleness that lies
> In other men, sleeping but never dead,
> Will rise in majesty to meet thine own."[4]

The act of forgiveness is the highest charity, the greatest kindness of man to his fellow. To give alms to the poor, to help the distressed, to be kind to the stranger are all easy and pleasant duties ;

[1] Lev. xix. 18.
[2] Prov. xx. 22.
[3] Ps. xviii. 25.
[4] Lowell.

but to love our enemy so far as to forego vengeance and bear him no grudge, is the highest form of virtue, because it is so much at variance with our strongest impulses.[1]

Kindness to Animals

The Bible tells us that God gave man " dominion over the fish of the sea, and over the fowl of the air, and over the cattle, and over every creeping thing that creepeth upon the earth." [2]

But in assigning to him this proud position, He imposed upon him certain duties and restrictions, intended to confine his power within reasonable limits. Man was to have control over the animal creation, but he was to remember that all birds and beasts and fishes and creeping things were yet God's creatures, all alike objects of His loving care.

Accordingly the Law impresses upon us the duty of kindness to animals. For seven days after birth, no animal was permitted to be taken away from its mother.[3] If an animal had to be slaughtered, it might not be killed on the same day as one of its young,[4] lest perchance the one might see the suffering of the other. An ox was not permitted to be muzzled while treading out the corn,[5] lest it might

[1] The Founder of Christianity, in a certain address to his disciples, is reported to have said : " Ye have heard that it hath been said, Thou shalt love thy neighbour and hate thine enemy. But I say unto you, Love your enemies." But nowhere in our Bible are we enjoined to hate our enemies ; on the contrary, we are ordered to forgive them. (See Prov. xxv. 21.)

[2] Gen. i. 26.   [3] Lev. xxii. 27.
[4] Lev. xxii. 28.   [5] Deut. xxv. 4.

be irritated at being prevented, in the presence of plenty, from satisfying its hunger. Nor was an ox permitted to be yoked with an ass at the plough,[1] lest the pace or tension of one animal might over-tax the strength of the other. No animal might be worked on the Sabbath-day, so that even the poor dumb brute might share with man the blessing of rest. It was commanded that any one seeing an animal fall beneath its burden must render help to raise it.[2] Even " if thou see the ass of him that hateth thee lying under his burden and wouldest forbear to help him, thou shalt surely help with him." [3] It is pronounced to be a duty to lead back an animal that has strayed,[4] even if it be owned by an enemy.[5]

During the wanderings of the Israelites in the wilderness, all animals that were slaughtered for food had to be brought for that purpose to the door of the tabernacle, and it was unlawful to slay an animal elsewhere. The blood of the slaughtered animal was sprinkled on the altar, and the fat was burnt.[6] In this manner the act of slaying an animal for food was dignified and promoted to a religious act, and there was no chance of any wanton cruelty. When the Israelites reached the Promised Land, this restriction was removed, and they were allowed to slay animals anywhere.

The law, which thus first gave to the priests the province of slayers of the cattle, probably gave rise to the custom always prevalent among the Jews,

[1] Deut. xxii. 10.   [2] Deut. xxii. 4.   [3] Exod. xxiii. 5.
[4] Deut. xxii. 1.   [5] Exod. xxiii. 4.   [6] Lev. xvii. 2-6.

even down to the present time, of appointing men of high religious character as slaughterers of animals used for food. The best guarantee was thus afforded that the prescribed rules should be conscientiously observed, and also that the animal should be slain with the least possible pain.

The Jew consequently does not indulge in that kind of sport which consists of killing. He does not shoot pigeons, grouse, and pheasants for the mere pleasure of taking deadly aim at them. The animals he requires for food he causes to be slain by the most expert, thus avoiding all needless torture.

If we are asked why we have so many laws for the protection of animals from cruelty, we may reply that the laws enjoining kindness to dumb animals form only part of the great Law of Love which the Pentateuch inculcates.[1] If man be taught by these laws to be kind to dumb animals, will he not all the more be kind to his fellow-men ? Will not he who spares pain to his ox, spare pain also to his servant, and treat his dependants with kindness and with brotherly love ?

[1] The same humane teaching is to be found in the Book of Proverbs : " A righteous man regardeth the life of his beast " (Prov. xii. 10).

CHAPTER XI

THE laws relating to health are too numerous to mention in detail; and it will be sufficient to treat of them in their broad outlines only.

The main principles of the laws of purification, as laid down in Leviticus and Numbers, appear to be that, as infectious diseases are mostly communicated by contact, all cases of infection are to be isolated; that all contact with any centre of infection is to be avoided; that when such contact has been unavoidable, there must be, first, segregation, to prevent the spread of infection, and finally purification, before the infected person is re-admitted into society.

Every corpse was considered a possible centre of infection. Hence, those who touched a corpse,[1] or who were under the same roof as a corpse,[2] or who touched a grave,[3] had to purify themselves on the third day, and it was not till the seventh day that they were declared clean, after having again purified themselves, washed their clothes, and bathed themselves in water.[4]

---

[1] Num. xix. 11, 12.   [2] Num. xix. 14.   [3] Num. xix. 16.
[4] It is quite likely that (as students of comparative religion have declared) some of these laws originated in previously

In quite recent time, medical men have come to the conclusion that infectious diseases can only be stamped out by the most careful system of isolation. Nevertheless, it will be seen that the sanitary laws of the Pentateuch clearly enforce this principle, and point to isolation as the first duty incumbent on a patient suffering from communicable disease, or on a person bearing the germs, or even the possible germs, of infection ; and it is declared that he who " purifieth not himself defileth the tabernacle of the Lord ; and that soul shall be cut off from Israel." [1]

The great scourge of the East was, and in many places still is, leprosy ; and in the thirteenth chapter of Leviticus will be found the most exact and stringent rules for the prevention of the spread of this malady by contagion or infection. Infected clothing was burnt ; [2] an infected house had to be first emptied, the infected parts of the building removed, and the walls scraped. Then, if the infection proved chronic, the whole house had to be razed to the ground, and the materials removed to an unclean place never to be used again.[3] The priest acted as physician. It was he who had to declare the patient, the garment, or the house clean or unclean. Before the re-admission of the leper into society, certain sacrificial rites had to be performed ; but, above all, certain ablutions had to

existing customs, some superstitious, and some arising from fear. If so, the Mosaic Code regulated those customs, and brought them within proper and useful limitations.

[1] Num. xix. 13.　　[2] Lev. xiii. 55, 57.　　[3] Lev. xiv. 33–45.

be made by the patient, and his hair had to be
shaved off.

In these times, when cleanliness is known to be
an essential condition of health, it will not be a
subject of surprise to find the washing of the clothes
and the bathing of the flesh with water ordained
as material acts of purification.[1] If these simple
remedies alone had been prescribed for the prevention of infection, they would doubtless have been
disregarded and neglected ; for there is a tendency
of the uneducated mind to respect a remedy of a
complex, and to disregard one of a simple, kind ;
just as we find that Naaman [2] doubted the efficacy
of the seven simple ablutions in the Jordan, prescribed by Elisha as a cure for his leprosy, because
the cure was not accompanied by any incantation
or ceremonial.

But probably this was not the only reason why
the ablutions were accompanied by priestly rites.
It must be remembered that many diseases take
their origin in intemperance, excess, and other in-
fractions of the moral law. So it was a salutary
act to bring the influences of religion to bear upon
the patient, not only with the object of impressing
upon him the need of an amended life, but of reminding him that, though God delegates His heal-
ing powers to man, the Great Physician is God

---

[1] It is worthy of note that the English adage, " Cleanliness is
next to godliness," has its parallel in the Mishnah, where we find
precisely the same sentiment in the proverb, נְקִיּוּת מְבִיאָה לִידֵי
טַהֲרָה, " Outward cleanliness leads to inward purity " (Sotah,
ix. 15).   [2] 2 Kings v. 11.

Himself, to whom we owe life and health and every blessing.

The law for the disposal of excremental matter [1] by burial in the earth is truly a remarkable one, and the most enlightened researches of modern science have proved its wisdom. The modern system which permits such matter to discharge into and pollute our rivers, though it has been scientifically carried out by a complex arrangement of drainage, and at an enormous cost, is now acknowledged to be a gigantic blunder ; and the best authorities are now of opinion—an opinion that has, in some places, been carried into practice—that, though storm-waters should be led into the rivers, sewage should be led into the earth, to enrich the soil, and reproduce the food whence it takes its origin—a recognition of the wisdom of the Mosaic ordinance last cited.

We have already referred to the law which declared unclean all who touched a corpse, or a grave, or who happened to be under the same roof as a corpse, and which required their purification before they could be re-admitted into society. But the law was much more stringent as regards the priests. These were not permitted to come near a corpse under any condition, except on the death of a near relative, namely, a parent, wife, child, brother, or unmarried sister ; [2] and, even in these exceptional circumstances, they had to be purified, and to remain apart for seven days. [3]

---

[1] Deut. xxiii. 12, 13.   [2] Lev. xxi. 1-3.

[3] Ezek. xliv. 26.

The sanitary importance of this rule must be clear, seeing that in the East the diseases most prevalent are contagious ; that a corpse, which in warm climates decomposes rapidly, is a highly probable source of infection ; and that the priests, being also the physicians, if allowed to touch the dead, might communicate mortal disease from the dead to the living. But these laws, which seem to regard the human corpse as a subject of uncleanness (a point of view rather repugnant to modern ideas), have a further meaning, far beyond their sanitary significance.

Our people have always regarded their dead with the greatest respect and veneration. The careful watching of the corpse from the moment of death till the funeral hour, the reverent ablution of the dead, the following of the remains to the grave with all marks of respect, regardless of the rank or station of the deceased, and the rule which assigns to each corpse, even to that of a pauper, a separate grave as an everlasting possession—all these customs, indicating an affectionate tenderness for the dead, seem strangely at variance with those Mosaic laws which treat the human corpse as a thing defiling him that touches it. What, then, can be the object of these laws, apart from their sanitary purpose ?

A glance at the history of certain ancient nations, and even at the customs of some religions of our own day, will furnish us with a reply. In ancient Egypt, the country where the Israelites had so long dwelt, the treatment of the dead was the great absorbing thought of the living. To build a grand tomb for himself was the first thought of every wealthy Egyptian. The greatest pains were taken to preserve the bodies of the dead. The more perishable parts were removed, and the body embalmed, wrapped tightly in bands of linen to prevent the access of air ; and the preservation of the body from decay was considered essential to the happiness of the departed soul. The chief books in the Egyptian literature were those relating to the funeral ritual. Before the tombs of the Egyptians, altars were erected, and on these altars their relatives offered sacrifices. In times of difficulty or danger they would consult the dead, and pray for their intervention, or for their advice. The privilege of burial was not allowed to all. According to Champollion, those who were declared by the forty-two judges, upon good evidence, unworthy of interment in the City of the Dead, were refused burial, and had to be kept for ever by their families, standing upright in closed coffins against a wall inside their houses, a lasting disgrace to their relatives. Poor people who died in debt were refused burial ; and, at one time, a creditor could make his debtor give as security the mummy of his father.[1] The City of the Dead was under the control of the priests of Egypt, who had high privileges, and possessed one-third of the land. Their influence over the people was enormous, chiefly derived from their power either to award honours or to offer indignities to the dead. At one period

[1] Herodotus, II. 136.

of Egyptian history they assumed to themselves the
rank and rights of gods. The huge burial-places
erected in Upper Egypt for the kings and priests
(and the kings of certain dynasties were always
priests) contained temples where the worship of
secondary gods took the place of the worship of
Amun-Ra, the God of gods—the primitive Egyptian
religion ; and thus we see the evil resulting from
the gigantic corpse-traffic, which became at last
apparently the aim and end of religion in Egypt.

No wonder that Jacob, fearful that his body
might become an object of worship for future
generations, exclaimed as a last request to his son,
" Bury me not, I pray thee, in Egypt ; " [1] or that
Joseph, with like apprehension, made the children
of Israel swear that they would carry his remains
from Egypt to Canaan.[2]

But you need not go back three thousand years
to learn to what " base uses " the dead human
body may be applied. In our own days there are
superstitions as bad, and perhaps more mischievous.
In the churches of Catholic countries will be found
bones of so-called saints, who lived centuries ago,
reverently preserved as relics, and kept as objects
of idolatry. Many of these are alleged by the
priests to be capable of working miraculous cures
even now ; and as the priests hold aloft these
human relics—perhaps a fleshless skull, or perhaps
a shrunken human hand, or perhaps only a single
bone—with great pomp and ceremony, the as-
sembled multitude bend the knee, and accord to

[1] Gen. xlvii. 29.   [2] Gen. l. 25.

these remains of frail mortality an adoration which should belong to the Supreme God alone.

No wonder, then, that God should bid His people to regard human remains and the graves of the dead as unclean. No wonder that He should forbid His priests even to go near a dead body. If the priests might not go near a corpse, how much less might they consult the dead, or offer a spurious worship at their tombs, or present sacrifices at their graves, or carry bits of old mortality before the eyes of an ignorant multitude, or work pretended miracles with the fragment of a corpse ?

When one calls to mind the fearful struggles that have taken place to obtain possession of the bodies of so-called saints, and to hold domination over certain sepulchres called by some " holy," one cannot but admire with rapt wonder the Divine foresight whereby *all* sepulchres were declared unholy and unclean, and whereby, when our great legislator, Moses, died, his burial was so arranged that " no man knoweth of his sepulchre unto this day." [1]

Not of the dead, as dead, are we to think.[2] Not upon the body, mouldering in corruption, are we to ponder ; for even the mummy, embalmed with

[1] Deut. xxxiv. 6.

[2] " I care not," said Socrates to his friends, " what you think of my body after death, if only you do not think that *I* am there."—PLATO'S *Phædon*.

Renan tells us that " when Mahomet expired, Omar quitted the tent, sword in hand, and threatened to strike the head off any one who dared to affirm that the prophet had ceased to live " (*Les Apôtres*).

costly care, and wrapped in richest cerements, must pass to dust ; but on the *spirit* of the departed are we to bestow our thoughts ; on their example and their influence ; on their worth and on their work ; [1] and if we would think of our beloved dead as they are, let us think of them as disembodied spirits, rejoicing in the presence of their Maker, working His will in the better world, as they worked His will in this.

The laws relating to food (although to some extent also laws of outward distinction) may be all classed under the head of sanitary laws ; for they may be fairly considered to have been ordained in the interests of health, moral and physical.

When, according to the early Bible narrative, God blessed Noah and his sons after the flood, He delivered into their hand the whole animal world,

---

[1] In the words of the Talmud, אֵין עוֹשִׂין נְפָשׁוֹת לַצַּדִּיקִים מַעֲשֵׂיהֶם הֵן הֵן זִכְרוֹנֵיהֶם, " The righteous need no monument : their deeds are their best memorials " (*Talm. Jerus. Shekalim*, 6). We may also quote here Dean Stanley's beautiful verses :—

> " O Life ! Thou too art sweet ;
>   Thou breath'st the fragrant breath
> Of those whom even the hope to meet
>   Can cheer the gate of Death.
>
> Life is the scene their presence lighted ;
>   Its every hour and place
> Is with dear thought of them united,
>   Irradiate with their grace.
>
> There lie the duties small and great
>   Which we from them inherit ;
> There spring the aims that lead us straight
>   To their celestial spirit."

and told them, " Every moving thing that liveth shall be food for you, even as the green herb, have I given you all things. But flesh with the life thereof, which is the blood thereof, shall ye not eat." [1] In those early days, there were no dietary restrictions but these two : a living animal might not be mutilated to afford food,[2] and the blood of an animal might not be eaten.

These laws were repeated by Moses, but with far greater detail and circumstance. We find in Leviticus,[3] " Moreover, ye shall eat no manner of blood, whether it be of fowl or of beast, in any of your dwellings. Whatsoever soul it be that eateth any manner of blood, even that soul shall be cut off from his people." With even greater stringency is the law repeated later : " Whatsoever man there be of the house of Israel, or of the strangers that sojourn among you, that eateth any manner of blood, I will even set my face against that soul that eateth blood, and will cut him off from among his people. For the life of the flesh is in the blood ; and I have given it to you upon the altar to make an atonement for your souls ; for it is the blood that maketh an atonement for the soul. Therefore I said unto the children of Israel, No soul of you shall eat blood, neither shall any stranger that sojourneth among you eat blood." [4] In Deutero-

---

[1] Gen. ix. 3, 4.

[2] Travellers relate that it is not uncommon for savage wandering tribes, reduced to hunger during a march, to cut out and eat slices of their beasts of burden. Even the Abyssinians still follow this odious practice.

[3] Lev. vii. 26, 27.   [4] Lev. xvii. 10, 11, 12.

nomy the same injunction is repeated : " Only ye
shall not eat the blood; ye shall pour it upon
the earth as water." [1]   And further in the same
chapter [2] we are told, " Only be sure that thou eat
not the blood, for the blood is the life, and thou
mayest not eat the life with the flesh.   Thou shalt
not eat it ; thou shalt pour it on the earth as water.
Thou shalt not eat it, that it may go well with
thee, and with thy children after thee."

What can be the object of this prohibition, so
stringently and so frequently repeated ?   The Bible
gives us as one reason that the blood was used
upon the altar as an atonement sacrifice ; but this
cannot be the sole, or even the chief, reason ; for
with regard to the bulk of the blood shed in the
slaughter of beasts for food, namely, the blood of
animals not killed at the door of the Tabernacle,[3]
the Israelites were told to pour it on the earth as
water.

The full, and absolutely certain, reason must
remain a mystery, until the great problem of life
is solved.[4]   We know nothing of the mystery of
vital action ; but we know that the blood is the
vehicle of life to the animal frame—the circulating
medium, maintaining vitality in every organ of the
body, and feeding the brain, the fountain of thought
and action.   We know, from the ascertained influence of certain narcotics, that what passes into the
blood after the processes of digestion, affects the

[1] Deut. xii. 16.   [2] Deut xii. 23, 24.
[3] Deut. xii. 15, 16.
[4] The footnote (4) to page 210 applies also to some extent to
the laws relating to blood.

brain ; sometimes acting on the intellectual, and sometimes on the moral, qualities of man ; sometimes weakening and sometimes stimulating those powers ; sometimes depriving him of volition, and converting him into a sort of sentient feather, the sport of the slightest impulse, without a will or a wish of his own. How the brain is acted upon, we know not ; but we know enough to feel sure that what we eat and drink does affect the mental and spiritual part of man. What, then, is more probable than that, if the blood of a brute animal—that blood which is its life—enters our frame, some of the qualities of that animal may become communicated to us through its blood, and that part of the nature of the animal may thus enter our nature, and debase and brutalise us ?

Experience lends a strong probability to this view ; and, if the view be correct, the precepts so strongly prohibiting blood are easily understood.

Our traditional mode of slaughtering cattle, by cutting the throat, was evidently ordained for the purpose of draining from the body of the animal the greatest possible quantity of blood ; and the custom adopted in observant Jewish households, of steeping meat in water for half-an-hour and keeping it afterwards strewn with salt for an hour before cooking it, has, doubtless, for its object the extraction of any blood still remaining.

When we further examine the laws prohibiting the use of certain animals for food, the leading principle of those laws seems to be that all animals which themselves feed on blood are pronounced unclean, and are prohibited. No quadruped might be eaten except such as had cloven feet, and also chewed the cud. Such animals as had only one of these characteristics (such as the camel, the *shaphan*,[1] the hare, and the swine) were regarded as unclean; their carcases might not even be touched, much less might they be used for food. The law, limiting the eatable animals to cloven-footed ruminants only, excluded the whole range of carnivora, or animals that eat flesh. Flesh-eating animals are, of necessity, blood-eating animals; so it is not difficult to see why they are prohibited.

No fish might be eaten except such as had fins and scales.[2] Twenty species of birds are also enumerated [3] as unclean, and forbidden as food. All worms and creeping things, and all insects, with the few exceptions enumerated,[4] are also prohibited; and it is quite possible, although not absolutely capable of proof, that nearly all those prohibited animals are, in some degree, carnivorous, and consequently sanguinivorous, or blood-eating.

It would be impossible, apart from this last consideration, and with our present limited knowledge, to assign a special sanitary reason for the prohibition of each one of these animals. We know but little of the habits of most animals, and we know absolutely nothing of their inner life. But, inasmuch as all the prohibited animals are described as unclean, there is probably something in their

---

[1] Probably the jerboa; mistranslated " coney " in the Authorised Version.

[2] Lev. xi. 9, 10.   [3] Lev. xi. 13–19.   [4] Lev. xi. 22.

structure and habits rendering them unwholesome
as objects of human food. The filthy habits of the
swine, and the shocking diseases to which it is
liable, and which it engenders in those who feed on
it, are very well known ; and in modern times it
has been thoroughly recognised by scientific medical
men that swine's flesh is unwholesome food, even
if the animal itself may have been healthy when
slain. Swine will eat any garbage, however decom-
posed, and they have even been known to devour
their own young. The forbidden birds include
several which are known to live on carrion of the
filthiest kind, and to delight in blood. Judging the
unknown from the known, all the forbidden animals
may be considered as unwholesome ; and the Law
wisely describes them as abominations, not even to
be touched, when dead, much less eaten.

Certain kinds of fat (חֵלֶב), specified by tradition,
and including the particular fat used for sacrifice,[1]
were forbidden to be eaten ; as was also the flesh
of any animal that was accidentally wounded, or
that died of disease.[2] This last precept has given
rise to the excellent traditional practice among the
Jewish people, that all animals slain for food must
be " searched "— the vitals being examined by
skilled persons, with the object of ascertaining
whether the animal was free from disease. In case
of disease being discovered, the animal is pronounced unfit for food (טְרֵפָה).

The law also forbids us to " seethe a kid in its
mother's milk." The word גְּדִי (gedi), translated

[1] Lev. iii. 17 ; vii. 23.   [2] Exod. xxii. 31 ; Deut. xiv. 21.

"kid," here means the young of any mammal. The command seems at first sight a strange one ; and its meaning has been questioned by many of the most learned commentators. It is repeated three times in the Pentateuch ; [1] in the first two places in connection with the offerings, and only in the last in connection with the dietary laws. It is not found among the dietary laws of Leviticus ; whence it has been supposed by some to have principally reference to a sacrificial rite. The great Maimonides (himself a physician of eminence) considers the prohibition to be solely a sanitary one, as he regards the mixture of flesh and milk too indigestible a food ; [2] but the more probable reason is that given by Abarbanel,[3] who represents that there is something cruel and repugnant to natural sentiment in boiling a young animal in the milk that was destined for its own nourishment ; and he sees an analogy between this precept and that which forbade the killing of any animal and its progeny on the same day.

Strange as it may appear, it is certain that even now it is a custom among the Arabs of the desert to eat kid boiled in goat's milk ; and Porter relates, in his " Giant Cities of Bashan," how this dish is offered to travellers as a great delicacy. It is also equally certain that the Jews have always abstained from such an unnatural mixture of food. According to traditional interpretation, the precept

---

[1] Exod. xxiii. 19 ; Exod. xxxiv. 26 ; and Deut. xiv. 21.
[2] *Moreh Nebuchim*, iii. 48.
[3] Commentary on Exod. xxiii. 19.

forbids the eating of meat or any preparation of meat with milk or anything prepared from milk.

Apart from the sanitary considerations, which most probably lie at the root of all the dietary restrictions of our people, there is another consideration—the moral influence which such laws exercise, by reason of the restraints which they place on our appetites. That the Jews are distinguished for temperance, is universally acknowledged. As social and convivial in their habits as any of their fellow-citizens, our people are yet moderate in their enjoyments; and drunkenness, the great and overwhelming curse of this country, finds no place among the vices of the Jews. For this immunity from the evil of intemperance, freedom from many of those diseases which affect other races, and a remarkable longevity, we may well regard ourselves as indebted to our dietary laws; which, while they permit us to enjoy in moderation the good things of life, place a curb on our appetites so habitually as to render moderation our second nature.

The " dietary laws " are indeed in the Bible part of the Law of Holiness which was enjoined on the people of Israel. In external habit and internal spirit Israel was to be holy. Judaism conceives of religion neither as something external only, nor as something spiritual only; it conceives of religion as both. Body and soul are to be united in the service of God.

P

CHAPTER XII

THE HISTORICAL FASTS AND FEASTS

EVERY nation that has a history has certain anniversaries which are marked as red-letter days in its calendar. But most nations willingly or wilfully forget their past misfortunes, their self-love and vanity prompting them to hold in remembrance only their glories.

With us it is different. Not that our self-love and vanity are less than our neighbours'. But our history is different. For since we lost the land of our inheritance, our history has been, with few and comparatively short exceptions, one long tale of persecution and humiliation. Now and then, indeed, the black clouds have broken, and the sun has burst resplendent through the mists, driving away for a little while the dark shadows which enveloped us ; but too soon the bright orb was hidden from view, and " a horror of great darkness," blacker than ever, fell upon us.

And now again, thanks to God, we Jews, in this happy country, and in other parts of the civilised world, luxuriate in the sunshine of fortune. We here live in peace and liberty, our lives and property secure, and, if it were not for the persecutions of our brethren in Russia and other barbarous countries, we should be apt to regard our past sad history almost as a frightful nightmare, scarcely as a series of real facts.

But in good and in evil times, it has been the custom of our people, as each anniversary came round, to praise God for good and evil alike,[1] to celebrate our past glories with heartfelt gratitude, and to call to mind our past sufferings with lamentations indeed, but equally with a voice of thanksgiving. For in darkness or in light, in sorrow or in joy, the Jew still felt himself the surviving heir to a precious heritage, and, confident in the future of his race, was grateful if he only lived—no matter how—lived to transmit to unborn generations that heritage in all its purity.

Four of these sad anniversaries are not only historical but biblical. They are mentioned as fasts in the Book of Zechariah[2]—the 17th day of *Tamuz* (שִׁבְעָה עָשָׂר בְּתַמּוּז),[3] the 9th day of *Ab* (תִּשְׁעָה בְּאָב), the 3rd day of *Tishri* (צוֹם גְּדַלְיָהוּ), and the 10th day of *Tebeth* (עֲשָׂרָה בְּטֵבֵת).

The fast of *Tamuz* commemorates the taking of Jerusalem by Nebuchadnezzar, King of Babylon; the fast of *Ab*—the saddest anniversary of all—the destruction of the First Temple by Nebuchad-

---

[1] חַיָב אָדָם לְבָרֵךְ עַל הָרָעָה כְּשֵׁם שֶׁמְּבָרֵךְ עַל הַטּוֹבָה: " It is our duty to praise God equally for the evil and for the good " (*Berachot*, 54, *a*).   [2] Zech. viii. 19.

[3] Although, according to Jeremiah (chap. xxxix. 2), the conquest of Jerusalem, prior to the destruction of the First Temple, took place on the ninth day of the fourth month, yet the fast is kept on the seventeenth, because on that day Jerusalem was taken by the Romans, just before the destruction of the Second Temple.

nezzar, and the destruction of the Second Temple
by Titus, the Roman General. The fast of Gedaliah on the 3rd day of *Tishri* is the anniversary of
the murder of Gedaliah, chief of the remnant of
our people, who clung to Judea after the destruction of the First Temple.[1]   From that date, the
independence of the Jews ceased, until the restoration in the days of Cyrus. The fast of *Tebeth*
commemorates the commencement of the siege of
Jerusalem by Nebuchadnezzar.

Reading these dry details, which seem a mere
catalogue of misfortunes, it is difficult to realise
their full import. But if you will read for yourselves the narrative of the destruction of the First
Temple, as detailed in the last chapter of the second
Book of Kings, and in the last chapter of the
second Book of Chronicles, and the history of the
siege of Jerusalem by Titus, as described by
Josephus, you may form some idea of the horrors
attending these national calamities, when the city
was consumed with famine, so that " there was no
bread for the people of the land," when the be-
siegers ruthlessly slew every one in the fated city,
" and had no compassion upon young man or
maiden, old man, or him that stooped for age."

Never in the world's history has such a siege
taken place as that which finally overthrew the
sacred city; never has a city been so completely
destroyed as was Jerusalem—destroyed so that
scarcely a vestige of its ancient glory now remains,
save a few cyclopean masses of masonry, the

[1] 2 Kings xxv. 25.

foundations of its outer walls, and a few under-
ground vaults, cisterns, and aqueducts, beneath or
near the site of the sacred Temple-enclosure.

Perhaps human nature is so constituted that we
may find it hard to lament the loss of what we, per-
sonally, never possessed ; and thus many thoughtless people may smile when they are told to mourn
for the loss of Jerusalem. But if you read in the
Bible and in works of history and antiquities what
Jerusalem was ; if you read descriptions of her
glorious Temple, and call to mind that that Temple
was *the* place on all the earth selected to be God's
Holy House, the religious centre of our people, the
admiration of surrounding nations, " beautiful for
situation, the joy of the whole earth " ;[1] when you
remember that all this would now be ours, but for
the sins of our forefathers and the tardiness of our
own repentance ; when you call to mind that,
instead of that glorious heritage, we have nothing
left to us but the Written Word—no land of our
own, no Temple of our own—and that, on the
site of the glorious Temple, mosques rear their
proud heads, but no House of God where the
Jew can worship the One and only God—then,
perhaps, if you are a fervent Jew, you may realise
what you have lost. And the fasts which recall
that loss may seem to you wisely ordained commemorations, inviting us to consider how best our
Religion may again find its centre in the City that
has been lost to us ; how best we may contribute
to our spiritual restoration by our recognition and

[1] Ps. xlviii. 2.

practice of all that is noblest in the teachings of
the prophets who foretold that restoration.

Our past history is not all gloom. Our history
is, indeed, too much a history of persecutions, but
it is also a history full of providential escapes.
Two of these marvellous escapes from dangers,
which might have utterly exterminated us, but for
the protecting hand of Providence, we celebrate by
festivals of joy and gladness—the feast of *Purim*,
and the feast of *Hanucah*.

Who can read the Book of Esther without dis-
cerning, in the wonderful chain of events therein
related, the guiding hand of an all-directing Providence ?   The historian has studiously avoided
inserting anywhere in his narrative the name of
God ; for he wrote the chronicle equally for Jews
and Persians ; and the latter, who worshipped
the sun-god Mithras, and paid allegiance to the
secondary divinities of good and evil, Ormuzd and
Ahriman, knew not the God of the Hebrews.   But,
though the Great Name is absent, we see everywhere in this marvellous chronicle the directing
Hand of Him who is the Guardian of Israel.

Of late there has sprung up a school of thinkers
and writers who, vainly seeking to erect history
into a science, would make every event, small or
great, an inevitable fact produced as a necessary
consequence of an unerring law, independent of
the will of man or the control of a governing
Providence.

But no one can read such a stirring history as

the Book of Esther presents, without feeling that this hard necessarian doctrine is at fault here, and that the ordinary sequence of events could never have produced the startling, and almost romantic, incidents to be found in the chronicle of Mordecai—incidents which crowd one on the other, till the climax at length brings the doomed children of Israel out of the depth of despair, and places them on the pinnacle of salvation and triumph. Many historians have remarked that the unexpected always occurs. Perhaps the " always " is an exaggeration ; but the aphorism, which is not so very far from the truth, shows the falsity of the necessarian doctrine, and points to the existence of a controlling Power, who shapes the destinies of men and nations, and who reigns superior to any fixed law of sequence understood by imperfect and short-sighted man.

Goethe truly says : " That which in the enterprises of human beings transcends all calculation, and which is apt to show its power most precisely when human nature is lifting itself most proudly—what men call CHANCE—this is just GOD, who in this incomprehensible way invades our little sphere with His Omnipotence, and disturbs our grandest plans, by the intrusion of what to us is a mere accident, but to Him is part of an all-embracing bond."

When, then, we celebrate the Feast of Purim, as did our rescued forefathers in Shushan, " with light and gladness, and joy and honour," we must keep foremost in our mind the recognition of God's government of the world ; and when we read the Book of Esther, we must note with wonder and admiration how a despised Jew and Jewess became, by rare acts of courage and self-devotion, the saviours of their nation ; how, when they had reached the summit of earthly fame and power, their great anxiety was to place on record an imperishable memorial of their marvellous escape ; and how, finally, the Jew Mordecai, raised to the post of first minister to the king of one hundred and twenty-seven provinces, though " next to the king," yet remained steadfast to his faith and race, " great among the Jews " and " seeking the welfare of his people." [1]

The events that gave rise to the Feast of *Hanucah*, or Dedication, are described in full detail in the Books of the Maccabees, which will be found in the Apocrypha. About the facts contained in the Books of the Maccabees there can be no doubt, as they receive ample confirmation from other historical sources.

About two centuries before the Romans destroyed the Second Temple, Judea was ravaged by the army of Antiochus Epiphanes, King of Syria, who penetrated to Jerusalem, and even took possession of the sanctuary. Resistance seemed useless. The priests fled from the Temple, and the Syrians there set up their idolatrous worship, with all its foul abominations. They then tried to convert the Jews to their own shameful religion. The ordinances of Judaism were proscribed, the

[1] Esther x. 3.

worship of God was forbidden, and all were ordered, upon pain of death, to bow down before the idols of the Syrians. Thousands of Jews died the death of martyrs, because they persisted in clinging to their own religion. Many, weakened by privations and torture, became, or pretended to become, converts to heathenism, and many fled to distant parts of Judea, taking refuge in the mountain caverns.

All seemed hopeless, and it appeared as if Jews and Judaism were about to vanish for ever from the face of the earth, when suddenly there arose a family of priests, who took upon themselves the apparently impossible task of resisting the idolatrous invaders. These heroes, consisting of an old man, named Mattathias, and his five sons, were the Maccabees,[1] or Hasmoneans; and they commenced their work of salvation for Israel by bidding defiance to the Syrians, when they invaded Modin, their village home. For at Modin the invaders had set up altars for the worship of their idols, and these the Maccabees, jealous for the True God, indignantly swept away.

The Syrians, accustomed everywhere to receive submission, were amazed at this boldness, and tried to bribe Mattathias and his sons, by promises of honours and riches, to yield to the king's com-

---

[1] The name Maccabee is said to have been derived from the initial letters of the words, מִי כָּמֹכָה בָּאֵלִים יְיָ, " Who is like unto Thee among the mighty, O Lord? "—the alleged inscription on the banner of Judas, son of Mattathias. Originally, only Judas himself bore the title, and it is generally assumed that it is derived from מַקָּבָה = *Hammer*. So Charles *Martel* was named from his battle-axe, and Edward I. was called " *Scotorum malleus.*"

mands, and to embrace the idolatrous religion. But the Maccabees indignantly refused ; and rallying around them a handful of villagers, whom they had inspired with a patriotism and religious fervour like their own, they engaged in battle with the hosts of Syria, and, though outnumbered to an enormous extent, conquered.

No sooner had they thus gained their first victory, than the Maccabees re-established the worship of the True God, and then proceeded to organise a small army with which to liberate their country. But the old priest, Mattathias, did not live to see the end of the conflict.   He died, leaving his sons to continue the task he had commenced, and inciting them by his last words to the work of regenerating and reviving the nation and the religion he loved so well.   The sons fought like lions.   Everywhere the little handful of Jewish patriots conquered.   Legion after legion of the Syrians, led by the most renowned generals of King Antiochus, fell in battle, struck down by the small band of Maccabee soldiers.   Nothing could withstand the prowess of these Jewish heroes ; and after a succession of victories, unbroken by a single reverse, they marched to Jerusalem, determined to crown their glories by rescuing the Holy City from the pagan hands that had desecrated the Sanctuary.   Here again they were victorious ; for they drove out the Syrians from Jerusalem, once more regained possession of the Sacred Temple ; and the remnants of the hosts of Antiochus gradually retired from Palestine.

Then, the soldiers' work over, the priests' work, the purification of the desecrated Temple, began. Every vestige of the idolatrous worship was removed ; new altars were built, new holy vessels were set up, the lights on the sacred candlestick were once more kindled, and the ancient worship of the Most High was re-established. Then was celebrated the first " Feast of Dedication " with great rejoicing. It lasted eight days ; and it was ordained that, for ever after, the Jews should celebrate as a festival this wonderful escape and the religious revival that followed it.

How it is celebrated, you all know. For eight nights observant Jews illumine their homes with festive lights ; commencing with one, and adding one daily till eight lights are reached ; and when these lights are kindled, joyful hymns of thanksgiving are sung to celebrate the salvation of Israel by the hands of the Maccabees.

The lesson taught by *Hanucah* is similar to that taught by *Purim*—the recognition of the Hand of God in human history and human destiny. One can well imagine the worldly-wise of the Maccabee age laughing at the temerity of Judas and his brothers, when they, with their handful of villagers, ill-clad, unpractised in the arts of war, and deficient in the implements of battle, went to fight the hosts of Syrian soldiers ; just as Goliath laughed at the stripling David, and just as, in the last century, the worldly-wise of many nations predicted failure to the small band of Italian patriots who undertook the liberation of their country.

But Providence is superior to earthly force, and skill, and numbers — Providence, whose guiding Hand we see in every page of History. This Providence rules the world—

> " with good
> Still overcoming evil, and by small
> Accomplishing great things ; by things deemed weak
> Subverting worldly strong and worldly wise."
>
> *—Milton.*

And thus, this wonderful episode of our deliverance from the Syrian yoke shows us how Providence selects as instruments, not always the powerful and strong, but sometimes even the weakest, humblest, and poorest, to work His Will. To regenerate an expiring nation, to revive the fast-dying embers of a glorious religion, and to restore its influence, He selects the poor, weak, old priest, and his five sons—inhabitants of an obscure village of Palestine. These were to be the saviours of their people. These were to inspire their followers with the courage of lions to meet and conquer an enemy many times stronger than they. These were to rekindle the fire of religious zeal among their fellow-Jews. These were to drive out the idolater and to restore the true religion. " Not by might, nor by power, but by my spirit, saith the Lord of Hosts." [1]

[1] Zech. iv. 6. I may here appropriately quote the words of the German philosopher-poet Herder : " Israel was and is the most remarkable people on the earth. In its fortunes and misfortunes, its failures and successes, in its glory and in its shame, it is alike so unique and wonderful, that I hold the history, the art, the existence of this people to be a most indubitable proof of the Providence of God in the world " (*Ideen*, II. p. 249).

CHAPTER XIII

THE FUTURE LIFE

No question concerns man more than the question of the future life. Life is so short, Eternity so long, that the one absorbing thought of life might well be, How shall we spend Eternity?

And yet, happily for ourselves, this is not the one absorbing thought. To every one, even to those on the brink of the grave, life has many interests; and the *present moment* is ever paramount in importance. When God made man of the dust of the earth, He meant him to have earthly interests, so that he might fulfil his mission as part of the work of creation.[1] If all men were to pass their lives like monks or fakirs, spending all their time in penance, prayer, and contemplation, neglectful of their duties as members of the human family, there would soon be an end to the human race, and the Divine project of creation would, so far as humanity is concerned, be frustrated.

Therefore, God endowed man with strong appetites, and tastes, and ambitions, that—held in proper restraint—they might serve as a spur to healthy action of heart and brain, giving a zest

[1] גַּם אֶת הָעוֹלָם נָתַן בְּלִבָּם "Also he hath set the world in their heart" (Eccles. iii. 11).

to life, and making life a thing to be enjoyed. An ever-present thought of death and futurity, would spoil that zest ; [1] and hence, happily for man, God has so constituted the human mind that the prevailing thought of life is life itself—life here on earth, with its needs, its duties and its enjoyments.

But, deeply implanted as is the love of life in every healthy human heart, it is not more deeply implanted than the hope and expectation of a future state. Hence, though eternity is not an ever-present subject for contemplation, it is one that crops up very frequently and persistently in every thinking mind ; and no religious person should suffer a day to depart without bestowing much more than a passing thought on the future of his soul.[2]

What does Religion tell you about ·the immortality of the soul ?   What Natural Religion teaches you, you already know.[3]   But what does Revealed Religion, what does the Bible tell you, about this all-important subject ?

Upon the future of the soul, the Pentateuch gives us no *direct* information.   But it tells us at the outset that " God created man in His own image ; " [4] that " He breathed into his nostrils the spirit of life ; and man became a living soul." [5]   Of no other being but man is it declared that " God

[1] " *Homo liber de nulla re minus quam de morte cogitat* " (The free man ponders on no subject less than on Death).—*Spinoza.*
[2] "*Omnem crede diem tibi diluxisse supremum* " (Think that each day that dawns on thee may be thy last).—*Horace,* Epist. I. 4 ; by no means a contradiction to the footnote above.
[3] Part I. chaps. v. and vi.   [4] Gen. i. 27.   [5] Gen. ii. 7.

breathed into his nostrils the spirit of life." These
very words indicate the kinship of the human soul
to the Divine Spirit. Again, when we are told
that God created man in His own image, it cannot
mean that man's bodily form is in the image of
God ; for we are repeatedly warned that God has
no bodily form or similitude. It can therefore only
mean that the soul of man is a reflection of the
Deity Himself, who is an eternal and spiritual
Being.

But, vague and indistinct as may be this indication of the soul's immortality, as derived from the
story of Creation,[1] the Pentateuch tells us enough
to show that its author must have been well versed
in the doctrine, and that the silence of the early
books of the Pentateuch upon the topic was due
only to the fact that the doctrine was taken for
granted—was, in fact, thoroughly established as an
axiom. Indeed, if one reads any work treating of
ancient Egypt, it is clear that at the time of the
Exodus, and even long before, the doctrine of a
future state was known to the Egyptians, and
played no small part in the inner and domestic life
of that nation. It is therefore absolutely impossible that Moses, who was trained at the court of
Pharaoh (and every Pharaoh was a learned priest),
could have been, as some have maintained, ignorant of the idea of the soul's immortality.

An investigation of a few passages in the Penta-

[1] The vagueness is increased by the ambiguity of the Hebrew
word for soul נֶפֶשׁ (*Nephesh*), which also means " person," and
sometimes " life."

teuch will clear up all doubt on this subject, and will show that in many cases the Law refers, although not directly, yet pointedly enough, to an after-life.

Quite early in the Bible we are told that " Enoch walked with God, and he was not, for God took him." [1]   If God took him, surely it could not have been for the destruction of his soul, but that his soul might live in a better and happier world to enjoy the reward of godliness.

We find another hint at the soul's immortality in the history of the patriarchs. God promised Abraham, " Thou shalt go to thy fathers in peace." [2] Now, this could not imply that he was to be buried with his fathers in peace ; for, as a matter of fact, he was buried in Canaan, at a great distance from the home and the graves of his ancestors at Haran. The promise could, therefore, only imply a reunion of the soul of Abraham with the souls of his relatives who had preceded him. A like phrase is adopted by the Bible historian in relating the death of Jacob. The patriarch charged his sons, " and said unto them, I am to be gathered unto my people ; " [3] and then he proceeds to tell them how they are to bury him with his fathers in the field of Machpelah ; and his death is described thus : " He gathered up his feet into his bed, and yielded up the ghost, and was gathered unto his people." [4] Now, the " being gathered to his people " could not imply his burial ; for the subsequent chapter con-

---

[1] Gen. v. 24.   [2] Gen. xv. 15.
[3] Gen. xlix. 29.   [4] Gen. xlix. 33.

tains a narrative of several events which preceded the actual burial ; namely, the embalming of the body, the forty days' mourning, the petition to Pharaoh for the removal of the remains to Canaan, the march of the funeral cavalcade, and the seven days' mourning at Atad ; and if it did not mean the burial, surely it must have meant the consummation of the hope of the righteous for the righteous soul—the reunion of that soul with the souls of those who had gone before.

In the narrative of the deaths of Aaron and of Moses the same phrase is used : " And die in the Mount whither thou goest up, and be gathered unto thy people ; as Aaron thy brother died in Mount Hor, and was gathered unto his people." [1] Now, both these great men had unknown, lonely, and separate burial-places in the wilderness, certainly far removed from the resting-places of their fathers ; and we are, therefore, irresistibly led to the conclusion that the phrase " to be gathered to their fathers " expressed the fact, or at least the belief of the historian, that the dead are reunited to their forefathers in a spiritual existence beyond the grave.

But it may be argued, Why did not God, through His servant Moses, clearly and distinctly propound the important doctrine of Immortality, promising undying happiness in a future existence as a reward of piety, and giving indications of the nature of those spiritual rewards, instead of promising long life and wealth, and all worldly blessings as the recompense of virtue ?

[1] Deut. xxxii. 50.

Q

" Truly a difficult question. But we may probably find a solution of the problem by imagining a converse state of things.

" Suppose that the Bible told us, without the slightest ambiguity, that there was an after-life, that the soul was an immortal part of man, which, released from its earthly bonds, would enjoy happiness or be doomed to misery in accordance with its deserts. What would be the result ?

" In the first place, not a single disinterested action would be left to be performed, even by the best of men. Every prudent man would calculate the effect of each good deed he performed, or of each temptation he resisted, and would, as it were, keep a debit and credit account with his Creator. Even as it is, there is not too much disinterestedness in the world. Intertwined with patriotism we see ambition ; intermixed with honesty we find policy—the fear of the law ; interwoven with religion we often find submission to fashion. The sterling good deed, the act of duty which is contrary to interest, to sentiment, to impulse, to fashion, and to inclination—this is the act which deserves eternal reward. But what act would be disinterested, if the promise of heavenly reward were unmistakably clear and distinct ? The cool, calculating man would be the best man. But he would not be a good man in the sense in which we now understand the term. He would be commercially good ; his good deeds would simply be good investments—investments of which the profit, though deferred, was certain—not only certain, but when attained, eternal.

" But there would be no merit in this kind of goodness. The object for which it would seem we are placed upon earth would be annulled. This world would be no test, no place of trial, to ascertain our worth. It might be a test of our sordid prudence—not of our moral worth. The aim and object of our existence in this world would be frustrated.

" Next, let us ask what end would have been served by a direct promise of immortality ? It would not have sufficed to have merely given the promise of a state of being which the mind cannot fully grasp. The mere promise of eternal happiness would have been to the majority the promise of a phrase—a mere vision—not a tangible, comprehensible reward. Our ideas of happiness are chiefly, if not entirely, derived from the physical world by which we are surrounded. What would have been the use of describing, as the recompense for goodness, a condition of spiritual happiness which the soul, wrapt in its mortal garb, could not have understood ? We could not appreciate a promise of pleasures which belong wholly and solely to a spiritual state of existence. But we can understand the pleasures of earth, because they are pleasures experienced by the agency of the senses. Every one can appreciate such pleasures ; and therefore it is that we find, in the Bible, material blessings held out as the recompense of well-doing. It would not have served to preach to the untutored people of ancient times, that Virtue is its own reward."[1]

Our ancestors, just delivered from the slavery of Egypt, were not a people with strong spiritual cravings. The Bible represents them as lamenting the flesh-pots of Egypt, looking back with fond regret to the time when they " did eat bread to the full,"[2] calling to mind, with greedy thoughts, " the fish which we did eat in Egypt freely, the cucumbers, and the melons, and the leeks, and the onions, and the garlick."[3] Men such as these would not have been attracted by promises of a spiritual happiness, long deferred. The spiritual idea of a happy future for the soul could only be developed by slow degrees. A different incentive had to be offered. They were therefore promised rich harvests and overflowing granaries, length of days and multitudinous progeny.

Lessing, the great philosopher-poet, who, through his intimate friendship with Moses Mendelssohn, had acquired a keen appreciation of Judaism, explains, in language of remarkable force, the reticence of the Pentateuch on the topic of the Soul's Immortality. He writes : " The Hebrews were a rude, unruly people, who had everything to learn. Only gradually could they rise from the conception of a patriarchal, national deity to the knowledge of the One God. So, too, could their moral education only be conducted on the plan of rewards and

---

[1] " The Bible and Immortality."　" Sabbath Readings." No. 71.

[2] Exod. xvi. 3.　　　[3] Num. xi. 5.

punishments, addressed to the senses. Their regards went no further than this earth; they
yearned for no life to come. To have revealed this
to them, before their reason was ripe to grasp it,
would have been the fault of the schoolmaster who
urges on his pupil too rapidly." [1]

But though the Pentateuch contains unmistak-
able hints as to the immortality of the soul,[2] the
later Scriptures contain much more than hints;
sufficiently showing that the doctrine was not first
learnt in the Babylonian exile, but that it was
accepted, if not by the masses, at least by culti-
vated minds.

The Psalmist, in many places, uses expressions
which show that to him the Soul's Immortality
was no unfamiliar doctrine. In the *Michtam*, that
beautiful psalm which is read in houses of mourning, he says, " My heart is glad and my glory
rejoiceth; my flesh also shall rest in hope. For
Thou wilt not leave my soul in the grave,[3] neither
wilt Thou suffer Thine holy one to see corruption.
Thou wilt show me the path of life; in Thy
presence is fulness of joys; at Thy right hand
there are pleasures for evermore " (Ps. xvi. 9-11).

Again, in the 17th Psalm, called the " Prayer of

---

[1] *Die Erziehung des Menschengeschlechts.* Maimonides uses
a similar argument in the Introduction to his Commentary on
the tenth chapter of *Sanhedrin.*

[2] The promised reward of " days of heaven upon earth "
(Deut. xi. 21) would have had no meaning, if a future life in
heaven had not been hoped for by those to whom the promise
was addressed.

[3] Wrongly translated " hell " in the Authorised Version
the Revised Version retains the Hebrew *sheol.*

David," after speaking with disdain of the prosperity of "men of the world which have their
portion in this life," [1] he closes with the words,
" As for me, I will behold thy face by righteousness. I shall be satisfied, when I awake, with thy
likeness." [2]

In the 49th Psalm, which contains so powerful
a homily on the vanity of wealth and fortune, the
Psalmist thus declares his belief in a future state :
" But God shall redeem my soul from the power
of the grave ; for He shall receive me." [3]

In the 103rd Psalm, he thus exhorts his soul to
bless the Lord who had endowed it with Immortality : " Bless the Lord, O my soul ; and all that
is within me, bless His holy name. Bless the Lord,
O my soul, and forget not all His benefits ; Who
forgiveth all thine iniquities ; who healeth all thy
diseases ; Who redeemeth thy life from destruction ; who crowneth thee with loving kindness and
tender mercies." [4]

And in the 73rd Psalm, in which the Psalmist
seeks to solve the problem of the prosperity of the
wicked and the trials of the righteous, and finds
the solution when he " went into the sanctuary of

---

[1] Ps. xvii. 14.

[2] Ps. xvii. 15. It is almost superfluous to state that such
phrases as " Thy face " and " Thy likeness " are not intended
to assign bodily similitude or form to the Deity. They are
mere anthropomorphisms, or figurative phrases adapted to the
common notions and language of man. To use a well-known
maxim of the Rabbis, דִּבְּרָה תוֹרָה כִּלְשׁוֹן בְּנֵי אָדָם, " The language of the Bible is the language of man."

[3] Ps. xlix. 15.   [4] Ps. ciii. 1–4.

God," and "understood their end," he exclaims, "Thou shalt guide me with Thy counsel, and afterward receive me to glory. Whom have I in heaven but Thee? and there is none upon earth that I desire beside Thee. My flesh and my heart faileth, but God is the strength of my heart, and my portion for ever." [1]

The prophet Isaiah declares the unknown glories of the future state in these words: "Since the beginning of the world men have not heard, nor perceived by the ear, neither hath the eye seen. O God, beside Thee, what He hath prepared for him that waiteth for Him." [2]

The last chapter of the Book of Ecclesiastes contains the most pointed assertion of the doctrine of the Soul's Immortality in the well-known words, "Then shall the dust return to the earth as it was; and the spirit shall return unto God who gave it." [3]

With such expressions as these in Holy Writ, who can, with any approach to truth, assert, as has been so repeatedly asserted, that the doctrine of Immortality was unknown to the ancient Hebrews, and that the Jews, at quite a late period of their history, derived their knowledge of that doctrine from Christian sources? [4] The doctrine must have been not only known to our people in olden times, but must have been so far recognised as a self-evident fact, and so far interwoven in their natural belief, as to have required

[1] Ps. lxxiii. 24–26.   [2] Isa. lxiv. 4.   [3] Eccles. xii. 7.
[4] The doctrine of immortality is clearly formulated in Jewish books (e.g. the "Wisdom of Solomon") long before the Christian era.

no enforcement by the authority of Divine Revelation.

" And if we would have a revelation of Immortality, what other need we have, what stronger can we have, than the inner voice (stronger than written or spoken words), which tells us of an eternal destiny ? ' The inward horror of falling into nought,' is the true revelation to the soul of the soul's eternity. Our own consciousness proclaims the great truth ; and if the Bible hints at it faintly and incidentally, instead of firmly, plainly, and dogmatically, it is because the object of the Bible is not to reveal the happiness of eternal life, but to teach us how to deserve and achieve that happiness." [1]

And who, with a gleam of reason, can talk of annihilation of the soul ?—who conceive its possibility ? Who ?—especially in these days, when philosophers declare even matter to be indestructible, and force, by the conservation of energy, eternal in its effects. Shall physical force be everlasting, and the Soul which, by the power of Will, gives life to force, itself lack immortality ? It cannot be.

> " What ! shall the trick of nostrils and of lips
> Descend through generations, and the soul
> That moves within our frame like God in worlds,
> Imprint no record, leave no documents
> Of her great history ?   Shall men bequeath
> The fancies of their palates to their sons,
> And shall the shudder of restraining awe,

---

[1] " The Bible and Immortality," before quoted.

The slow-wept tears of contrite memory,
Faith's prayerful labour, and the food divine
Of fasts ecstatic—shall these pass away
Like wind upon the waters tracklessly ? " [1]

" The thought of Death," writes the aged Goethe, " leaves me in a state of perfect peace ; for I have the most assured conviction that our soul is of an essence absolutely indestructible, an essence that works on from eternity to eternity. It is like the sun, which to our earthly eyes sinks and sets, but in reality never sinks, but shines on unceasingly."

Then with the natural revelation of the Soul's Immortality, and the Bible's strong hints of a future state, how should we regard Life and Death ? We should regard *Life as a mere incident in Eternity, and Death a mere incident in Life*—the opening of the door of Immortal Life.

" There is no death ; what seems so is transition.
    This life of mortal breath
Is but a suburb of the Life Elysian,
    Whose portal we call Death." [2]

Lord Bacon says, " Men fear death, as children fear to go in the dark ; and as that natural fear in children is increased by tales, so is the other." [3]

And truly those superstitious tales of hell and its torments, the inventions of the priests of other religions, who have traded on the fears of men,

[1] George Eliot.
[2] Longfellow's "Resignation."
[3] " Bacon's Essays," II. (" On Death "). Lucretius (Book III. 78) makes a similar remark—" For even as children dread all things in the thick darkness, thus we in the daylight fear at times things not a whit more to be dreaded than what children shudder at in the dark."

have done the greatest mischief to Religion, and
have, by painting Death as a hideous monster,
robbed life of what should be one of its purest joys,
the placid contemplation of our earthly end, the
happy anticipation of reunion with those we love,[1]
and with the loving God from whom our spirit
came. For who, believing in the boundless goodness of God, can look upon death, despite the
sufferings which precede it, as anything but a
blessing—the last and final blessing which He
bestows upon man on earth?[2] We hail as a
sweet blessing the repose of sleep. Why fear the
sleep which hushes to eternal rest the weary, aching
heart and brain, and awakens to a life of freedom
the imprisoned soul? It is conscience that makes
us cowards. It is a sense of unworthiness that
makes us lend a ready ear to those who dissemi-
nate the vile idea of utter perdition and eternal
punishment.

But though conscience may make us cowards, it
need not make us unbelievers. Mindful of the

---

[1] " Who can conceive," says Sherlock in his " Discourse on
Death," " the joyous reunion of two souls in Paradise ? What
are all the trash and trifles, the bubbles, bawbles, and gewgaws
of this life to such a meeting ? This is a hope which no reasoning shall ever argue me out of, nor millions of such worlds as
this should purchase. Nor can any man show me its absolute
impossibility, till he can demonstrate that it is not in the power
of the Almighty to bestow it on me."

[2] A Rabbi made the striking remark on the words of Scripture וְהִנֵּה טוֹב מְאֹד זֶה מָוֶת, " ' And God saw everything that He
had made, and behold it was very good '—aye even Death "
(Midrash, Bereshith Rabbah, ch. ix.). And similarly Seneca classes
Death among the great boons of Nature, " inter munera naturæ."

endless goodness of Him who made us, conscience
may tell us that we are unworthy of God's loving
countenance in the world to come ; but conscience
should not place a limit to God's loving kindness,
forgiveness, and tolerance of His erring creatures.
In the words of the philosopher last quoted : " It
were better to have no opinion of God at all, than
such an opinion as is unworthy of Him ; for though
the one is unbelief, the other is contumely." [1]
Judging from all our past experience, we can only
think of God as infinite, unlimited Mercy. The
Midrash [2] tells us that when the Supreme Being,
asked by Moses to show him His glory, caused all
His goodness to pass before him,[3] He opened to
his astonished gaze the treasure-houses of Heaven,
pointing out to him, one after the other, the rewards in store for the righteous ; but that when
at length He exposed to view one treasure-house
larger than all the rest, piled up with precious things
beyond number, and Moses, in rapt astonishment,
exclaimed, " Lord, what is this great storehouse ? "
God answered him, " This is the storehouse of happiness for those who have no merit of their own."

Such is the Jewish view of God's mercy to the
undeserving. And surely it is no extravagant idea,
when we call to mind man's career on earth. He
enters the world helpless and naked. Loving hands
receive him, tend him, clothe him, and feed him ;
loving hearts educate him ; and however great the

---

[1] " Bacon's Essays," XVII. (" On Superstition ").

[2] *Midrash, Shemoth Rabbah*, ch. xlv.

[3] Exod. xxxiii. 18, 19.

struggle of life, there is evidence, at every step and
stage, of a Providence that guides him, unworthy
though he be. Unworthy, indeed ; for since none
are free from sin, if God were a vindictive Being,
as some religions would represent Him, even the
best of us would be struck dead long before we
attained manhood. But He has no vindictiveness.
He has declared through His prophet that His ways
are not as our ways ; that as the heavens are
higher than the earth, His ways are higher than
our ways, and His thoughts higher than our
thoughts.[1] And He has declared Himself " merciful and gracious, long-suffering, and abundant in
goodness and truth, keeping mercy for thousands,
forgiving iniquity, transgression, and sin." Surely
He who provided gentle hands and hearts to receive
us on entering this world, will provide a loving wel-
come for the soul, released from its earthly envelope,
whether it be the soul of the sinner trembling for
its future, or the soul of the pious, yearning for
that perfection which the earth forbade.

Think not that such mercy, infinite and universal, is inconsistent with justice. He who fashioned
the heavens, and balanced the countless suns and
planets in boundless space, can surely adjust rewards according to our deserts. " The great, the
mighty God, the Lord of Hosts is His name. Great
in counsel and mighty in work ; for Thine eyes are
upon all the ways of the sons of men ; to give
every one according to his ways, and according to
the fruit of his doings." [2] But Justice does not

[1] Isa. lv. 8, 9.   [2] Jer. xxxii. 18, 19.

require annihilation, perdition, or eternal punishment. Justice to weak, faulty, erring, and imperfect man, rather requires mercy—mercy illimitable
from the Perfect Being who created us. And so
when the time will come—as come it must to all—
when death approaches, though the parting from
loved ones may be with tears, and the severance of
earthly ties may be with lamentations, yet let there
be no fear in the soul as it enters the presence of its
Maker; for, merited or not, the loving mercy of
God is the sure passport of every soul to heaven
and happiness.

And yet the good will have the reward of their
goodness; and yet the wicked will be requited for
their wickedness; for God will by no means wholly
clear the guilty.[1] Man cannot be saved from the
natural consequences of his sin. Of the reward in
a future state we know nothing here; and still we
may, perhaps, gain some slight foretaste of its
nature from the sense of spiritual delight we experience after the performance of a truly good,
unselfish act, involving heavy sacrifice. Of the
punishment in a future state we can know nothing
here; and still we may, perhaps, have some slight
foreshadowing of its nature from the sense of
remorse which follows the commission of a sin.
Just as the grown man looks back on the foibles of
his childhood and youth with contempt, and perhaps disgust, so may we well imagine the soul,
released from its earthly envelope, burdened with
remorse at the sins of its worldly career, until the

[1] Exod. xxxiv. 7.

Great " God of the spirits of all flesh " shall have
purified it from its earthly stains.

And as to the shares and proportions of reward
meted out to each, though there will be Heaven for
all, immortality for all, happiness for all, through
the boundless mercy of God, the happiness will,
perhaps, be greater or less, not according to the
measure in which it is *bestowed*, but according to
the measure in which it is *deserved*.

Perhaps that happiness, whatever it be, will be
the purer, because God, in His revealed Word, has
not made it a matter of bargain with man; [1]
because the promised guerdon is vague and indistinct ; because the acme of happiness comes as the
consequence of virtue, not as the *reward* of virtue.
For it is the unselfish, disinterested work that is
truly godly—satisfying God and satisfying the soul
by its purity and lack of motive—the labour done
without hope of profit, fame, or reward—the work
wrought for the glory of God and the good of man.

[1] Antigonus of Socho used to say : " Be not like servants who
serve their master in consideration of receiving a reward ; but
be like servants who serve their master without any hope of
receiving a reward ; and let the fear of Heaven be upon you "
(*Aboth*, i. 3).

And so speaks Browning :—

> " God whom I praise ; how could I praise,
>   If such as I might understand,
>   Make out and reckon on His ways,
>   And bargain for His love ? "

CHAPTER XIV

PROPHECY AND ISRAEL'S HOPE

WHAT do we mean by Prophecy ? Why are we to believe in the prophets ? What do the prophets teach us ?

You all know that the Bible is divided into three great sections—the Law, the Prophets, and the Sacred Writings. Now, the Prophets contain much that is by no means prophetic, and that is distinctly historical. Indeed, there are many of the so-called prophets who never prophesied, in the common sense of the word—that is, they never foretold coming events ; but they were the scholars, sages, and statesmen of the people ; they excelled in poetry, oratory, and music ; they were the guardians of the Law, the interpreters of God's will, the chroniclers, moralists, and preachers of biblical times.

Those who attained the faculty of foretelling future events were but few in number. Withdrawing themselves from the occupations and pleasures of the world ; sanctifying themselves to the service of God, whose works and ways they were ever studying with awe and reverence ; possessed of the highest spiritual longings ; and looking down upon the earth and earthly things from an eminence far

above, and, as it were, outside this world, these few
select men became the messengers of God to man.

Theirs was not merely the insight acquired by
the astute historian, who reads the future by the
light of the past, and who, making History a
science, traces a faint outline of coming events
from the parallel records of bygone times. Theirs
was not the mere warning voice of worldly wisdom,
nor the sage counsel of human genius, nor the sad
foreboding of the anxious patriot. Their prophecies were messages from God, delivered in His
name, because under His inspiration, and bearing
all the tokens of Divine authority.

Nor were these prophecies mere presages of
future history. Interspersed with their predictions
of good and evil, were golden words of wisdom,
joyous songs of prayer and praise, stirring exhorta-
tions to duty, mournful dirges for glory lost and
gone, glowing thoughts of the Divine Majesty,
visions of heavenly hosts, dreams of celestial bliss ;
and all portrayed in the winged words of sweetest
poetry. But interwoven with the main fabric of
this poetry, we find the Divine Word, as promulgated in our Code ; its teachings are never lost
sight of ; no contradictions, no inconsistencies, no
new covenants superseding the old ; but a unity
of thought, design, and feeling, a consistency of
principle, showing that One Mind inspired all the
Prophets—the Mind Divine that gave us our Law,
through His servant Moses.

We, living in these days of materialism, when
many in all honesty, but with all reverence, doubt

the possibility of miracles, because such miracles
as the Bible relates do not now happen, may perhaps feel, if not doubt, at least wonder, that the
Great Maker of the Universe should choose a few
obscure men in one of the tiniest of His planets (a
planet however large to us, yet infinitely small
compared with any of the countless suns that be-
spangle the wide heavens), and should make those
men the exponents of His Will to their fellow-
mortals on that little planet. The mind, with its
finite ideas, cannot grasp the notion of a Being
infinitely great condescending to the infinitely
small ; and this is the cause of the difficulty experienced by some. But once admit the Divine
Government of the World, which all Religion
teaches, once admit that God in His mercy does
concern Himself with the welfare of His creatures,
infinitely small though they may be compared with
Himself—and the difficulty vanishes. Why should
not God, who witnesses every act of our lives,
single out His own agents to work or to proclaim
His Will on earth ? Why should not He who
breathes the spirit of genius into one, the spirit
of poetry into another, the spirit of invention and
discovery into a third, inspire others in dreams or
visions, or even in their waking hours, with the
spirit of prophecy, as a warning to the wicked, and
a hope and encouragement to the righteous ? He
makes all the forces of Nature His servants ; He
" makes the winds His messengers." Where, then,
is the improbability in His choosing the best of
men and inspiring them to declare His Will to the

R

creatures whom He loves ? If we extend the
meaning of the term prophecy to the teaching of
the Unknown by the inspired genius, then even
these our times have in truth witnessed the advent
of many great prophets who have enriched our
souls by their prophecies.

Chief and first among the prophets of old was
Moses, unlike all others as the expositor of the
Law of God.[1] You know well how he proved his
Divine mission by working for his people's good,
acting as their protector and advocate, and con-
ducting them out of the land of bondage. You
know the part he took in the Divine Revelation,
how he became the Lawgiver, Teacher, Judge, and
Leader of his nation during the forty years' wanderings.   Before his death, he gave his people a
prophetic insight into their future, first in that
remarkable chapter of blessings and curses,[2] then in
his dying song, full of fervid eloquence,[3] and lastly
in his parting blessing to the tribes.[4]

The prophets who came after Moses could never
hope to vie with him in position and influence.
Yet they, too, were to have their credentials ; and
the people were not to listen to their voice before
those credentials had been produced. For Moses
commanded his people [5] not to listen to every one
who pretended to be the bearer of a message from
God.   Still, they were told that prophecy was not
to cease ; that a prophet, one of themselves, would
be raised up, in whose mouth God would put His

---

[1] Deut. xxxiv. 10.   [2] Deut. xxviii.   [3] Deut. xxxii. 1–43.
[4] Deut. xxxiii.   [5] Deut. xviii. 14.

words ; who should speak all that God would command him ; and to this prophet they were to hearken.[1]

And what was to be the test of a true prophet ? It was to be twofold. " When a prophet speaketh in the name of the Lord, if the thing follow not, nor come to pass, that is the thing which the Lord hath not spoken, but the prophet hath spoken it presumptuously ; thou shalt not be afraid of him." [2] The test of true prophecy is, thus, first, the common-sense test—fulfilment. There is no demand for blind belief, no call upon credulity, a credulity so often mistermed faith ; but the test was to be the evidence of the senses. Next, the word of the prophet, if it is to be believed, must be consistent with the revealed Word of God. " The prophet which shall presume to speak a word in My name which I have not commanded him to speak, or that shall speak in the name of other gods, even that prophet shall die." [3]

When, therefore, we read in the Bible the words of the prophets, we may rest assured that those who regarded them as prophets, in their own times, had good and valid reasons for so regarding them, and that they did not blindly accept their statements on trust, without some evidence of their prophetic gift.

But we, living in an age far distant from the time when these prophetic warnings and promises were uttered, have the best evidence of their truth ;

[1] Deut. xviii. 18, 19.   [2] Deut. xviii. 22.
[3] Deut. xviii. 20.

for time has verified nearly all of them in so
wondrous a fashion, that we sometimes stand
amazed at the coincidence of prophecy, in all its
smallest details, with accomplished facts. The prophecies relating to Palestine, Assyria, Babylon, and
Egypt have been fulfilled in the main. Yet some
prophecies remain unfulfilled ; and what shall we
say to them ? If nine out of ten prophecies of one
prophet have been realised, shall we discredit the
tenth ? Shall we not rather say that the tenth is
not yet ripe for fulfilment ? And when we find
the same unfulfilled prophecy foretold equally by
several other prophets, the majority of whose predictions have also come true, is it not reasonable
to conclude that, in the fulness of time, the as yet
unrealised prediction in which so many prophets
concur, will also come to pass ?

To us Jews, the question is momentous ; for
the unfulfilled prediction to which I refer is that
of the spiritual restoration of Israel. We Jews,
who love our religion, have hopes apart from the
hopes of worldly success. Wherever the Jew is
domiciled, he lives two lives—his life as a citizen,
and his life as a Jew. He loves with tender love
the land of his adoption, whose laws protect him
and his property, and shield him from persecution.
He is a patriot to the land which gave him birth,
and gladly bears the burdens of citizenship, faithfully obeys the laws, and shares in his nation's joys
and tribulation. But the fervent Jew has another
country that he loves without detriment to his
love for the land of his birth. He loves that land

which was the cradle of his Faith, the home of
the patriarchs, the glory of his nation ; the land
which contains Zion and Jerusalem. He thinks of
it, not as it is, desolate, barren, and forsaken, its
towns ruinous, many of its mountain-sides un-
tilled, its holy places in Gentile hands ; he thinks
of it as it was in the days of its pristine glory, and
as it will be when all the prophecies regarding it
shall have been fulfilled.

Nor is his hope for the restoration of his people
merely an insensate longing to re-possess the land
of his inheritance ; for this world has fairer homes
than Palestine ; more fertile fields than its ill-
watered plains ; more verdant slopes than its rocky
hills ; but the hope of Israel is for a spiritual
restoration, which shall make Palestine once again
the religious focus of the world, Jerusalem again
the Holy City of the earth, Zion once more the
mount of God—a spiritual restoration, which shall
make the essence of his Faith—the belief in the
One and only God, and submission to His will—
the religion of the world.

Let us hear what the prophets tell us concerning
the future of Israel, and Israel's land.

First of all, Moses foretells to repentant Israel a
happy return to the Land of Promise, in clear language, free from doubt or oracular ambiguity, in
these words : " And it shall come to pass when all
these things shall come upon thee, the blessing and
the curse, which I have set before thee, and thou
shalt call them to mind among all the nations,
whither the Lord thy God hath driven thee, And

shalt return unto the Lord thy God, and shalt obey
His voice according to all that I command thee this
day, thou and thy children, with all thine heart,
and with all thy soul ; That then the Lord thy
God will turn thy captivity, and have compassion
upon thee, and will return and gather thee from
all the nations whither the Lord thy God hath
scattered thee. If any of thine be driven out unto
the utmost parts of heaven, from thence will the
Lord thy God gather thee, and from thence will
He fetch thee. And the Lord thy God will bring
thee unto the land which thy fathers possessed, and
thou shalt possess it ; and He will do thee good,
and multiply thee above thy fathers." [1]

This prophecy is as yet unfulfilled. It did not
come to pass at the close of the Babylonish captivity ; for the ten tribes of the kingdom of Israel
were not included in the restoration under Ezra
and Nehemiah. It must, therefore, have reference
to a restoration yet to come.

Next, let us hear what Isaiah reveals to us on
the same subject. Isaiah, though his thoughts are
mostly clad in the resplendent garb of brilliant
imagery, or in the fiery mantle of impassioned
poetry, when he prophesies the second restoration,
is perfectly clear and circumstantial : " And it shall
come to pass in that day, that the Lord shall set
His hand again the second time to recover the
remnant of His people, which shall be left, from
Assyria, and from Egypt, and from Pathros, and
from Cush, and from Elam, and from Shinar, and

[1] Deut. xxx. 1-5.

from Hamath, and from the islands of the sea. And He shall set up an ensign for the nations, and shall assemble the outcasts of Israel, and gather together the dispersed of Judah from the four corners of the earth." [1]

Israel, whose lost ten tribes are yet undiscovered, is to join with Judah in the happy restoration. And when is this marvellous event to take place ? The restoration is to be heralded by the previous advent of him whom we style the Messiah, or the Anointed, not a god, but a man, a descendant of David, a man filled with the spirit of God, worthy of being the harbinger of a glorious restoration ; and thus does Isaiah describe him : " And there shall come forth a rod out of the stem of Jesse, and a branch shall grow out of his roots. And the spirit of the Lord shall rest upon him, the spirit of wisdom and understanding, the spirit of counsel and might, the spirit of knowledge and of the fear of the Lord : And shall make him of quick under-standing in the fear of the Lord ; and he shall not judge after the sight of his eyes, neither reprove after the hearing of his ears : But with righteous-ness shall he judge the poor, and reprove with equity for the meek of the earth ; and he shall smite the earth with the rod of his mouth, and with the breath of his lips shall he slay the wicked. And righteousness shall be the girdle of his loins, and faithfulness the girdle of his reins." [2] . . . In those days, " The earth shall be full of the know-ledge of the Lord, as the waters cover the sea." [3]

[1] Isa. xi. 11, 12.　　[2] Isa. xi. 1–5.　　[3] Isa. xi. 9.

For this restoration will not affect Israel and Judah alone ; it will affect the whole world. At the advent of the Messiah, there will be a time not only of knowledge, but of peace : " And it shall come to pass in the last days, that the mountain of the Lord's house shall be established in the top of the mountains, and shall be exalted above the hills, and all nations shall flow unto it. And many people shall go and say, Come ye, and let us go up to the mountain of the Lord, to the house of the God of Jacob ; and He will teach us of His ways, and we will walk in His paths ; for out of Zion shall go forth the law, and the word of the Lord from Jerusalem. And He shall judge among the nations, and shall rebuke many people, and they shall beat their swords into ploughshares, and their spears into pruning-hooks ; nation shall not lift up sword against nation, neither shall they learn war any more." [1]

At this epoch the oppression of tyrants will come to an end, and the pride of kings will be humbled. *Religions* will be abolished, and *Religion* will reign supreme. " And the loftiness of man shall be bowed down, and the haughtiness of man shall be made low, and the Lord alone shall be exalted in that day. And the idols he shall utterly abolish." [2]

But though the whole world will thus profit by the spiritual restoration of Israel, our people are still to remain the depositaries of God's Holy Law, and through them the earth is to be enlightened. " And a Redeemer shall come unto Zion, and

---

[1] Isa. ii. 2–4.   [2] Isa. ii. 17, 18.

unto them that turn from transgression in Jacob, saith the Lord. As for Me, this is My covenant with them, saith the Lord : My spirit that is upon thee, and My words which I have put in thy mouth shall not depart out of thy mouth, nor out of the mouth of thy seed, nor out of the mouth of thy seed's seed, saith the Lord, from henceforth and for ever." [1] "And the Gentiles shall come to thy light, and kings to the brightness of thy rising." [2]

Jeremiah, the priest, who had prophesied in several successive reigns the downfall of Jerusalem and Judah, and who became himself a witness of, and sufferer by, that terrible calamity ; whose wail over the captivity of his people finds an echo in those Lamentations, which seem written in scalding tears—Jeremiah, too, foretells the coming of the Messiah, and the happy restoration of his race : " Behold the days come, saith the Lord, that I will raise unto David a righteous Branch, and a King shall reign and prosper, and shall execute judgment and justice in the earth. In his days Judah shall be saved, and Israel shall dwell safely." [3] . . . " And they shall dwell in their own land." [4]

Even out of the darkness of the dungeon, where the wicked king Zedekiah had imprisoned him, thinking to stifle his prophetic utterances, there came to Jeremiah, coupled with the presage of immediate evil, the promise of the great and permanent restoration of his people in distant days : " Behold, I will gather them out of all countries,

---

[1] Isa. lix. 20, 21.
[2] Isa. lx. 3.
[3] Jer. xxiii. 5, 6.
[4] Jer. xxiii. 8.

whither I have driven them in Mine anger, and in My fury, and in great wrath : and I will bring them again to this place, and I will cause them to dwell safely. And they shall be My people, and I will be their God : and I will give them one heart and one way, that they may fear Me for ever, for the good of them and of their children after them : and I will make an everlasting covenant with them, that I will not turn away from them to do them good ; but I will put My fear in their hearts, that they shall not depart from Me." [1]

Ezekiel, whose spirit of prophecy seems to have sprung out of the miseries of the captivity, but who, more than any other prophet, gives us, as it were, a glimpse of the transcendent glories of heaven, prophesies in like terms the return of his nation from their long exile, their renewed obedience to their Divine Ruler, and the permanency of Israel's settlement in the Holy Land. " Thus saith the Lord God : Behold, I will take the children of Israel from among the heathen, whither they be gone, and will gather them on every side, and bring them into their own land. . . . Moreover, I will make a covenant of peace with them ; it shall be an everlasting covenant with them ; and I will place them and multiply them, and will set My sanctuary in the midst of them for evermore." [2]

The Minor Prophets [3] join in these good tidings

[1] Jer. xxxii. 37–40.

[2] Ezek. xxxvii. 21, 26.

[3] The Minor Prophets are so called by biblical scholars, not because these prophets were inferior in prophetic gift to Isaiah, Jeremiah, or Ezekiel, nor because their predictions were of

of our future restoration, and there is a remarkable
coincidence everywhere in the terms of their prophecies. The prophet Zechariah, who delivered to
the captives of Babylon the message of their speedy
return, and who encouraged them to proceed with
the rebuilding of the Temple in spite of their ad-
versaries,[1] foretells the concourse of the nations
to Jerusalem to join in the true worship : " Thus
saith the Lord of Hosts ; it shall yet come to pass
that there shall come people and the inhabitants
of many cities. And the inhabitants of one city
shall go to another, saying, Let us go speedily to
pray before the Lord, and to seek the Lord of
Hosts ; I will go also. Yea, many people and
strong nations shall come to seek the Lord of
Hosts in Jerusalem, and to pray before the Lord." [2]
In all these prophecies, the same note prevails—the
spiritual triumph of Judaism and of its great principle, the monotheistic idea.

And in these times, when we see how the world
is gradually recognising the marvellous wisdom of
our Law in all its bearings, and acknowledging its
debt to the Jew who has observed, and, by observing, preserved that code through ages of persecution ; when we see the honoured position which our
people are achieving in every country where they
have enjoyed liberty and fair play for their talents,
it seems as if this prophecy, too, is not far from
fulfilment : " In those days it shall come to pass

minor value ; but because their writings are smaller in bulk and
quantity. In Hebrew they are called תְּרֵי עָשָׂר, " the Twelve,"
and are counted as one book.

[1] Ezra v. 1. [2] Zech. viii. 20–22.

that ten men shall take hold out of all languages of the nations, even shall take hold of the skirt of him that is a Jew, saying, We will go with you; for we have heard that God is with you." [1]   In those days the mythologies of now dominant religions will have become curiosities of human history, and will give place to the pure monotheism of Israel.   " The Lord shall be king over all the earth ; in that day shall there be one Lord, and His name ONE." [2]

To us, living in a free and happy country, not only tolerated but respected by our fellow-citizens of other creeds, and admitted to the honours and dignities of the State ; to us, enjoying full liberty, religious and civil, the question may fairly suggest itself, why should any of us long for a restoration of our Temple or wish to return to Jerusalem ? Why pray for the termination of a captivity in which we are free men ?   Why repine at a misfortune nearly two thousand years old, which lost to us our own country, but which, after long and bitter misfortunes honourably borne by our ancestors, has given to us another country which we have reason to love so dearly ?

But to the Jew who understands the mission of Judaism, Palestine, his mother-country, is not dead —is but in a trance.   She will surely awake, and yet claim him as her own.   To the Jew, the restoration of the Holy Land is no vain phrase, for his prayers for the renewed glory of Zion aim at the spiritual glories of the Messianic era and the

[1] Zech. viii. 23.   [2] Zech. xiv. 9.

regeneration of the entire human race ; and thus
he prays not in selfish prayer for his own good, or
even for the good of his people alone, but, in the
broadest spirit of philanthropy, prays for a condition of things which will embrace the happiness of
all mankind, when " wickedness shall be consumed
like smoke, and the dominion of oppression shall
pass away from the earth," when " the world will
be perfected under the kingdom of the Almighty,
and all the children of flesh will call upon His
name "—an era of *one religion, One God.*

For he reads the dismal page of History, and
there sees how, though Religion was given to man
as the greatest blessing, Religions have proved his
greatest curse. He reads of wars waged for centuries between Mahometan and Christian, hatred
between these two creeds surviving even now, and
lasting even to our own times. He reads of the
persecutions of Christian by Christian, feuds between
Greek Church and Latin Church, between Protes-
tants and Catholics, the *autos-da-fé* of the Inquisi-
tion, the burnings of Smithfield and of Oxford.
He reads of creeds split up into every possible
form of dissent, its priests quarrelling about candles
and vestments and postures and other like trifles,
till he feels inclined to exclaim with the Psalmist,
" He that sitteth in the Heavens shall laugh ; the
Lord shall have them in derision." [1]

And then he turns to his own glorious History,
and finds his Religion outliving all the rest, un-
changed, unsullied, evergreen through the long

[1] Ps. ii. 4.

lapse of ages, surviving still with all the most important forms, prayers, ceremonies, and beliefs of ancient Bible-times. He asks himself : Wherefore this sempiternal life of Israel's Creed ? Why this ever-renewed youth of his Religion, in spite of persecution and oppression, in spite of the law of change and decay, whose influence is to be traced in all things else ? And he thinks it must be the fulfilment of the Divine law of Nature, " the survival of the fittest "—the survival of that creed destined to be the Creed of the World.

For the Jew alone remains as he was, in spite of his lost nationality. Other nations springing from obscurity, rose, achieved greatness, became dictators of the world, then fell into decay and perished utterly, their grandeur and their monuments mingling with the dust. But the Jew survives them all.

He sees, in the history of the past, his people exiled, plundered, tortured, massacred ; but he sees also how Judaism outlived its persecutors, and even derived from persecution new vitality. Driven hither and thither about the world, first tolerated, then banished, then recalled, then driven again into exile, the Jew leaves his trace everywhere, like the wandering thistle-down, blown about from field to field, the sport of the winds, the plaything of the gales. Driven out by persecution, he takes root in every land and clime, so that in every corner of the inhabited globe there rises a fane where the God of Israel, the One and only God, is worshipped ; and wherever he has found a

rest for the sole of his feet, he has achieved a high
position. But his greatest achievement has been
that everywhere in his exile, through ages of persecution, he has held aloft the pure, unalloyed
Word of God as the standard of morality, and his
pure belief in One sole God, to whom man is
responsible, as the standard of Religion.

This last has been his mission in bygone days,
and it remains his mission yet. For now, standing
on his lofty eminence, he witnesses the battles of
the creeds, and pities the combatants. He sees
them fighting about the shadows of which he
proudly holds the substance—shadows of the Bible-
creed prolonged in irrecognisable distortion, as the
bright sun of truth advances, directing men to
believe only the credible.

Standing on this lofty eminence of credible belief,
he thinks he sees the world in time to come, wiser
with age, turning to the One True Faith to which
he, as custodian, has so long clung ; and amid the
ruins of exploded superstitions, amid the ashes of
burnt-out beliefs, amid the wreck of irreligion,
amid the crash of creeds, he thinks he sees his
creed emerge triumphant—THE RELIGION OF THE
WORLD.

APPENDICES

APPENDIX I

EVOLUTION AND DESIGN

MANY have expressed the opinion, that the " Argument from Design " in proof of the Existence of a God, which Paley was the first to popularise,[1] and which I have here [2] attempted by familiar examples to adapt to the comprehension of the young, has become weakened, if not wholly invalidated, by the recent theory of Evolution.

According to this theory, now accepted by most philosophers, being powerfully supported by well-established facts of science, the Earth and its contents did not come into their present state of existence by a series of separate and distinct, or, so to speak, arbitrary acts of creation, by so many fits and starts of creative energy, but are the results of certain natural forces, acting upon matter according to fixed laws, causing gradual changes and developments in living things, and, by slow degrees, during the course of countless ages, transforming the simplest into the most complex

[1] Paley is by no means original in his " Argument from Design." Cicero stated the argument in these words : " Whoever thinks that the wonderful order and incredible constancy of the heavenly bodies are not governed by an Intelligent Being, is himself void of understanding. For shall we, when we see an artificial machine, a sphere or a dial, acknowledge at first sight that it is a work of art and understanding, and make any doubt that the heavens are the work not only of reason, but of an Excellent and Divine Reason ? "—*De Natura Deorum*, II. 38.

[2] Part I. chap. i.

and varying forms of life, till the present climax was reached ; and that climax itself no final climax, but itself, like many that preceded it, a starting point for a gradual decline of some, and for an equally gradual higher development of other forms of life.

If this theory be true, " every organic being has a place in a chain of events. It is not an isolated, a capricious fact, but an unavoidable phenomenon. It has its place in that vast, orderly concourse which has successively risen in the past, has introduced the present, and is preparing the way for a predestined future. From point to point in this vast progression, there has been a gradual, a definite, a continuous unfolding, a resistless order of evolution. But in the midst of these mighty changes stand forth immutable the laws that are dominating over all." [1]

But if this theory of Evolution be true, if a slow and gradual transformation from one living form to another —a transformation obedient to fixed law—is, in our belief or mental vision, to take the place of that sudden calling forth of life, which we have hitherto associated with the idea of Creation, what, it is asked, becomes of the " Argument from Design " ? Can a living thing be said to have been designed, if it arose in the ordinary course of events, if its coming into life was not only not specially designed, but was even an unavoidable event ?

I would answer, that the " Argument from Design " is vastly intensified in force if the theory of Evolution be true. For if it be true, as the Evolutionists tell us, that all living creatures have gradually descended from a low organic form known as protoplasm, acted upon by forces which have ever remained subject to the same invariable laws, what must be said of the Origin of such protoplasm, such force, and such law, as could produce such results as the living creatures which

[1] Prof. Draper's " Conflict between Religion and Science."

people our world ? Are not the marks of design all the more striking, if, with a foresight which the human mind can scarcely grasp or realise to the faintest degree, the matter, force, and law were so ordained, countless ages ago, as to produce, *without intervention in the interval* (as the Evolutionists would have us believe), a world teeming with all forms of life, as we see it now ?

I would maintain, that if the doctrine of Evolution be true (and much yet remains to be proved before it can be regarded in any other light than that of a highly probable theory), the scheme of primal creation is thereby immeasurably ennobled, that the presence of Design is *ipso facto* proved—design of a kind so far-sighted, so multifarious, so full of numberless nascent and unborn conditions of life, each productive of countless forms of life, actual and potential, that the mind, contemplating the huge gap between the protoplasmic form and the complex vertebrates of to-day, quails beneath the burden of the developmental idea ; and we feel that language is poor and weak, nay, powerless, since DESIGN is the strongest word we have to cover the far-sighted Creative Intention, which started into life a world of germs, that, after countless ages, could produce the wondrous world of life now surrounding us ! [1]

[1] Darwin concludes his " Origin of Species " with these words : " There is a grandeur in this view of life with its several powers having been originally breathed by the Creator into a few forms or into one ; and that, while this planet has gone cycling on according to the fixed law of gravity, from so simple a beginning, endless forms most beautiful and most wonderful have been, and are being, evolved."

It is remarked by Sir John B. Byles (" Foundations of Religion," page 26) that, in the latter part of Voltaire's life, the argument from design was that which most impressed the philosopher, and seems to have removed from his mind not only all doubt, but all fear of ever doubting again : " J'admets cette Intelligence Suprême, sans craindre que jamais on puisse me faire changer d'opinion. Rien n'ebranle en moi cet axiome—tout ouvrage démontre un ouvrier."

APPENDIX II

LIMITS OF FAITH AND INQUIRY [1]

FAITH, *but not credulity*. Where shall we draw the line between the two ? Where does faith leave off and credulity begin ? What shall he that has faith believe, and what shall he discredit ? When shall Reason bend its head to Faith, and how shall it, without abdicating its sway ? These are questions which affect every religion, and ours perhaps more closely than any, because our religion can afford inquiry.

Let us, then, attempt to define the limits, on the one hand, beyond which no religion should claim our belief ; and, on the other hand, the limits beyond which no logic should dare to tread.

No religion should tax our faith to such an extent as to ask us to believe in an incongruity. Any religion that would tell us that, by one of its miracles, a part became greater than the whole, or that two and two made five, or that a thing was right and wrong at the same time, or that past time would come back again, would be wholly unworthy of belief ; for such statements would involve moral impossibilities, incongruities, contradictions in terms.

But perhaps the reader may ask why we take such pains to demonstrate what every rational person must see to be a truism. We shall show that we are not contending with a mere shadow.

There is a religion which represents that there is a

---

[1] Reprinted, with alterations, from " Sabbath Readings."

Deity, consisting of three distinct personages acting independently of each other, but yet forming one Deity, one and indivisible. Of course, any rational man would say that a being cannot be *one* being and *three* beings at the same time; that if a being be indivisible, it cannot consist of three independent parts; that the whole theory is a contradiction in terms.

But those who profess the creed which propounds this remarkable doctrine tell us, in reply, that we cannot reason upon such a matter, and that men only require faith to believe in it.

We answer that though credulity can make a man believe a contradiction in terms, faith cannot; faith is the credit which the mind lends willingly *to that which has been tested and found trustworthy ;* while credulity is the blind surrender of mind and reason to the untried scheme, or dreamy phantasy, or senseless theory, or cloudy mystery.

Why does the child have faith in his parents, and believe what they tell him ? Because he has had experience of their kindness and of their love. He trusts them because he always finds them true to him. Childlike faith is not a blind faith, as some would maintain. It is a faith born of experience ; and it is the stronger, the stronger its origin.

When Abraham left his native land, his kindred, and his father's house, at the bidding of God, was it blind faith that dictated obedience ? Was it not rather the strong belief in the mission that was before him, the strong abhorrence of the idolatry of Haran, the strong confidence in the God who had saved him from the flames of the fire-worshippers, that made him believe in the Lord, so that " it was accounted to him for righteousness " ? His faith was not blind credulity. It was *belief*, the offspring of experience. It had fed on the broad pastures of reason, and drunk from the deep wells of thought.

And even with Abraham, the father of the faithful, faith required to be fed and nursed. " Lord God," he exclaimed, when he had been told that his seed would possess the land of Canaan, " whereby shall I know that I shall inherit it ? " and God solved his doubts in a vision.   Later yet, when a son was promised to him in his old age, he fell upon his face and laughed, and his wife exclaimed, " Shall I of a surety bear a child ? " scarcely believing such an improbable event. God asks him, " Is anything too hard for the Lord ? "   And, still later, when he feared lest with the sinners of Sodom his kinsman Lot might be destroyed, and seemed to question the Divine justice in the words, " Shall not the Judge of all the earth do right ? " he shows that his faith even then was not quite complete.

But when the promise is fulfilled, and in his old age the longed-for son is born, and the prospect of a multi-tudinous progeny dawns upon him, we see a change. His faith is complete.   Steadfast in that faith, he binds his son on Mount Moriah, for he knows that the command of the All-just, the All-merciful Ruler of the Universe must have been prompted by some wise and holy purpose.

Later yet, when he sends away his servant to seek a wife for his son from amongst his own kindred, he is confident that God will favour his mission ; and, addressing the trusty Eleazar, he says, " The Lord God of Heaven, who took me from my father's house, and from the land of my kindred, and who spake unto me and sware unto me, saying, Unto thy seed will I give this land, He shall send His angel before thee." Abraham's faith is perfect.   It had grown with a natural growth ; experience had strengthened it ; and, in his old age, his faith in God was ripe.

Let us now turn from the early Pentateuch history to the Mosaic Code itself, and we shall there see that the same standard of experience is set up as the only trustworthy basis of belief. Moses points out to the people in the following words the test whereby the false prophet may be detected : " When a prophet speaketh in the name of the Lord, if the thing follow not, nor come to pass, that is the thing which the Lord hath not spoken, but the prophet hath spoken it presumptuously." [1] Belief in a prophet was not to be that mere mental effort which some call faith ; it was to be founded upon some fact within the experience of the believer.

But though the revelations of prophecy are to be thus tested by evidence and experience, we are not to allow ourselves to be led away to believe in that which is repugnant to reason, and at variance with the divine command. We are told,[2] " If there arise among you a prophet or a dreamer of dreams, and he giveth thee a sign or a wonder, and the sign or the wonder come to pass whereof he spake unto thee saying, Let us go after other gods which thou hast not known, and let us serve them, thou shalt not hearken unto the words of that prophet or that dreamer of dreams, for the Lord your God proveth you to know whether ye love the Lord your God with all your heart and with all your soul." [3]

The fulfilment of the prophecy or portent, then, is not to be the only test. There may be jugglery or chicanery ; even the prophecy may verily be fulfilled, or the sign and the wonder may truly take place ; but if the prophet bring a strange religion " which thou hast not known," a religion full of mystery and incon-

[1] Deut. xviii. 22.   [2] Deut. xiii. 1–3.
[3] The line of argument and biblical illustrations here given are to a certain extent coincident with those in Chapter xiv. But it is thought desirable not to omit them in this reprint.

gruity, a religion inconsistent with the behests of God, such a prophet is not to be believed.

No matter, then, if at the foundation of a new creed its exponent or prophet gave signs and wonders which came to pass. Even assuming (which we do not grant) that those alleged miracles were historically true, we should not be justified in obeying him, when he bids us " follow after other gods," whom we neither know nor comprehend.

That God, who is unchangeable, did not, through Moses, in one day make a covenant with His people, and through that people with the whole earth, revealing His will, His behests, and His attributes, to abrogate and repeal that covenant on another day; substituting for a clear, simple, and comprehensible religion, a religion which is all mystery, all incongruity, credible only by excessive credulity. The revelation was not given to be revoked by a new covenant at a future epoch of the world's history. True, it did not reveal everything to our finite senses. It did not solve at once every problem in nature, for " the secret things belong to the Lord our God " ; but those things which it did reveal are the eternal heritage of our race ; they are clear, credible, comprehensible, even to our children ; they " belong to us and to our children for ever, that we may do all the words of God's Law." [1]

Thus far we have endeavoured to define the limits beyond which no religion should claim our belief. Let us now seek to discover the limits beyond which no reasoning should dare to tread.

When and where is Reason to stand still, and hand us over to the guardianship of Faith ? Logic must not travel alone into the regions of the unseen, the illimitable, the eternal. In matters of religion, logic may deal only with what we see, and feel, and know, found-

[1] Deut. xxix. 29.

ing all its reasonings upon axioms known and indisputable. Nor may we in our thoughts and reasonings about God, His ways and works, judge of Him and them by our own petty human standard ; " for My thoughts are not your thoughts, neither are your ways My ways, saith the Lord." [1]

Nor may we waste our mental energies in vain attempts to reconcile conflicting points, which in this life never will be reconciled.[2]   What is the use, or where our right, to seek to reconcile the foreknowledge of God with the free-will of man, or any other such conflicting questions ? What right have we to institute a suit between the two, and then to seek in vain to reconcile the suitors ?

Predestination and free-will !   Free-will we *think* we understand ; but when we trace volition to the brain, and ask how free-will acts, all certain knowledge ends. We know the brain gives impulse to the nerves and muscles ; but how, in what manner, no mind can comprehend.   We *think* we have free-will ; but find volition modified by circumstance of time and place, weather, health, and fancy, and a thousand trifles which we would scarcely own.

Predestination ! What mind can fathom to its depth the meaning of Divine foreknowledge, defining that one word Omniscience ? Omniscience ! knowledge of all events to all eternity, knowledge, too, extending back, and back, and back to that eternity, which is past and gone ! Whose mind can grasp this one idea, even the shadow of omniscience ? And yet men talk so glibly of predestination and free-will, and seek to reconcile the two !

[1] Isa. lv. 8.
[2] " Man is not born to solve the problems of the Universe, but to find out where the problem begins, and then to restrain himself within the limits of the comprehensible. His faculties are not sufficient to measure the activities of the universe ; and an attempt to explain the outer world by reason, from his narrow point of view, is a vain endeavour."—*Goethe.*

On the fatal rock of attempted reconciliation, many have wrecked their faith. The busy brains of shallow reasoners work hard to reconcile. They twist and turn the facts, distorting truth, till truth appears a falsehood. To their shallow minds all is beautifully reconciled and deftly fitted ; but thoughtful men are not so satisfied. They see religionists build up religion on shifty quicksands of specious quibbles. " Is this religion ? " they ask ; and their questions end in doubts, their doubts in unbelief.

A sad result. Not that we must therefore suppress reason and underrate its powers. But reason must not proudly rear its head, and deem itself antagonist to faith. It is in truth a marvel. In all nature, reason has no parallel ; and yet the mightiest effort of the greatest human mind must be of petty insignificance in the sight of Him who rules all mind and matter. Perhaps the infant's soul in heaven knows more than Newton ever knew on earth ; perchance, transplanted to the realms above, the idiot's soul set free, may look down upon the master-work of masterminds on earth ; and in its high pre-eminence of thought, may scorn to laugh at those small minds which laughed to scorn his own.

Such thoughts as these should check our small conceits, our overweening pride of reason which would weigh all things in the balance of logic, and seek to make religion, virtue, and futurity demonstrable like Euclid's elements. There must be a point where reason must bend its head to faith, and bid it take up the thread of a half-finished argument.[1]

Reason shows us not infallibly the aim and end of life and living things. The great problem—why do we live and die ?—reason will never solve with cer-

[1] " A man who would be all head is as great a monster as he who would be all heart. The wholly sound man is both."—*Herder*.

tainty. All it can do is to lead us to surmises from
known facts and ascertained analogies ; to prove to us
what we all feel true without such proof : that there
is a God, and that that God is good and works for our
good. Then faith, not credulous and blind belief, but
faith built upon the sure foundation of experience of
God's mercies, tells us all the rest ; tells us of the future
we all hope to gain, and of the immortality we all hope
to inherit.

Here Reason bends its head to Faith without abdicating its sway. It says, " So far, no farther can I
guide you. Those dizzy heights of future, that dark
abyss of past, no human mind can penetrate. Eternity,
infinity, omnipotence, are only *words* to men. Through
those broad plains of the illimitable ask me not to
lead you. But you may read the future from the
past. The sun which rose to-day will rise again
to-morrow ; and so the God who always has been
good, tender, and loving to His creatures, will be the
same to you for ever. Act well and righteously, and
await the end with trustful, loving faith."

Wise men will learn to wait. We have not long to
wait. It needs no mighty strain on faith to feel and
know that when the soul returns to Him from whom
it came, all problems will be solved, all doubts removed
without the adventitious aid of those misguided and
misguiding folks who seek to reconcile.

Till then let Truth remain. Seek not to hide the
fact. You cannot stay the progress of discovery, nor
put a skid upon the wheels of science ; and even if
you could, the *truth* would yet remain. The truth is
our heritage. The " things which are revealed belong
to us, and to our children for ever."

APPENDIX III

THE TITHE [1]

" Will a man rob God ?   Yet ye have robbed Me.   But ye say, Wherein have we robbed Thee ?   In tithes and offerings " (Mal. iii. 8).

THERE is this remarkable inconsistency in the practice of our religion, that while some of the Divine Commands are most scrupulously obeyed, others are totally neglected and ignored.

No more flagrant example of a neglected precept could be adduced than the law of Tithe.   We have no excuse for forgetting it, for we read it in our synagogues three times a year ; the precept is enjoined over and over again in the most solemn terms, and the prophets denounce those who neglect this command.   And yet how few, nowadays, give tithe ?   Indeed, many who read this will be startled at hearing that it is at all a religious duty ; a few may have heard of tithe as some sort of a burden on property like a rate or a tax ; but most will think it some old and obsolete custom, belonging to an age long passed away ; while some really pious people will complacently persuade themselves that it may be neglected with impunity now, since we are exiles from the Holy Land.

The words of the prophet quoted as a text will show in a sufficiently strong light the nature of the obligation involved in this important law.   In Israel's palmy days, the tithes took the place of rates and taxes.   Every one was bound to bring the tenth of his

[1] Reprinted from " Sabbath Readings."

produce for the support of those who had no means—
the Levites (who had no inheritance) and the poor.
The first poor-law was made at Sinai, and an assess-
ment was made then and for all time. It declared,
" At the end of three years, thou shalt bring forth all
the tithe of thine increase the same year, and shalt lay it
up within thy gates. And the Levite (because he hath
no part nor inheritance with thee), and the stranger, and
the fatherless, and the widow, which are within thy
gates, shall come and shall eat and be satisfied." [1]

In those days, there was no workhouse ; but poverty,
as well as property, had its rights. The poor had the
right to live, not by starvation doles, which make life
only a lingering death, but by the open-handed gift of
sufficient charity. The poor-law of Sinai proclaimed :
" The poor shall never cease out of the land, therefore, I command thee saying, ' Thou shalt open thine
hand wide unto thy brother, to thy poor, and to thy
needy, in thy land.' " [2]

But the institution of the Tithe possesses even a
more remote antiquity than the Mosaic Code. We find
that Abraham gave Melchizedek, the king-priest, tithe
of all he possessed,[3] and that Jacob, in his prayer at
Bethel, promised God, " Of all that Thou givest me, I
will surely give the tenth to Thee." [4] In those early
days there was no sacrificial system requiring support,
nor was there any elaborate state-establishment needing maintenance ; so the tithe given by the patriarchs
must have been bestowed on the poor alone.

The Mosaic law of tithe, however, was of a three-
fold character. One tithe was devoted to the service
of the tabernacle or temple, and was given to the
Priests and Levites for the maintenance of the state-
establishment. It comprised " the tithe of the land,

---

[1] Deut. xiv. 28, 29.   [2] Deut. xv. 11.
[3] Gen. xiv, 20.   [4] Gen. xxviii. 22.

whether of the seed of the land or of the fruit of the tree, the tithe of the herd or of the flock," [1] and this tithe was declared " holy unto the Lord."

Then, there was the yearly tithe of which the giver was also the recipient. We read in Deut. xiv. 22, 23 : " Thou shalt truly tithe all the increase of thy seed, that the field bringeth forth year by year," " the tithe of thy corn, of thy wine and thine oil, and the firstlings of thy herds and of thy flocks." This tithe was not to be given away ; but every man had to take it to Jerusalem, and was there to eat it, " that thou mayest learn to fear the Lord thy God always." Or, if he lived at a distance from the Holy City, he was told to carry thither the money-value of the tithe, and to expend it for whatsoever his soul lusted after, and he was to eat this before the Lord God, and rejoice, he and his household. This tithe made Jerusalem not only a great religious centre, but also an important commercial centre ; for one tenth of the whole produce of Palestine had thus to be brought to the Holy City, and was either there consumed, or it changed hands in the ordinary course of commerce ; and the Israelite was thus taught to spiritualise his worldly prosperity and enjoyments, by eating the tithe of his produce " before the Lord."

Lastly, there was the tithe of the third year. Every third year the Israelite had to bring forth the tenth part of his profits, and in that same year to lay it up in reserve for the service of the poor. " At the end of three years thou shalt bring forth all the tithe of thine increase the same year, and shalt lay it up within thy gates : And the Levite (because he hath no part or inheritance with thee), and the stranger and the fatherless and the widow which are within thy gates shall come and shall eat and be satisfied ; that the

[1] Lev. xxvii. 30, 32.

Lord thy God may bless thee in all the work of thine hand which thou doest." [1]

In that remarkable book of the Apocrypha, Tobit, we find the three tithes thus practically described : " The first tenth part of all increase I gave to the sons of Aaron, another tenth part I sold away, and went and spent it every year at Jerusalem, and the third I gave unto them it was meet." [2]

Our Ritual Code, too, in distinct terms, enacts the law of tithe, declaring that " a man should give in charity at least one tenth of his income." [3]

As we have no longer Priests, nor Levites, nor sacrifices, we cannot bring the first tithe. As we have no Jerusalem, wherein we can rejoice before the Lord, we cannot bring the second tithe. But the privilege of the third tithe, the tithe of the third year, the tithe of the poor, yet remains to us, and it is with this command that we are at present chiefly concerned.

The tithe of the third year was to be brought by every Israelite, and laid up within the gates of his city. It was to be a reserve fund, on which the needy were to draw as occasion required. All who were in distress, the stranger, the widow, and the orphan, were to partake of its bounty, and " eat and be satisfied." There were storehouses for the tithe, and we find that there were times when it was collected in such abundance that even a special organisation was needed for its distribution. [4]

And when it was duly stored, each man bringing tithe made a solemn declaration before God that he had truly assessed his profit, and had given the exact tenth to the poor, and he craved the blessing of the Almighty as a reward for his faithful stewardship.

The Bible, and especially the Pentateuch, is very

---

[1] Deut. xiv. 28, 29. [2] Tobit i. 7. [3] Yore Deah, 249, § 1.
[4] 2 Chron. xxxi. 5, 6, 12 ; Neh. xiii. 12.

sparing in imposing prayer-formulas ; but, with regard
to the tithe, the Law prescribes a special prayer to
accompany it, so lending to the observance a significance sufficiently indicative of its importance. And
this is the prayer : " I have brought away the hallowed
things out of mine house, and also have given them to
the Levite, and unto the stranger, to the fatherless and
to the widow, according to all the commandments
which Thou hast given me. Neither have I trans-
gressed Thy commandments, neither have I forgotten
them. I have not eaten thereof in my mourning,
neither have I taken away aught thereof for any unclean use, nor given aught thereof for the dead ; but
I have hearkened to the voice of the Lord my God,
and have done according to all that Thou hast commanded me. Look down from Thy holy habitation,
from heaven, and bless Thy people Israel, and the land
which Thou hast given us, as Thou swarest unto our
fathers, a land that floweth with milk and honey." [1]
No more powerful declaration could be imagined than
that contained in this prayer. It says in plain language : " Inasmuch as I have fulfilled Thy command
by giving truly tithe to the poor, so fulfil Thy gracious
promise, and grant us the blessing of plenty ! "

How the blessing was fulfilled, all readers of Sacred
History know well. Difficult though it may be for the
modern traveller to conceive the present arid plains
and rocky crags of Palestine ever to have been otherwise than they now are, we all know that in the days
of Israel's greatness the Holy Land was truly a land
flowing with milk and honey. But it was the tithe
that brought the blessing. " Bring ye all the tithes
into the storehouse," said the prophet Malachi, " that
there may be meat in Mine house, and prove me now
herewith, saith the Lord of Hosts, if I will not open

[1] Deut. xxvi. 13, 14, 15.

you the windows of Heaven, and pour you out a blessing, that there shall not be room enough to receive it." [1]

In these days of materialism and infidelity, people find it difficult to realise any connection between the giving of tithe and a good harvest; and these words of the prophet, if spoken now, would probably fall on deaf ears. But the same prophet spoke those startling words which we have cited as our text, and they possess a force even greater than the promise of a miraculous harvest. For they appeal to our sense of honour. We all pride ourselves on our sense of honour. The idea of robbing any one is repugnant to every right-minded man. Who would think of robbing even his enemy? Who would dream of robbing his best friend? Then "shall a man rob God?" Yet, says God, "ye *have* robbed Me, in the tithes and offerings."

If we could but appreciate the full purport of this imputation—an imputation which holds good against many, nay, most of us, in these our times—how different would be the standard of our liberality to the poor, and how different would be the condition of suffering humanity! To God we owe all we have, be it much or little. He gives it to us with generous hand, but bids us return Him one tenth, only one tenth, for His poor, for the widow, the orphan, and the stranger: and yet that small tenth we withhold from Him! Shall a man rob God? Yet we do rob Him when, instead of giving, freely and fully, the fair tithe of our income, we bestow our niggardly gifts on the poor, and call that charity.

There is much cant abroad in our times, and there is no more rampant specimen of this cant than the cant of social economists, with reference to the question of charity. They would organise charity to such

[1] Mal. iii. 10.

refined perfection that, in the end, there would be no
occasion to give, for there would be no one to receive.
They would only give to the " deserving poor," to
those who can help themselves. All other gifts would
be contrary to the rules of social economy; and God
forbid that, in helping the poor, they should break
the laws of supply and demand! They would stamp
out pauperism by stamping out the poor. That one
and the same poor man should receive a little aid from
two sources, is hateful to their souls; that two charities
should do like work, like two rivers running in parallel
courses and fertilising the same soil, is sacrilege in
their sight. They are charitable, but their charity is
an abstract idea, and it is so much cheaper to talk
charity than to practise it.

But, as our religion is the religion of action, so is
our charity the charity of action; and the dreams of
sociologists will never stamp out pauperism, nor stem
the overflowing tide of poverty. The true cause of
chronic pauperism is the insufficiency of our charitable
aid. It is said there are too many charities, and too
little organisation. We would reply, there is too little
charity, and nothing to organise. The first condition
of organisation is, that there must be enough subject-
matter to organise.

What is our charity? The small doles received by
our poor are barely enough to meet their pressing
necessities, to ward off for the moment the pangs of
hunger or of cold; and who can evoke in them
prudence for to-morrow, when they have not even
the bread of to-day? Who can arouse a spirit of
self-reliant hope in the starving soul, or incite to industry and action the ill-nourished, attenuated frame?
The small dole pauperises, because it is a hand-to-
mouth relief; the large gift founds new hope, starts
new efforts, new activity, new industry, new work.

T

It gives the poor man a to-morrow; it revives his strength for a fresh start, for a new struggle, to wipe out past sufferings, humiliations, and despair.

But whence are to be obtained the means for these large gifts? How find the capital for the poor, small though it be for each, out of the niggardly income of our charities? It can never be done, and the poor can never be adequately, successfully, and permanently relieved, while men give as they now give, fitfully, sparingly, grudgingly; never till men give the full tithe of their income to works of benevolence. Then there will be enough, and to spare; and charitable relief will mean not a mere stop-gap, but a permanent benefit to the large majority of the relieved. True, even unlimited means cannot insure invariable success, and the poor will never entirely cease out of the land; but miseries can be alleviated, and the helpful can be helped, and the falling aided before they have fallen, if only adequate means be at hand.

We Jews pride ourselves on our charity; and, perhaps, compared with our neighbours, we are charitable indeed. But even our standard is low, miserably low, compared with that which our Divine Law has ordained for us, the standard of the Tithe. We give fitfully, without system, without principle; we give as creatures of impulse. Charity should be a deliberate act, and it can only become such by our devoting thereto a fixed proportion of our means.

It must not be imagined that the law of Tithe applies only to the opulent. It applies to all classes. Even the poor Levite who had no inheritance in Israel had to bring a tithe of his tithe.[1] And so the poor, when they made a profit, were expected to devote the due proportion to works of benevolence. "If thou hast abundance, give alms accordingly; if thou hast

[1] Num. xviii. 26.

but little, be not afraid to give according to that
little." [1]   The same God, who ordained the tithe,
promised a certain reward—even a material reward—
for the fulfilment of this command ; and surely no
one with a spark of religion will doubt the Divine Will
or Divine Power so to reward the trustful poor, who
give from their scanty resources, already burdened by
their own needs. These—the alms eked out from
daily necessities—make charity the highest of virtues.
These, though they may be but crumbs compared with
the rich man's gifts, are more precious than showers of
gold cast off from the superfluities of wealth.   Probably
with us Jews, the poor give tithe more often than do
the rich ; for among the less fortunate of our brethren,
nothing is more frequent than to find poverty aiding a
greater poverty, forgetting self in ministering to the
sufferings of others.

The poor helping the poor is truly a sight that im-
parts a halo of romance even to sordid poverty.   For
who can look upon such acts of self-denial without a
thankful recognition of the divine power of pity and
love, implanted in the human breast, making every
man, however humble, an angel—a messenger of God
—to him he succours ?

We live in dangerous times—dangerous because
education is becoming general, and education makes
men think ; and thinking men ask, wherefore those
frightful social contrasts which civilised life presents
—the contrasts between the two extremes of wealth
and indigence ?   Wherefore the contrast between the
multitude, who live a struggling, starving life, and
the few, who live a useless, aimless, luxurious life,
embarrassed with riches that they know not how to
spend ?   For who can look beneath the thin film of
that skin-deep civilisation which modern society pre-

[1] Tobit iv. 8.

sents, and not be appalled at the seething mass of
poverty, suffering, and wretchedness, which seems
ready to break the bounds of law, like lava bursting
the volcano's crust ?

Heaven has ordained that there must ever be rich
and poor, master and servant, and all those grades of
social rank which wealth creates. But Heaven never
ordained poverty to be hopeless, chronic, and without
remedy, nor meant it to be, as it is to thousands,
another name for death. The rich were to help the
poor, help them wisely, tenderly, sufficiently—not with
the niggard hand that drops a stray copper to the
starving wretch, who roams about the streets weak
with hunger ; nor with the half-grudged guineas, given
by hard persuasion, to ill-supported charities, which
leave their work undone, ill-done, half-done, for want
of means—but with the systematic share, well and
truly meted, of the wealth that God has given.

And if this sacred duty were honourably fulfilled by
all, how different would be the world ! We should not
find those shocking scenes of poverty that assail the
senses in every great city ; those hideous hovels,
reeking with filth and squalor, that constitute the poor
man's home ; nor the pale, emaciated forms of children,
old in their early youth from want of sustenance ; nor
the gaunt, white spectres of men and women, wan
with want and suffering, pinched and withered in the
struggle for their daily bread. From those murky
social swamps, where the poor wither and die before
their time, springs the will-o'-the-wisp of communism,
and those other godless pestilential creeds, which
threaten society. In its own defence society should
help the poor. It cannot last long with such contrasts as it now presents.

And in so many ways can the poor be helped, not
merely helped but raised, if only there were forth-

coming sufficient means and earnest workers, and if to each worker were apportioned his fair share of the gigantic task. Then, indeed, would wealth be adorned and glorified ; for the rich would have the glorious work of raising the indigent from the deep abyss of suffering and sorrow—a mission worthy of angels.

To all of us, soon or late, the time must come when this world and all its charms and blandishments will fade away from our gaze, and all our worldly hopes and aims and ends, all our ambitions, will be as nought. Nothing then will seem or be to us of value, save the small handful of godly goodly works, that we have wrought for others. In that supreme hour, how poor may be the rich, how rich the poor !

Whatever be our means, great or small, in that dread hour our wealth will be what we ourselves have stored in works of goodness, kindness, mercy to others ; they will be our riches, for no other coin is current before the Throne of Mercy but deeds of mercy. To the merciful, God will show Himself Merciful.[1]

At such an hour, would you have it forced on your unwilling, but too vivid, memory, that you have fallen short of your duty to the poor, that you have withheld from them their fair share of God's great bounty to yourself, that you have robbed the widow and orphan of their due, that you have withheld from God his tithe ?

Then, while you have life and health and means, give—give to God the tithe which is His ; for the sake of the poor, that they may live ; for the sake of society, that it may endure ; for your own sake, that the work of your hands may be blessed ; for the sake of duty, honesty, and honour !

For " shall a man rob God " ?

[1] Ps. xviii. 25.

APPENDIX IV

THE SANHEDRIN, AND THE ORIGIN OF THE TALMUD [1]

WE have already seen [2] how, at the instance of Jethro, the first local Israelitish courts of justice were established by the appointment of "rulers of thousands, rulers of hundreds, rulers of fifties, and rulers of tens," who "judged the people at all seasons." But the Supreme Court, which, later in Jewish history, acquired the Greek name *Sanhedrin*, is said to have had its origin in the events related in the eleventh chapter of Numbers.

"And the Lord said unto Moses, Gather unto Me seventy men of the elders of Israel, whom thou knowest to be the elders of the people, and officers over them ; and bring them unto the Tent of Meeting, that they may stand there with thee. And I will come down, and talk with thee there ; and I will take of the spirit which is upon thee, and will put it upon them ; and they shall bear the burden of the people with thee, that thou bear it not thyself alone." [3]

Moses found the task of governing and controlling the people too burdensome for him. He was accordingly directed to associate with him seventy elders, to share with him the burden of the people. The Bible does not tell us clearly how the selection was made ; but tradition tells us that it was made in this fashion :

[1] Much of the material for this Appendix was kindly supplied for the original edition by the Rev. Dr. Hermann Adler, the present Chief Rabbi.

[2] Page 171. [3] Num. xi. 16, 17.

Six candidates, known for their prudence and worth, were selected from each tribe, thus making seventy-two, or two in excess of the required number. Seventy pieces of parchment were marked with a certain sign, and two pieces were left blank. The seventy-two then drew lots. Eldad and Medad are supposed to have been the two who drew blanks, and their peculiar position is described in a later part of the same chapter.[1] The remaining seventy were duly installed, " and when the spirit rested upon them, they prophesied."

The functions of the august assembly thus constituted were, the maintenance of order and the instruction of the people, more especially the solution of difficult points of law, beyond the powers of the tribal or local courts ; and thus appears to have originated an institution which, in later times, exercised the greatest influence upon the development of Judaism —the Sanhedrin.

In post-biblical history, the Great Sanhedrin is constantly mentioned as a body which constituted a common centre of religious authority to all the children of Israel, throughout their dispersion. Much has been written on the subject. An Englishman, John Selden, who lived in the reign of Charles I., wrote a Dissertation in Latin, entitled *De Synedriis et Præfecturis Juridicis veterum Ebræorum.* An elaborate Treatise on the subject has been published by Dr. Hoffmann, entitled *Der oberste Gerichtshof in der Stadt des Heiligthums.* Some scholars suppose that this great council did not arise until the days of Ezra, and that it was a new institution devised by this sage. But the weight of probability is against this view. It is not likely that the council of seventy elders, established by Moses, should have been merely a temporary tribunal. There had been previously a temporary

[1] Num. xi. 26–29.

appointment of elders, who, together with Aaron and Hur, were to rule the people, while Moses was absent for forty days on the mount of God,[1] but, judging from the sequel—the history of the worship of the golden calf—these delegates could have had little influence over the people. The spirit of Moses was not upon them.

But with the tribunal of Seventy ordained in the eleventh chapter of Numbers it was far different. Moses had been so wearied by the strain of his burden, that he had begged God to take his life rather than permit him to continue in his wretchedness.[2] No temporary appointment would have given to Moses the necessary relief. It is not credible that the transfer of the spirit of the great Legislator to the Seventy Elders would have been effected as a mere temporary expedient, and the Bible does not mention any special exigency needing the special and temporary work of the Elders. Indeed, the whole language of the text indicates the permanency of the institution. " When the spirit rested upon them, they prophesied, and did not cease." [3]

It is true that we do not find the Tribunal of Seventy again referred to in the Pentateuch in distinct terms ; but such an omission would be quite in accordance with the biblical style of narrative, which, while most explicit in some passages, contents itself with mere hints and allusions in others. Thus, when we find in the narrative of the rebellion of Korah, that the elders of Israel followed Moses,[4] there can be no doubt that reference is made to the Council of Seventy, who aided him in communicating to the people the Divine behest. Again, in the twenty-seventh chapter of Deuteronomy, where we find [5] that Moses with the Elders of Israel charged the people to keep the commandments, it was

<hr/>

[1] Exod. xxiv. 1–14. [2] Num. xi. 15. [3] Num. xi. 25.
[4] Num. xvi. 25. [5] Deut. xxvii. 1.

doubtless again the Council of Seventy who acted as assessors to the great Legislator. We again meet with allusions to the Elders in the time of Joshua and the Judges, and we may readily understand that if Moses had needed the support of a tribunal to share with him the duties and responsibilities of government, his successors would still more urgently need such aid.

It is probable that the Tribunal of Seventy fell into abeyance during the reign of some of the Kings, who desired to rule despotically, unchecked by representatives of legally constituted authority. But there can be no doubt that King Jehoshaphat strove to reorganise it, for we are told,[1] " Moreover in Jerusalem did Jehoshaphat set of the Levites and of the priests, and of the chief of the fathers of Israel, for the judgment of the Lord, and for controversies," and he appears to have imparted to the tribunal a twofold character, by appointing two presidents, one, the high-priest, for religious matters, and the other the ruler of the house of Judah for civil causes.

When our fathers returned from the Babylonian captivity, the Institution was revived by Ezra, the Seventy Elders in all probability forming a part of the " men of the Great Synagogue." [2] But it is at the time of the Maccabees that we find the Tribunal of Seventy flourishing in all its vigour, as the Supreme Council of State. It is mentioned in all the most important State documents. Thus, when Jonathan makes a league with the Lacedæmonians, he writes : " Jonathan the High Priest and the Elders of the nation, and the priests and the other people of the Jews unto the Lacedæmonians, their brethren, send greeting." [3]

[1] 2 Chron. xix. 8.
[2] These were 120 in number, and were the first compilers of a Jewish liturgy, on which our present prayer-book is based.
[3] 1 Macc. xii. 6.

The Talmud gives full particulars of the mode in which members of the Sanhedrin were appointed, and as to the functions the tribunal had to fulfil. The tribunal was originally called *Beth-din haggadol* (בֵּית דִּין הַגָּדוֹל), "the Great House of Judgment," but it acquired the name Sanhedrin (סַנְהֶדְרִין) from the Greek συνέδριον, which simply means "assembly," at the time of the Macedonian supremacy, the senators of that state being called συνέδροι or assembly-men.

The Sanhedrin consisted of seventy members, besides the president, *Nassi* (נְשִׂיא), prince or patriarch ; and thus it exactly corresponded with the Assembly in the Wilderness, which consisted of seventy Elders, with Moses as president. Each member of the Great Sanhedrin was called to his high office by ordination (סְמִיכָה) or imposition of hands, and this ceremony connected him, through a long chain of prophets and judges, with Joshua, whom Moses himself had ordained.

The members were selected, not from the privileged or wealthy classes, but exclusively from those who were distinguished for their personal worth and high attainments. The king was not eligible, lest his opinion, backed by his lofty authority, might carry too much weight. It is stated that the moral qualifications necessary for admission to the august assembly were wisdom, modesty, the fear of God, disinterestedness, the love of truth, humanity, and an unstained reputation. Moreover, the Israelite admitted to a seat in the Great Council was required to be profoundly versed in the Law, and was also obliged to show himself well acquainted with a wide range of studies not theological, such as astronomy, physics, and medicine. He had likewise to be a good linguist, so as to be able to understand evidence in foreign tongues without the aid of an interpreter, and he was also expected to be acquainted with the philosophies, opinions, practices, and superstitions of the heathens. The High Priest himself could not *claim* to be a member of the Sanhedrin ; but preference was given to him, as well as to the ordinary priests, if they possessed the necessary qualifications.

The *Nassi*, or president, was chosen entirely on account of his pre-eminent worth and wisdom. The senior member of the Seventy, called the *Ab Beth-din* (אַב בֵּית דִּין), "father of the house of judgment," sat at the right hand of the president, and the rest of the Seventy sat before them in the form of a semicircle.

The place where the sessions of the Sanhedrin were ordinarily held, was the *Lishchath Hagazith* (לִשְׁכַּת הַגָּזִית), a hall in one of the courts of the Temple.

The functions of the Tribunal were twofold, executive and legislative. It constituted the Supreme Court of Judicature, which tried all cases of national importance, such as cases of false prophets, a traitor high-priest, an idolatrous tribe or city, and, generally, all capital cases. It should be added that the Talmud distinctly asserts that the power of inflicting capital punishment was taken away from the Tribunal by the Romans forty years before the destruction of the Second Temple, and that it was only the Roman procurator who could confirm and execute the sentence of the Sanhedrin. This fact is an important one, as it rebuts the charge, which has been the cause of so much persecution, that the Jews crucified Jesus. He was certainly arraigned before the Sanhedrin as a false prophet, but the punishment was executed not by Jews, but by Romans, and according to Roman custom ; for crucifixion was not one of the Jewish modes of capital punishment.

The legislative function of the Sanhedrin was derived from its judicial function. Like all supreme courts of appeal, it gradually built up a system of " case law " upon the broad substructure of statute law; the statute law being, in the present instance, the Mosaic Code with its traditional interpretation. Deriving its authority from the precept in Deut. xvii. 8–10, to which we have already referred,[1] the Sanhedrin did not permit its system of " case law " to drift gradually into chaotic confusion, as is the custom in many modern communities, and notably in England; but, sitting permanently, it collected and collated ancient traditions, judgments, and decisions, gave coherence and system to them, and thus enabled many enactments of the Pentateuch, otherwise obscure, to be carried out in practical life.

These decisions were voluntarily accepted by the people. At first they were traditional, handed down from Sanhedrin to Sanhedrin, from teacher to pupil by word of mouth, codified, but not allowed to be reduced to writing, lest the traditional law which, in certain circumstances, could be modified by subsequent decisions, should be confounded with the immutable written law promulgated on Sinai. But later on, about 150 years after the destruction of the Second Temple, when the nation was dispersed in many countries, Rabbi Judah, the Prince, or the Holy, fearing that the traditions might be lost or forgotten amid the many trials to which our people were subjected, determined to reduce to writing the entire bulk of the traditional law, a work already commenced a century back by the disciples of the renowned Hillel. Aided by his sons Simon and Gamliel, and by other sages and scholars of his time, he accomplished this work, condensing the tradition into six divisions, which he styled the *Mishna* (מִשְׁנָה) (Learning).

The traditions once codified and reduced to writing, no new laws or decisions were permitted to be added

---

[1] Page 160, " Laws of Government."

to them. But, as time went on, the Mishna itself became a starting point and basis for further development and commentary ; and, the two centuries succeeding its codification being a period of great mental activity among the remnant of our nation, an enormous mass of commentary was at length accumulated, which was, in course of time, collected by Rabina and Rab Ashi, and formed the work now known as the *Gemara* (נְמָרָא), *i.e.* Tradition. The *Mishna* was completed about the year 200, the *Gemara* about the year 500 of the common era. These two works together constitute the *Talmud* (תַּלְמוּד), or Study of the Law.

There are two recensions of the Talmud—the Jerusalemean and the Babylonian ; the latter being the more comprehensive work, and that generally referred to when the term " Talmud " is used.

INDEX

U

THE END

Printed by BALLANTYNE, HANSON & CO.
Edinburgh & London